What Readers Are Saying About *Web Design for Developers*

This is the book I wish I had had when I started to build my first website. It covers web development from A to Z and will answer many of your questions while improving the quality of the sites you produce.

► **Shae Murphy**
CTO, Social Brokerage

As a web developer, I thought I knew HTML and CSS. This book helped me understand that even though I may know the basics, there's more to web design than changing font colors and adding margins.

► **Mike Weber**
Web application developer

If you're ready to step into the wonderful world of web design, this book explains the key concepts clearly and effectively. The comfortable, fun writing style makes this book as enjoyable as it is enlightening.

► **Jeff Cohen**
Founder, Purple Workshops

This book has something for everyone, from novice to experienced designers. As a developer, I found it extremely helpful for my day-to-day work, causing me to think before just putting content on a page.

► **Chris Johnson**
Solutions developer

From conception to launch, Mr. Hogan offers a complete experience and expertly navigates his audience though every phase of development. Anyone from beginners to seasoned veterans will gain valuable insight from this polished work that is much more than a technical guide.

► **Neal Rudnik**
Web and multimedia production manager, Aspect

This book arms application developers with the knowledge to help blur the line that some companies place between a design team and a development team. After all, just because someone is a "coder" doesn't mean he or she can't create an attractive and usable site.

► **Jon Kinney**
Ruby on Rails architect, Avastone Technologies

Web Design for Developers emphasizes practical, easy-to-master techniques. Achieving a professional look is possible, even by those whose idea of symmetry is a balanced set of curly braces.

► **Craig Castelaz**
Principle software engineer, at a mind-boggling immense software company

Web Design for Developers

A Programmer's Guide
to Design Tools and Techniques

Web Design for Developers

A Programmer's Guide
to Design Tools and Techniques

Brian P. Hogan

The Pragmatic Bookshelf
Raleigh, North Carolina   Dallas, Texas

Pragmatic Bookshelf

Many of the designations used by manufacturers and sellers to distinguish their products are claimed as trademarks. Where those designations appear in this book, and The Pragmatic Programmers, LLC was aware of a trademark claim, the designations have been printed in initial capital letters or in all capitals. The Pragmatic Starter Kit, The Pragmatic Programmer, Pragmatic Programming, Pragmatic Bookshelf and the linking *g* device are trademarks of The Pragmatic Programmers, LLC.

Every precaution was taken in the preparation of this book. However, the publisher assumes no responsibility for errors or omissions, or for damages that may result from the use of information (including program listings) contained herein.

Our Pragmatic courses, workshops, and other products can help you and your team create better software and have more fun. For more information, as well as the latest Pragmatic titles, please visit us at

http://www.pragprog.com

Printed in Canada.

ISBN-10: 1-934356-13-1
ISBN-13: 978-1-9343561-3-5
Printed on acid-free paper.
P1.0 printing, December 2009
Version: 2009-11-19

Contents

Chapter 1

Introduction

If you've ever written an application and wished it looked a little better, then this book is for you. If you've ever looked at your favorite website and tried to pull apart the CSS to figure out how it works, you're reading the right book. If you've ever wondered how many licks it takes to get to the center of a Tootsie Pop, then you should consult Wikipedia because this book doesn't cover that.

This book covers the web-design process for programmers who have little to no design background. Underneath all the pretty colors and nice layouts, websites require an awful lot of programming to get just right. You must follow rules and best practices when working with Java, Ruby, or C#; the same is true of designing websites if you want to achieve the desired result.

1.1 Before We Get Started...

Good web design is about much more than creating pretty pages. Basic concepts such as color theory, typography, layout, and usability are all part of a good design. These things work together to make the site succeed for users. You could pick all the right colors and use smooth gradients, but if you don't use a readable font, your site isn't designed well. You could whip up something awesome in Photoshop or GIMP, but you'll never be able to make it look good in a browser if you don't know how HTML and CSS work. If you have sloppy markup, your JavaScript won't work as you expect it to work. If you don't optimize your content, search engines will hate your site. And if you take accessibility and usability for granted, your users will hate your site even more.

> ### There Is No One True Way
>
> This book is aimed at the programmer who wants to learn about web design. The method this book uses is an effective entry-level web-design process, and although it's certainly not the only way to build websites, the techniques described in this book will make you well prepared to explore other techniques so that you can develop your own workflow.
>
> As you work through our example, you will find many places in which you might have made a different decision than I did or used a different technique. That's great! I've made these choices to help you get started as a designer. Over time, you'll change, and so will popular tastes. I look forward to seeing the sites you create.

Another key aspect to good web design is creativity. I want you to focus on your own creativity when you work through the exercises in this book. I will show you how to build a site in this book to illustrate the design process, but my hope is that you won't completely follow every example exactly as shown. I want you to pick your own colors and fonts, using this book as a guide to make your own design. As you implement your own design, you'll learn a lot about the theory behind web design. It is my hope that the site you design will look completely different from the example shown at the end of the book.

Your programming experience will help you build an attractive web page. For the first half of this book, you will live in the world of the designer. You will learn about colors and fonts because they are important parts of creating a good design. You'll also learn how to use the tools and techniques that designers prefer. Once we cover the appropriate theory, you'll have some code to write. After all, that's what you expect from a book for programmers, right?

1.2 The Design Process in Action

A good way to understand the typical web-design process is to follow Ron, a busy web developer, as he works with a client to create a small web page.

Joe Asks...

Do People Still Do Mock-ups in Photoshop?

Designers do. If you're not seeing it where you work, you probably spend a lot of your time around skilled CSS coders, not designers. I know tons of programmers who routinely receive a Photoshop file (PSD) from a graphic artist. Part of a developer's job is to incorporate that design into a web application, and learning how to handle PSDs is part of the design process.

We will use Photoshop mock-ups in this book for two reasons. They are good vehicles for describing many parts of the design process, and it's easier to learn CSS concepts when you have working color mock-ups to follow.

Gathering Requirements

Ron has a new client, a real-estate agent. The agent needs a simple content system to manage her property listings. After an initial meeting with Kim, the realtor, Ron grabs a pen and sheet of paper, and he starts sketching the home page. He draws many different designs and then picks the three designs that he thinks will work best, given Kim's needs.

He meets again with Kim to discuss the three designs. Kim selects one of the sketches and makes some suggestions. When Ron brings up colors, Kim decides on a color scheme of blue, gray, and white because these colors are similar to the ones on her business card.

Photoshop Time

Later that day, Ron sits down at his computer, opens Photoshop, and quickly mocks up the home page using the finished sketch and Kim's preferred colors as his guide. He grabs a few royalty-free stock images and places them on the mock-up. He spends a little time looking at various shades of blues and grays until he gets something he likes. Once he's done, he exports the document and sends it off to Kim to get some feedback.

After waiting a week, Ron calls up Kim to get her opinion on what he's done so far. She tells him she'll take a look at it when she gets back from her vacation in a week.

Time to Get Coding

Another week goes by, and Ron finally gets a call from Kim. She says she likes how it looks, and she wants to move forward. Relieved, Ron fires up his trusty text editor and begins the transition from mock-up to web page.

Ron begins by creating a simple HTML document that defines the structure and content for the page. Next, he uses Photoshop to slice up his mock-up so he can extract the banner graphics and other images, which he then inserts into the HTML document.

Next, he carefully codes some CSS to pull the whole thing together. The style sheets transform the linear-page skeleton into a brightly colored, two-column layout.

Ron opens up the new web page in Firefox, and everything looks great, just like his mock-up. He then fires up Internet Explorer 6 and winces at the ugly page staring back at him.

Fortunately, Ron has seen this kind of thing before, so he quickly throws in a few extra style definitions in an IE-only style sheet. Presto! He's ready to show Kim the finished page.

Good to Go

Kim loves the site, and Ron is ready to start building the rest of the pages for the site. Now that Ron has worked out the colors, the images, and the style sheets, it will be easy to produce the rest of the site. Ron can take pride in the fact that he's made his new client happy.

It's Not Always That Easy

Ron got lucky this time. He got an easy-to-please client. Unfortunately, clients are not always so easy to please, as you'll see when dealing with the stakeholders of the Foodbox website that we'll use as a running example in this book.

1.3 YourFoodbox.com

You just finished a website for a company that has obtained financial backing to build the ultimate recipe-sharing website. The site will allow users to search thousands of recipes, contribute their own recipes, and offer variations on existing ones. You're supposed to launch the site next week, but you've just shown the finished product to the stakeholders, and although they think the functionality is intact, they can't stand how it looks. They don't think it "feels right," and they would like something more eye-catching. Of course, they can't give you any concrete ideas, and you will need to use your experience at gathering requirements to figure out what they want so you can make them happier.

The chapters in this book will guide you through this all-too-common scenario. You'll learn about the process of picking colors, choosing fonts, creating buttons, optimizing images, and using a grid to build the template for the site. You'll learn how to make web forms look a little nicer, and you'll learn assorted tips and tricks to make your site work across multiple browsers and platforms. After you finish building the site, you'll learn how to make it friendlier to search engines, as well as how to squeeze a few more drops of performance out of your pages.

You'll also find that it's important to me that your website be accessible to the widest possible audience. We'll try to make sure that people with disabilities can easily work with the site. This is a good business decision for you and personally important to me because I, along with my father and daughter, was born with congenital cataracts that affect my vision. We won't tackle accessibility issues in depth until later in the book, but I will make references to various accessibility and usability topics as we work through the examples.

1.4 Ready to Go?

We know where we're going, and we have a long way ahead of us. Let's start by looking at the original site and finding out what the shareholders want us to fix.

1.5 Acknowledgments

No one writes a book alone. In fact, it turns out that writing is only a small part of what brings a book like this to completion. The feedback, criticism, friendship, and moral support from colleagues, friends, and family made this book possible.

First, to Dave Thomas and Andy Hunt, thank you for signing this book, for believing in this project from the beginning, and for seeing it through to completion. I have learned from you and the books you've supported through the Pragmatic Bookshelf, and I am honored to have had the opportunity to work for you.

Next, I want to thank my patient, wise, and incredibly supportive editor, Daniel Steinberg. I'm a much better writer than I ever thought I could be thanks to you and your excellent feedback and well-placed criticism.

Thanks to my awesome technical reviewers Jeremy Sydik, Jon Kinney, Chris Johnson, Ben Kimball, Josh Peot, Mike Mangino, Lyle Johnson, James Wylder, Jeff Cohen, and Mike Weber. Thank you all for taking the time to provide excellent feedback and for challenging me to explain myself and my ideas better.

A special thank you to the folks at iStockphoto.com for letting me use their stock images in the examples in this book.

Thank you, Bruce Tate, for single-handedly changing my career.

Thank you to Lillian Hillis, Erich Tesky, and Marian Ritland at the University of Wisconsin-Eau Claire, for their friendship, support, questions, and answers. Special thanks goes to Marian for fostering an environment where we can all learn, grow, and be challenged.

Thanks to Bobby Pitts for teaching me how to really use design tools. When I reach for the Pen tool, I remember the classes.

Thank you Chris Warren, Kevin Gisi, Gary Crabtree, Carl Hoover, Josh Anderson, and Adam Ludwig for allowing me the opportunity to mentor you and help you grow. Your successes always make me proud.

Thank you, Dad and Claudia, for your advice and support, and thank you, Mom, for making me who I am. I'm sorry you missed this book.

Finally, there's no way I could have done this without the love and support of my wonderful wife, Carissa, and my daughters, Ana and Lisa. I am blessed to have such a wonderful family cheering me on even when it meant a weekend of writing instead of a weekend of family time. Thank you all for being so wonderful and supportive. I do it all for you.

Part I

The Basics of Design

## Chapter 2

The Basics of Site (Re)design: Redesigning Foodbox

Foodbox, our example site, is an online community where users can post recipes and share them with the world. It's intended to be one of those trendy social-networking sites where users can tag recipes, leave comments, and build their own cookbooks.

The site has financial backing and a talented group of application developers. Steve, your fellow developer, has just finished presenting the demo to the stakeholders. He tosses a notepad on your desk filled with bullet points from the meeting.

"They hate the home page," Steve says. "They hate the banner. They hate the colors. They think it's too bland, and they want to see the things on this list addressed before they'll even look at the rest of the site."

2.1 The Existing Site

Begin by looking at the current web page (see Figure 2.1, on page 11). Next, read the list of suggestions from your stakeholders:

- "Can we get some nicer-looking buttons, maybe something shiny or glossy?"

- "Let's make our logo look like it's reflecting on something, you know, like those other Web 2.0 sites do."

Joe Asks...

How Do I Look at This Foodbox Site?

Take a look at http://www.yourfoodbox.com. You'll notice we're aiming for a simple, straightforward design that is perfect for demonstrating the techniques in this book. This design might not please every reader, but it's simple enough for a beginner to implement.

It's also important to realize that in the world of design, one person's masterpiece is another person's terrible design. Your challenge is to take what's in this book and put your own spin on it. Pick your own fonts, colors, and design, using this book as a guide.

Finally, you should reserve your domain names as soon as you think of them. You'll notice that our Foodbox site has the http://www.yourfoodbox.com URL and that http://www.foodbox.com is a different site. A domain name is cheap if you're the initial buyer, but it can be expensive if you have to buy it from someone who already owns it! In our case, someone else already owns the http://www.foodbox.com site.

- "We need some colors that will attract people. We don't want the site to be bland."

- "I want to see the forms look nicer. Everything looks too much like an application."

- "I'm not really sure what I'm looking for, but I want it to look more...*fun*."

- "We need pictures of food throughout the site—that will make people hungry."

- "I really like what Amazon does—can't you just do that? Except lose the tabbed navigation, use more colors, and maybe not have so much clutter. That should be easy, right?"

This list has a lot of strange requests from the people who sign the checks. Your job is to come up with something that will make them happy.

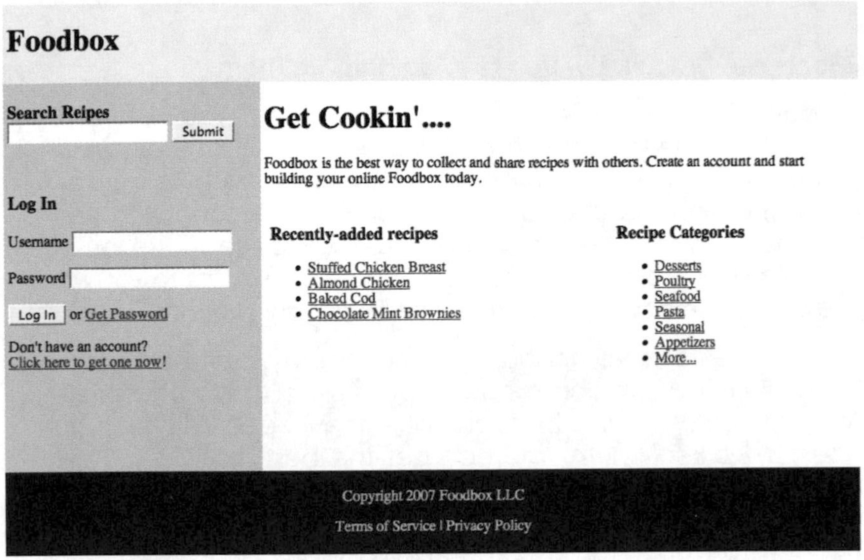

Figure 2.1: OUR STAKEHOLDERS DEEMED THIS DESIGN TOO BORING. WE'LL IMPROVE ON THIS DESIGN OVER THE COURSE OF THIS BOOK.

Where do you start? First, try to understand what your clients think they want from the site you are designing. The feedback you got is a good starting point, but often a list like this means you did not do enough discovery the first time around. Gathering requirements is as important to design as it is to development. You need to use your experience as a developer to get the answers you need to solve your customers' problems.

Second, make sure you understand the real purpose of the site and that you have a feel for the intended audience. Different audiences will have different expectations and interact with sites differently. So, find out who your client's target audience is, and then research the competition to learn its strengths and weaknesses. This research will help you ask your clients all-important questions such as, "Have you thought about this?"

Finally, once you get a list of requirements together, start sketching while you process all this information. Yes, I said sketch, as in pen and paper. We'll get into why in a bit, but first let's talk about how to extract the information we need from the clients.

> ### Clients Are Difficult, but Don't Be Too Hard on Them
>
> It's can be tough to deal with the odd requests you get from your clients. The thing you have to remember is that they hired you for your expertise. It's your job to figure out what they truly want. They don't know how to tell you what's wrong with the site, so they do the best they can. You have to use your experience to listen beyond what they are able to express to you so you can understand what's really bothering them.
>
> Many developers say that clients don't know what they want. I'd say that they just don't know how to tell you, and what they want becomes clear to them only after they see something that doesn't work for them. You can get the best results by constantly communicating and showing things to your clients so that they can tell you whether or not you're on the right track. This constant communication works as well in design as it does when building an application.

2.2 Gathering Requirements

If you were to redesign an existing application, you'd need to know exactly what it is that the app is supposed to do. You'd interview the stakeholders and users. You'd also dig into the source code and play around with the current system. You might also investigate what the competition is doing. You need to follow the same process that you use when redesigning a website.

Start by gathering requirements, as you would for any other project. In this case, you can look back at the list of notes that Steve has dumped on your desk from Section 2.1, *The Existing Site*, on page 9. You should start to see some basic requirements for your design.

You can see that you'll need to learn how to make buttons and other graphics. You will use some of the buttons as links; you might need to use others to replace form buttons.

You want to be careful not to follow all the latest fads, but you also want to balance that against the desires of your clients. Reflective text and images are popular, and your client wants them. You need to learn how to reflect things, something we can do easily in Photoshop. You'll also need to draw a digital copy of the logo for the site, which will give you a chance to learn how to create scalable vector graphics.

The color requirements mean that you'll need to learn some basic color theory and learn how to select appropriate colors. Also, you can soften the look of a website or web application by using images, color, and some CSS tricks. This will address the concerns the client has with the look of the forms.

This is a food site, so you'll need to get your hands on pictures of food. Competing recipe websites are adorned with imagery that makes people hungry. When you do manage to find some pictures, you might have to modify them to work with your site. This will involve doing some photo retouching, lightening, darkening, and resampling.

Some requests might not seem clear or reasonable. Don't feel overwhelmed when clients say they want the site to look more *fun*. Having heard this one myself many times, I can say only that you'll accomplish this one by brute force, trial and error, and a little luck. If you accomplish the rest of these requirements, then you'll be in good shape.

Even worse is when the client asks you to create something exactly like an established site, except different. At least that request conveys useful information; look back to Steve's list, and you'll see that the last stakeholder in his list basically leaves you sitting there without a clue about how to respond. So don't. It might seem like a bad idea at first, but a comment like this is one that you should quietly ignore. Follow good design principles and solicit constant feedback from your clients, and these kinds of requests should work themselves out.

2.3 Know Your Purpose

As you design this site, keep your focus on serving your target audience. One useful approach is to get the clients to list a few websites they would like you to use as a reference. You don't want to use these as a model, but knowing about them can help you gauge what elements your clients like. Usually, clients will look at what their direct competition is doing, but others will try to design their site based on sites in an unrelated field. It's common for people to say things like, "Do it just like eBay does it." Your clients want these features because they are familiar to them.

As you work on the design for Foodbox, be sure you make the site for your client and her users, not for yourself so that you can show off to your colleagues. Don't throw in some flashy new technique you just learned so that you can impress your co-workers. The client and her users come first.

Keep Your Focus on Your Audience

I had a client a few years ago who hired me to redesign a site of about 100 pages. He wanted something that would help him sell his services more effectively. The original site was something a family friend had developed for him, and it consisted of a few stolen images from other sites, a couple of animated icons, neon colors on a black background, and a bit of JavaScript that placed the company's phone number on the end of the mouse cursor, so it waved around as you moved the mouse.

This client ran a respectable business, but he had a website that did nothing to project that image. When I presented my first design, it was immediately rejected because it wasn't *fun* enough. The client kept asking me to look at a few radio-station sites that he liked, and I had to explain to him that he was in a completely different market. After many hours of negotiating, gentle prodding, and careful compromise, we ended up with a great site that kicked his company into high gear. Within a couple of years, his sales multiplied several times, and he continues to thank me for steering him in the right direction.

The point here is to remember that, above all else, you need to design your sites with the intended audience and the goals of the site firmly in mind. You'll probably need to give in on a few things, but the end result will be a better site.

Make sure everyone understands the site's purpose. Is the site meant to present information, encourage consumers to purchase products, entertain users, or collect data? For example, you would design and present a website for an upcoming summer blockbuster differently than you would for an online retailer.

You'll also need to learn as much as you can about the site's audience. You will need to ask all sorts of questions. Will these be casual visitors who will occasionally use the site, or will they be experts in the field who will use this site on a daily basis to get their work done? Knowing your audience will help you plan the scope of your design. For example, you would design a site for younger children much differently than you would a site for real-estate agents.

Figure 2.2: OUR FIRST SKETCH: A SITE WITH FEW GRAPHICS OTHER THAN THE LOGO

2.4 Where to Go from Here

You've gathered the requirements, and you have a good understanding of the site that you're trying to build. Now it's time to come up with an implementation plan. If you break the requirements into logical steps, they might look like this:

1. Sketch some basic designs and get one approved.

2. Select colors.

3. Select fonts.

4. Implement the basic design in Photoshop.

5. Create images for the banner, buttons, and other elements.

6. Create an HTML and CSS template.

7. Test your designs for compatibility and accessibility.

The rest of this book will walk you through this process, teaching you various techniques and the theory behind them along the way.

Joe Asks. . .

Why Can't I Just Start with Photoshop or Building HTML Mock-Ups?

Pencil and paper are important to the creative process, and you can draw much more quickly with these tools than you can with a computer. Also, it's easier for you to throw away early designs because you have so little invested in them.

If you've been a programmer for a while, you probably have access to a whiteboard, and I'd be willing to bet that you draw simple diagrams on that to communicate with the rest of your team. Apply this same approach to your meetings with your clients. A nontechnical client might be put off if you pull out your laptop and start typing and clicking away on a design, but pencil and paper can be a great interpersonal communication tool. Sketch your ideas in front of your client, and then hand your client the pencil to see what ideas he has for the site.

The point of this is to facilitate communication with your team and your clients. Your initial designs might end up looking nothing like your final product, but any designer will tell you that's normal. You could spend hours on digital versions, or you could spend minutes with a pencil and some paper.

The pencil and paper are part of your design team; use them to help get the ideas flowing.

2.5 Sketching Your Ideas

You should draw your designs on paper to capture your ideas quickly. Doing so makes it easy to share your ideas with others or to make adjustments to them. You can even get your client to help.

Now go grab a piece of paper and a pencil. I'll wait.

Ready? Good.

To sketch a design, you need to know what the site's layout should contain. What links need to be present from the home page? What elements should the home page contain? You can see the current home page in Figure 2.1, on page 11; it contains the following items:

- The site name
- A search field

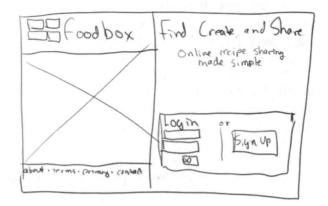

Figure 2.3: A SKETCH OF A MORE GRAPHICAL VERSION. THIS EXAMPLE MODIFIES THE FIRST BY PROVIDING A SPACE FOR A LARGE, ATTRACTIVE IMAGE ON THE LEFT.

- A login form
- A brief introductory paragraph about what the site does
- A list of the most recently submitted recipes
- A list of categories

In addition to these elements, the home page also contains links to various informational pages, including the following:

- Terms and conditions
- Sign-up text
- The privacy policy
- Contact information

Let's throw together a few sketches.

Layout Conventions

You've probably noticed that websites tend to have many things in common. Most have a header region that displays the site's name or logo. Many sites also have their main content region divided into columns, and at least one of those columns is often used as a sidebar region that might contain navigation elements or additional information. It's also likely that the site has a navigation bar either across the top of the page or along the left side. Finally, you can usually find a footer region that contains copyright information and maybe some additional links.

The most obvious reason for this similarity between sites is that designers and developers imitate what works. It's no coincidence that many news sites look the same. In fact, most newspapers follow the same layout.

Over time, users have come to expect these similarities. To design a functional website, you have to make sure that your users can find what they want immediately, without having to hunt around or dig too deeply. Your site should be easy to navigate, and following conventions goes a long way toward achieving that goal. You start confusing users when you do things unconventionally.

Before you start sketching your designs, browse the Web for ideas. Look at sites that are in the same market as your intended site. Look at some examples in unrelated fields to see whether your competition is missing something you could use to your advantage. Most of all, work toward developing a layout that conveys information but is immediately familiar to your audience.

Three Sketches

Come up with at least three designs for your clients on every project. Provide a simple, conservative design; a complex design; and a design that aims for the middle, something mostly conservative that also has some splashes of flair.

Don't worry if you're not a great artist. A sketch of a site layout doesn't have to be pretty. The main purpose is to get your ideas on paper so you can share them easily with other people.

Let's walk through three sketches I whipped up based on the requirements we have so far. The first sketch features a minimalist design, and it isn't meant to look pretty (see Figure 2.2, on page 15). This page doesn't have much functionality other than the sign-up button and the login box. It's a text-heavy version of the site that will most likely rely on color, gradients, and shading to draw attention to the various sections. An advantage to this design is that more text content can help

Figure 2.4: OUR THIRD SKETCH: A MUCH MORE FUNCTIONAL VERSION OF THE SITE. IT USES ELEMENTS FROM THE CURRENT HOME PAGE AND ADDS SOME NEW CONCEPTS.

with your search engine rankings. Of course, it can also be boring to look at.

The second sketch shows a more graphical design, with a large space for a photograph on the left and the login and sign-up boxes on the right (see Figure 2.3, on page 17). This page should be a bit more attractive than the first design, but it won't have as much information to tell the users why they should proceed any further than the home page.

The final sketch shows a more functional design that incorporates elements of the current home page but turns the original site's categories list into a tag cloud (see Figure 2.4). This design keeps the search box and the rest of the links but leaves the login and sign-up boxes off the home page, replacing the boxes with buttons. It's similar to the original design, but it incorporates some graphical elements, and it leaves space for us to explain to users what we're about and why they should use what we offer.

> ### Getting Your Clients to Help
>
> When your clients comes to you asking for a new site design, get them to do some of the legwork for you. Ask them to identify a few websites they like. Get them to tell you what they like about them. You want to hear things such as, "I like the colors that Blinksale* uses." Or, "Amazon's tabbed navigation bar works well for me." You won't rip off these ideas, but you will to get a feel for what your clients want. You can then use this feedback, along with your judgment and experience, to come up with something that works well.
>
> ---
> *. http://blinksale.com

When presenting designs, I like to show a design that's conservative, another that's pretty artistic, and a third that contains elements of both the simple and complex designs. Generally, the client tends to pick the design that falls in the middle but then mixes in a few elements from the other two designs, resulting in a bit of a hybrid. When you show up with design sketches or mock-ups, you're not presenting the final version of the site; instead, you're presenting ideas to get the discussion going. Don't be disappointed if the client wants to change your design around. You have to remember that it's the client's site, not yours.

You should almost never come to the table with only one design. Clients like to make choices and feel involved. A few clients want you to tell them what to do, but you need to *let them tell you that*. You don't want to make that assumption yourself because that borders on arrogance, and it can hurt your relationship with your clients.

Your sketches are done; it's time to share them with the stakeholders.

2.6 Sketch Selection

Steve came back from his meeting with the stakeholders with a big grin on his face, holding up one of the sketches. It turns out that they have selected the third sketch (see Figure 2.4, on the preceding page); however, they would like to see it mocked up as a color image as soon as possible.

> **It's an Iterative Process**
>
> I once heard a great presentation from Robert Martin about how writing software was like writing a book. You'll do a first draft and then a few revisions, refactoring until you get it just right, and that's your final draft. Design is kind of like that, except that after you go through all those stages, your client will see it and tell you that he hates it. You'll make concessions in your design. You'll change the colors to something you don't like because that's what the client wants. One thing that frustrates designers is having their creative vision destroyed by client requirements. As a developer, you're already all too familiar with how requirements drive projects. Think of the design phase as another set of requirements for your app, and keep refining, rewriting, and refactoring.

2.7 Summary

The redesign process boils down to communication with your clients. Some clients know what they want, but most need you to guide them through it. Follow conventions, ask the right questions, and listen. You'll end up with a successful redesign plan.

The stakeholders want to see a color mock-up. To do that, you need to learn about picking colors and choosing fonts so you can build a nice-looking digital mock-up for the next meeting.

Chapter 3

Choosing Colors

We have our sketch in hand and our marching orders to mock up a design; the next step is to pick out some colors and build a color scheme.

Colors can make or break your application depending on how you use them and blend them together. They evoke emotions and draw attention to important details. This is one of the most important chapters in this book because it helps you build the foundation of a great-looking site.

Great designers seem to have an eye for color. Their experience and intuition often guide them when it comes to creating a color scheme for a website. Certain color schemes, or combinations of colors, are based on tried-and-true strategies similar to the design patterns that developers use. If you know how colors relate to each other, you can pick colors that go together just as easily as you can pick the right design pattern for a web-based application.

3.1 The Basics of Color

In our everyday, three-dimensional world, objects absorb some wavelengths of light and reflect others, and our eyes perceive the reflected light from objects as color. A color is described by its name, its level of saturation, and its brightness.

You have a lot of things to think about when working with colors. You have to think about the shade of the color, the amount of color, and how the color looks alongside other colors. You also need to think about how the color might be interpreted by your audience. In this section, you'll learn how this all works together.

Hue, Saturation, and Brightness

When people talk about an object's color, they're referring to the *hue*. You've been trained to use hue all the time, whether you're shopping for bananas (the green ones aren't ripe yet!) or trying to beat that yellow traffic light.

Saturation is the amount of color in the image. A saturated color is vibrant, whereas a desaturated color looks dull and gray. If you reduce the saturation, you make the colors look more *washed out*. In some cases, this is a good thing because it takes the edge off some otherwise harsh or shocking colors.

Altering the *brightness* of a color can make the overall appearance of the colors darker or lighter. As you add cream to your coffee, you alter the brightness of the brown coffee, making it change from dark brown to light brown.

Changing the brightness and saturation lets you alter the color's appearance (see Figure 3.1, on the next page, for some examples).

Additive and Subtractive Color Mixing

Colors you see on your screen might not be the same as those that you print. There is a fundamental difference between the way color works on paper or in nature, where the light is reflected, and the way color works on a screen, where it is projected. On your screen, the color mixing is *additive*; in print, it is *subtractive*. You can see this difference best by comparing colors in paints and colors on a computer screen.

When you're working with paints, crayons, and markers, you deal with the primary colors of yellow, blue, and red. You start with all the colors of light mixed together (white) and filter out what you don't want to get the color you're looking for. When you color with a red crayon, you're actually causing all the other colors to be absorbed or subtracted, except for red, which is reflected back to your eyes.

You see the subtractive method in action when you mix paints. You know that if you mix yellow and blue, you get green. If you mix blue and red, you get purple. If you mix all the colors together, you get black because the object absorbs the entire visible spectrum; you no longer have any light left to hit your eyes. A banana doesn't actually have any color. It doesn't have any light energy to produce color. Instead, a banana appears to be yellow because it reflects all the light waves that cause us to see yellow, while absorbing all the other waves.

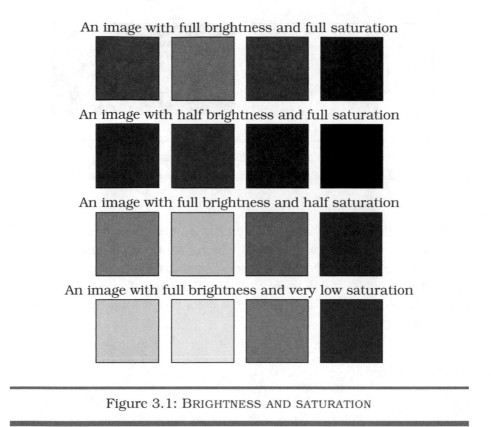

Figure 3.1: BRIGHTNESS AND SATURATION

Computer screens display colors using the additive color system. The primary colors you've grown up with are replaced by red, green, and blue. These colors are mixed together and projected, creating the light. Unlike the banana, the image on a computer screen is generating light waves rather than reflecting them. You start with nothing (the black of your monitor) and start adding colors. When you mix red, green, and blue together, you end up with white. When you don't mix any colors together, you get black. This process is additive color mixing. Your eyes are absorbing the colors coming from the screen. Here, you get yellow by mixing green and red.[1]

So, what does all this have to do with web design? It's important for you to know that there are different color modes out there. When you

---

1. The terms *additive* and *subtractive* can sometimes confuse people. In this setting, I'm talking about color reflection—pigment-based subtractive color mixing. When I mix yellow and blue to make green, I am adding the colors. But this process is not called *additive* because I'm subtracting a different set of wavelengths.

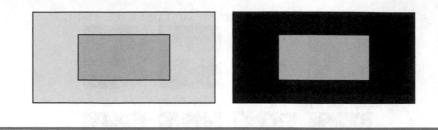

Figure 3.2: WHICH BLUE BOX IS DARKER?

work with color on the computer, you have a choice between RGB, the additive color method; and CMYK, which stands for Cyan, Magenta, Yellow, and Key (usually black), the subtractive method. You usually want RGB if you're working on the Web. However, if you plan to print something, you want to use CMYK, the color mode used by many four-color printing systems.

3.2 Color Context

Look closely at the images in Figure 3.2. The blue rectangle on the left probably appears to be darker, even though both rectangles are exactly the same color. This trick your eyes played on you is called *color context*, and it can be extremely frustrating.

I was working for a client on an update for his company's home page. The client wanted to put some red lettering over a light blue background in the banner, and he wanted to make sure I used the same red that we used throughout the rest of the site.

As a developer, you can see the problem. The customer was suggesting the implementation. The client wanted the red to *look* like the red used throughout the site. It was up to me to know that to achieve that goal we needed to use a brighter red.

When I used the same red—just as the client had specified—he didn't like the result. The red didn't look right. When I changed the red color to something a little brighter, it *appeared* to be the same color as the rest of the reds in the site, and the client was happy.

The context of a color can greatly influence how it appears in your application. Even if you technically pick the correct colors, you might have to make additional adjustments to make them *look* right.

Adjacent colors with fewer steps make the transition more obvious.

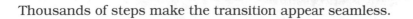

If we increase the number of steps, our brain starts to blend the colors.

Thousands of steps make the transition appear seamless.

Figure 3.3: EXAMPLES OF COLOR FLUTING

This effect is caused by *fluting*, which is the technical term for the way your eyes blend adjacent colors together. You can use color fluting to your advantage (see Figure 3.3). As the example illustrates, fluting is what makes gradients possible. If you don't do the transitions gradually enough, you get the banding effect. However, if you do the transitions with lots of slight variations, your eyes ignore them and blend everything together.

3.3 Evoking Emotion with Color

We are taught from birth to associate colors with emotions, moods, or feelings. When choosing colors for your application, it's important to think about the various responses your choices might trigger. Using red or blue improperly could trigger an undesired response or could even create confusion.

Your choice of color influences your users' perspectives, and simply applying a different color scheme to a website completely changes the user experience.

Warm Colors

As the name suggests, warm colors make you think of warmth, sunlight, and heat. Some people believe that you feel warmer if you look at these colors.

Red

Red is a strong color that can stand for love, joy, happiness, and romance. It can also represent lust, anger, war, an emergency, or danger. Its use in applications is almost always to show a warning or an error message. Red attracts a user's eyes immediately.

Yellow

It's hard for a user to focus on yellow, but the color can evoke feelings of intelligence and happiness when used correctly. Many applications use some sort of *yellow fade effect* to let you know that the action you just took was successful.

Orange

Orange can be cheerful like yellow, but it can also be arrogant and superior, depending on the amount of red. Some experts claim that the red contained within orange can stimulate the brain.

Cool Colors

Cool colors have a cooling or calming effect on people. They're comforting, and you can use them to tone down a site. Cool colors include blue, green, and purple.

Blue

Blue can be calming, soothing, and cool. It has a tendency to make users relax when it's desaturated. However, as the shades of blue get darker, they can cause feelings of sadness and depression.

Green

People tend to associate green with nature, hope, health, and responsiveness. However, if used incorrectly, green can also trigger feelings of envy (most likely because of the expression "green with envy"). In addition to envy, green can evoke feelings of greed, guilt, and disorder. Certain shades of green allow the eyes to rest, which can have a soothing effect on your users. The wrong mixture of colors can make your users feel sick or disgusted.

Black and White: The "Noncolors"

Black and white are not technically colors. When you're talking about images on a computer screen, black is the absence of color, while white is a mixture of all color in the spectrum. Remember from the discussion of additive vs. subtractive color mixing that the inverse is true when you're working with paints, so be careful!

Though not technically colors, black and white still evoke emotion and should be considered as colors when building a color scheme.

Purple

Purple is one of those odd colors that doesn't appear in nature very often. You might see it on the petals of flowers, but you see it mostly in things that people create. Purple is often associated with royalty and mysticism, mainly because it was extremely difficult to produce in ancient times. Purple is a mixture of red and blue, which means you get some of the attributes of each color. Light purple is often associated with nature, peace, tranquility, and spirituality. Dark purple can evoke feelings of depression. Large amounts of purple can be difficult on the eyes.

Neutral Colors

Black, white, silver, gray, beige, and brown are unifying colors. They help bridge the gap between cool and warm colors. When used as background colors, they help other colors stand out.

Black

Black can represent prestige and elegance, and it can be really powerful if used in the right context. However, black is also associated with mourning, death, despair, and brooding. When you use black in a design, you must make sure you target your audience carefully.

White

White evokes feelings of purity and perfection. It's a perfect color for a clean website. Too much white can be boring and sterile, but it makes every other color stand out that much more.

Brown

Brown can stimulate hunger, health, and simplicity. On the flip side, some people perceive brown to be a dirty color, and it can evoke feelings of uncleanliness, which is definitely not something you want for your site.

Beige

Beige makes people relax. It is a conservative color that borrows from brown and white. It's a great choice for a background because it can be calming, and it will allow other colors to stand out well.

Gray

This color seldom evokes an emotion, but when it does, it's usually associated with feelings of gloom, mourning, and moodiness, much like a cloudy day. It leans toward the cool side of the color spectrum.

Gray is a funny color; if you make it dark, you get to borrow some of the elegance of black. If you make it light, you get to borrow some of white's traits.

Colors and Your Users

Remember that a person's personal biases will have some effect on how your color choices affect his or her emotions. This bias might be because of an association created by an experience or memory, but more often, it's cultural.

For example, although we might find that red is a lustful, angry, or passionate color, it's a color of good luck and celebration in China. In parts of India, red can mean triumph or success. Red can also symbolize socialism and communism; in South Africa, it's the color of mourning. Black is a color of mourning in the Western world, but the Chinese use black to symbolize high quality.

Brandcurve has an excellent article[2] outlining color meanings in different cultures. If your site is going to be used by an international audience, then don't forget to localize your colors, just as you localize your text.

---

2. http://www.brandcurve.com/color-meanings-around-the-world/

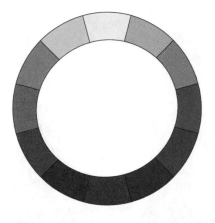

Figure 3.4: In the mixing color wheel, the primary colors are red, yellow, and blue. This is often referred to as the *RYB color wheel*.

3.4 Color Schemes

Some colors just don't look good next to each other, and some do. Color schemes are groups of colors that work together to create a visually appealing result. Let's take a brief tour of the different types of color schemes and how we can apply them.

You need to understand a little bit about color theory before you pick a color scheme, and the best way to do that is by taking a look at the *color wheel*. A color wheel helps show relationships between various colors. I've drawn a simple RYB wheel, or *mixing color wheel*, that uses red, yellow, and blue as the primary colors (see Figure 3.4). I'll use the mixing wheel throughout this chapter to show examples of various color schemes.

Monochromatic Scheme

The monochromatic scheme is made up of just one hue (see Figure 3.5, on the next page). You create the scheme by altering the brightness and saturation of the hue and adding that variation to the scheme.

This scheme adds form and depth to a design. When you use it in your site, your other elements, such as photographs or icons, really stand out. This scheme is ridiculously easy to create, but it works best for sites where the content is the most important element.

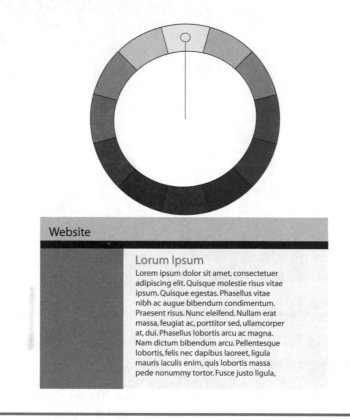

Figure 3.5: MONOCHROMATIC COLOR SCHEME

Analogous Scheme

The two colors on either side of a color on the color wheel are referred to as *analogous* colors. Take all three colors—the base color and its two neighbors—and use them to build a scheme (see Figure 3.6, on the facing page). The scheme is subdued, but the adjacent colors accent the scheme a bit.

This color scheme involves picking colors that appear directly adjacent to each other on the color wheel. One color dominates this scheme, and other, similar colors are used for impact.

This scheme is as easy to create as the monochromatic scheme, but you get richer results because you use different colors instead of just different shades of the same color. These additional colors can help accent the main color, drawing your users' eyes toward important content.

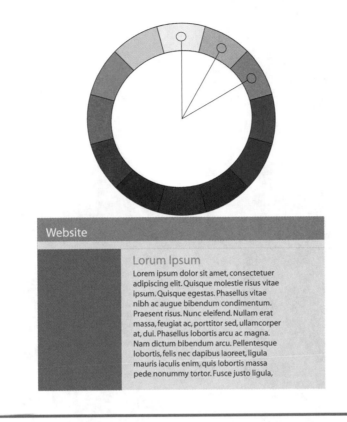

Figure 3.6: ANALOGOUS COLOR SCHEME

One major problem you might run into is that this scheme lacks any real color contrast, so you don't get as much contrast as you would with a complementary scheme. It does tend to be the best-looking scheme for beginners, though, because it's not hard to create, and it gives you a nice, safe range of colors to choose from that won't clash.

Complementary Scheme

A complementary color scheme uses two colors that appear on opposite sides of the color wheel as the base colors. These colors are said to *complement* each other directly. Purple and yellow are great colors for this scheme, as are red and green. You can see an example of a complementary scheme in Figure 3.7, on the next page.

Complementary color schemes are often difficult to balance because the colors can be extremely bright, and you need to do a lot of tweaking to tone things down. Some combinations, such as orange and indigo, can

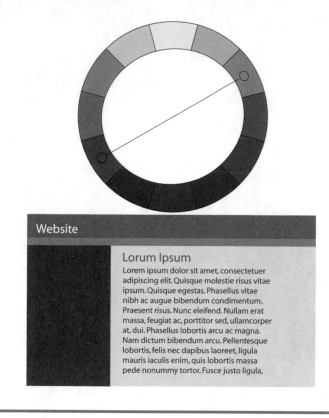

Figure 3.7: COMPLEMENTARY COLOR SCHEME

be extremely difficult to balance. When used improperly, those colors can be very shocking and intense; however, you can get a nice effect if you desaturate the cool colors and saturate the warm ones. One of the best ways to make the most of this scheme is to use your base color as the main color and use its complement as an accent color.

Be careful when placing your text. Using a color for your text and its complement for your background can make things difficult to read if you don't make the proper saturation adjustments.

Split-Complementary Scheme

The split-complementary color scheme is interesting because it's a little more difficult to use, but like the complementary scheme, it can be quite attractive if you make the proper adjustments to saturation and brightness. I encourage you to experiment with this scheme the most

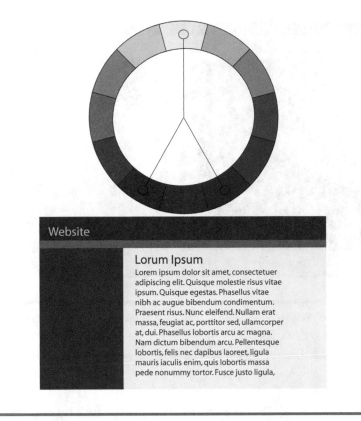

Figure 3.8: SPLIT-COMPLEMENTARY COLOR SCHEME

because it's not used very often, which means it can give you a chance to make certain features of a design stand out.

This scheme involves picking a color on the color wheel and then picking the two colors adjacent to the first color's complementary color, rather than its direct complement.

This approach allows for strong contrast while adding some different color variations. You'll end up with a scheme that is less extreme or shocking than a complementary scheme.

Be especially careful not to use a lot of dull colors because that will subtract from the overall effect.

You should try working with all these color schemes to get a feel for how they work. I tend to use monochromatic in a lot of my design work because I like how much photographs pop out. You might discover you

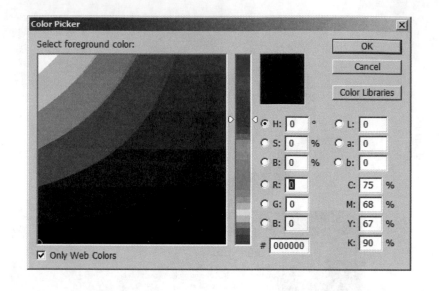

Figure 3.9: PHOTOSHOP'S COLOR PICKER PROVIDES AN OPTION TO SHOW ONLY WEB-SAFE COLORS.

favor a different one. The important thing is to understand the advantages and disadvantages of each scheme.

3.5 The Web-Safe Color Palette

The web-safe color palette consists of only 216 colors that are supposed to look exactly the same across all operating systems. It was designed at a time when video cards were limited. Designers working on a Mac wanted to be sure that PC users could see the images as the designers intended. Unfortunately, this color palette was quite bland and extremely limiting. It consisted of six shades of blue, six shades of green, and six shades of red mixed together in various amounts.

Designers are abandoning the web-safe palette now that the majority of users have computer displays that can render millions of colors. You still might see slight variations from machine to machine, but these variations are minor in most cases.

A few experienced web designers, as well as some organizations, still insist on working in this palette, and many graphics packages provide options that will help you stay within the web-safe palette. You can

The Three-Color Rule

My grandfather sold men's clothing for many years. When I was little, I remember him talking about the *three-color rule*. His idea was that a man should dress using three colors: the first two colors should complement each other, and the third color should be completely different. For example, a man might wear a white shirt, black pants, and a tie with some black, a little white, and maybe some yellow to liven things up.

When I'm working on a website, I always come back to that rule. I'll pick a background color and a foreground color, but then I'll find another color that I can use as an accent, something that really pops. For example, you could choose blue and gray for your main colors, and then use yellow as your accent color. Throughout the site, you could use varying shades of blue and gray to define objects and make them stand out.

Note that I'm not advocating that you stick to exactly three colors in your application.

see the Color Picker from Photoshop in Figure 3.9, on the facing page (notice the Only Web Colors checkbox in the bottom-left corner). If you decide (or are forced) to use a color that's not web safe, you need to be aware that it might not look the same everywhere.

3.6 Building Color Schemes

Now that you have some background on how colors work, you can start thinking about various color choices for Foodbox. You already know how to use the color wheel to find color combinations, but I'm going to show you a couple of techniques I use when picking out colors.

As we did in the site designs, we want to come to the table with several color options for our stakeholders to review. We'll use two different methods to select colors: the *technical method* and the *natural method.*

Selecting Colors Using the Technical Method

The technical method uses color theory to build a color scheme. You pick a base color and then combine it with one of the color schemes we discussed in Section 3.4, *Color Schemes*, on page 31, to get additional

---

HTML Color Codes

HTML color codes are hexadecimal triplets. The first number represents red, the second represents green, and the third represents blue.

For example, #FF0000 will be red because all the bits are on for the first number and off for the other two numbers. Each grouping contains a value from 0 to 255, so red would be FF (full red), 00 (no green), and 00 (no blue).

---

colors that work well with the base color. You then adjust brightness, saturation, and contrast to create the right mix of colors. That might sound hard, but it's much simpler than you'd think thanks to the existence of some great software tools.

We're using color theory to build our color palette when we use this method. We're not relying on intuition as much as algorithms and rules. This is a good method to start with if you don't think you're artistically inclined. It's also the method I use when I don't have any photos for inspiration and I just need a quick color scheme.

When we write programs, we tend to use things like IDEs to make our jobs as programmers much easier. You could write code by hand using Notepad, but that's just crazy when you're working on large projects. Along the same lines, you could get out a color wheel and develop a scheme manually, or you could use some color tools to help you define a scheme.

You can find a lot of tools on the Web that will help you build color schemes, but in my opinion none of them even comes close to ColorSchemeDesigner.com.[3] It provides an interface for you to build a scheme quickly and save the output to various formats, including a Photoshop color palette. Pull that site up in your browser now.

Choosing a Color Wheel

Take a look at Figure 3.10, on page 40, which shows the traditional RYB color wheel on the left and the additive, or RGB color wheel, on

---

3. http://www.colorschemedesigner.com/

Macs and Color

PC monitors tend to default to a 2.2 gamma, while Mac monitors have traditionally used a gamma of 1.8. This difference in gamma can cause colors to look more washed out on a Mac. However, beginning with Snow Leopard, Mac monitors are set to use the same default gamma setting as a PC monitor. If you are using an earlier release of Mac OS X, you should consider altering your gamma settings to the 2.2 default using the Display properties in System Preferences.

Even with this change, you should definitely test your colors on both types of systems to make sure that your colors aren't too washed out or too saturated.

---

the right. When designing a scheme, you need to choose which wheel you want to use. Can you see the difference?

The complementary colors on these wheels are *different*! If you developed a complementary scheme using the RYB wheel with a base color of yellow, the complement would be purple. If you used the RGB wheel, yellow's complement would be blue. This difference can be a big source of frustration to developers and designers, especially if they fail to realize the difference between the two wheels or, worse, use them interchangeably.

Designers argue quite a bit about which one you should use when developing your own color scheme. Some believe that the color schemes created with the RYB wheel are more pleasing to the eye because this is the color wheel used by painters and traditional designers, so it's more familiar. Others believe that you should use the RGB wheel to display web pages because the colors on this wheel display more accurately on a computer screen.

So, which wheel do you use? The simple answer is that it doesn't matter too much for web design if you choose your colors using a color wheel that's on your screen. The schemes you saw earlier in this chapter were all developed using the RYB color wheel, but you'd still get great results using the RGB wheel. Even web-based color tools differ on which color wheel to use. The color picker from ColorSchemeDesigner.com, which we'll use to create our site, uses the RYB color wheel; Adobe Kuler uses

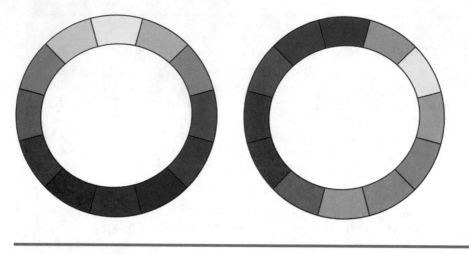

Figure 3.10: RYB AND RGB COLOR WHEELS

the RGB wheel. Feel free to experiment, but when you pick one, use it consistently across the site!

Building a Scheme

If you're new to building color schemes, you might wonder what color you should use as your starting point. You can begin by using the associations you learned about in Section 3.3, *Evoking Emotion with Color*, on page 27. When you think about food, consider what colors naturally come to mind: oranges, greens, reds, and yellows. Let's start by using a variant of yellow for the base color.

You can control the base color for the scheme by selecting a point on the color wheel on the left side of the interface. As you select a color, you'll notice that the color squares on the right side change, giving you a rough idea of how colors within the scheme work together.

If you already know the hex code of the color you want to use, you can set it manually by clicking the RGB color code on the lower-right corner of the wheel and entering the code into the dialog box that appears. This is useful if you've selected a base color from another source, such as a photograph or a web page, and you want to build a scheme quickly from that.[4] We'll use a base color of #FFE500 for this scheme, which is

---

4. There's a little bit of color conversion that happens here because you can't convert RGB color codes to RYB colors with absolute accuracy; however, these "RYB" colors are rendered on the screen and not on paper, so you'll hardly notice the color conversion.

an orange-yellow color. Feel free to build your own scheme or to follow along with my colors by entering that hex code into the wheel.

Green, yellow, and orange are adjacent to each other on the color wheel. As you learned earlier, you can use the analogous color scheme to build a theme around adjacent colors. One of the nicer benefits of using the analogous color scheme is that it helps you build a scheme that adheres to the aforementioned three-color rule. Change the scheme from Mono to Analogic, which gives a color scheme composed of various shades of yellow, orange, and green.

The adjacent colors are, by default, 30 degrees away from the base color on the wheel; however, you can adjust this angle by dragging one of the adjacent colors closer or farther away. The larger the angle, the more contrast you'll see between your colors. Experiment with the angles if you're having a difficult time finding just the right color to grab the attention of your users.

You should also adjust the saturation and brightness here, so you can see how it affects the entire scheme. By default, this color picker selects various levels of brightness and saturation. You can modify this by selecting the Adjust Scheme tab. Move the sliders around, or play with any of the default color options. Remember that reducing saturation washes out your colors, and reducing brightness makes them darker. Any variation of saturation or brightness for a given hue is fair game for use in your scheme from a technical standpoint.

You can see an example of this in Figure 3.11, on the following page.

You might want to adjust a color scheme a bit if something doesn't look right to you. You don't want to rely entirely on the computer to pick your colors, just as you wouldn't want to rely completely on autogenerated code in one of your applications.

Once you finish playing around with the various color options, you should save the scheme so you can refer to it later when it comes time to decide how you want to use these colors in your design.

Select the Export tab of the color picker, and choose one of the export options. I recommend selecting ACO (Photoshop Palette) so you can use these colors as swatches when you do your mock-ups.[5]

---

5. The Photoshop ACO file I used is also available for download at http://www. webdesignfordevelopers.com/colors/.

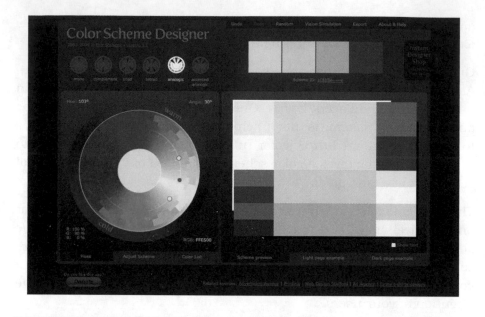

Figure 3.11: THE COLORSCHEMEDESIGNER.COM COLOR PICKER, USING
AN ANALOGOUS COLOR SCHEME

Each scheme has a URL associated with it so you can return to the
scheme later. If you want to use the colors I chose for the book's example, you can grab them from the ColorSchemeDesigner.com website.[6]
Of course, you can also just refer to Figure 3.18, on page 51.

Further Exploration with Adobe Kuler

If you want to use a color picker that relies on the RGB color wheel
to build schemes, you should give Adobe Kuler a look.[7] Using Kuler,
you can select a base color, choose a color scheme, and then have
Kuler generate a five-color palette for your site. You can then adjust
the brightness and saturation for each color in the palette. Finally, you
can save your palette for later use, or you can share it with others.

Note that you can find other tools online for building color palettes for
your site. Before proceeding to the next step, let's look at the other
approach to choosing a color scheme: the natural method.

---

6. http://colorschemedesigner.com/#1C51Tyi-----y
7. http://kuler.adobe.com

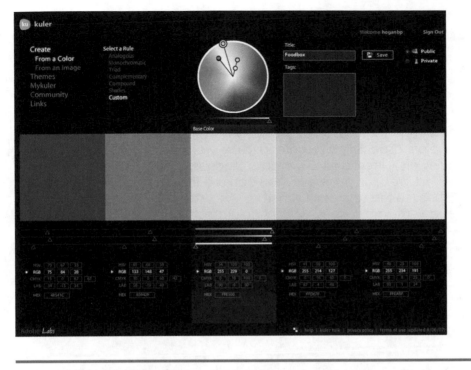

Figure 3.12: USING ADOBE KULER TO PICK COLORS

Selecting Colors Using the Natural Method

Color theory is great, but sometimes you end up with colors that look too dull or too technical. The natural method of color selection, or *matching*, is a popular alternative in which you develop a color scheme by selecting colors from various sections of some reference material, usually a photograph. You can get some great results from this method, but it relies on having the right photograph or inspiration. It also helps to be familiar with color theory so you can comfortably make adjustments to your scheme. It does take more time and planning to make it look just right because it's really easy to select bad or inappropriate colors from the source image.

The biggest strength of the natural method is that you're working with nature itself. If you're working with a photograph of food, the colors in that picture already work together. People's minds don't have a hard time interpreting the colors of nature. Green grass and blue skies go together. The next time you go outside, take a careful look at the colors that make up your front yard.

Joe Asks...

What About Color-Blind Users?

It's important to consider color-blind users when you pick your colors, especially if you intend to use your colors to capture your viewers' attention. I cover colorblindness in Section 16.2, *Color-Blind Users*, on page 235. You can use the techniques outlined there to test your color schemes. Also, the color picker we used can simulate various types of colorblindness.

Finding Colors

Grab a digital camera and go on a bit of a field trip. These places offer a great opportunity to explore how colors work together:

- Flower gardens

  Visit university campuses, public parks, and even public botanical gardens. The abundance and variety of flowers in these places give you the best way to explore nature's colors.

- The zoo

  Take some pictures of animals at the zoo. Tigers, leopards, peacocks, and other animals are often a lot more colorful than you think.

- A busy street

  Take pictures of cars, signs, and buildings. A gray city street often has a lot more color than you might notice on your walk to work.

This exercise has two goals: to force yourself to look at the world around you and to let the colors you find in nature inspire you.

Figure 3.13: COLORS SAMPLED FROM AN IMAGE. THE ORIGINAL IMAGE IS COURTESY OF MORGUEFILE (HTTP://WWW.MORGUEFILE.COM), AND IT IS USED IN ACCORDANCE WITH THAT SITE'S TERMS AND CONDITIONS.

Let's go through this method so you can see how you'd apply it in a design. I snagged an image[8] from MorgueFile.com, a great place to get some free reference photographs for your compositions.[9]

Look at the various colors you can use in this image. You can see the bright green and red of the strawberry, the darker colors of the blueberries, the light color of the crust, and even some grays you can pull from the background of the image.

You can pull colors manually, or you can cheat and use software to do it for you. You can see the colors I manually selected using the Eyedropper tool in Adobe Illustrator (see Figure 3.13). Selecting colors manually can be a frustrating process because it can be slow. First, you first need to select the region with the Eyedropper tool, and then you need to find out what color it selected by looking at the value of the color in the color selection palette. Fortunately, there's an easier way.

---

8. http://www.morguefile.com/archive/?display=111353
9. If you want to use an image from MorgueFile in your finished product, you need to look at the MorgueFile licenses. Although it doesn't explicitly say you need the photographer's permission, it's always a good idea contact the author of the photograph.

Figure 3.14: THE PICTURE I TOOK FOR THIS PROJECT

Using ColorSchemer Studio to Grab a Color Palette Easily

ColorSchemer Studio has a feature called the PhotoSchemer that will automatically build a color scheme based on a photograph you provide. A closer examination of the colors available in the picture of strawberries reveals that the picture contains too much red. It might be better to try to find something with more yellows and oranges because those colors are less harsh. This time, I went out and took my own photograph of some grapes, cheese, and carrots. The green grapes and the yellow and cream colors of the cheese might help us create a very nice color scheme for our site.

Visit this site[10] to bring up the image shown in Figure 3.14. Right-click the image, choose the Save Image As option, and then save the image to your desktop so it's easy to find.

Now you're ready to try the PhotoSchemer feature in ColorSchemer Studio:

1. Launch ColorSchemer Studio, and then click the QuickPreview button in the toolbar (or press Ctrl+P).

---

10. http://www.webdesignfordevelopers.com/files/color/grapes_cheese_carrots.jpg

2. Click the PhotoSchemer icon in the toolbar (or press $\boxed{\text{Ctrl}}$+$\boxed{\text{H}}$) to bring up the PhotoSchemer.

3. Click the Open button, and load the photo you downloaded. Photo-Schemer displays the image and shows you a color scheme made up of four colors.

4. You can drag each of the color squares to a region in the Quick-Preview window to see how it would look as a color scheme. You can also increase the number of color points on the image to as many as nine.

   You can manually adjust the selected colors as well. Move around each of the selection points that each color box points to, and the color in the color box will change.

5. Play around with the color scheme a bit until you find a combination that works well for you. Remember to use what you learned about color contrast to select the color scheme. You can see mine by looking at Figure 3.15, on the next page.

6. When you have colors that you like, click the Add to Favorites button. This adds your colors to the ColorSchemer Studio main window (see Figure 3.16, on page 49).

7. Select View > Color Wheel Mode, and make sure that you see a check mark next to the Computer Color Wheel (RGB) option. This will ensure that the appropriate color codes are created for you.

At this point, you should have all the colors and their HTML color codes on the screen. You can copy these to your clipboard, or you can use ColorSchemer Studio to help you build additional schemes based on that color. For now, save the color scheme by selecting File > Save so you can use it later.

Combining the Natural and Technical Methods

You can combine both of these methods to build a nice color scheme. Use ColorSchemer Studio to snag a color off an image, and use that color as the base color for your color scheme either in ColorSchemer Studio or in one of the online tools. It so happens that Adobe Kuler can extract colors from any image you upload; you can then tweak those colors to build a scheme. You can see this feature in action in Figure 3.17, on page 50.

Figure 3.15: USING COLORSCHEMER STUDIO'S PHOTOSCHEMER TO SNAG COLORS FROM A PHOTOGRAPH

This is a more experimental way of developing a color scheme because the end result could be many times removed from the original color you chose. The more you practice, the better you'll get. Eventually, you'll start to rely less on your tools and more on your intuition.

3.7 Choosing Your Scheme

You've seen that you can easily and successfully follow two paths to create a color scheme for a site. Now you have to choose one of these approaches before you can start working on the digital mock-up. In this case, I think the brighter scheme created by the technical method works best, so that's the one we'll use in the rest of this book's examples. Before you can move on, you need to make some decisions about how you will use these colors on your site.

Foreground and Background Colors

You must choose the color of your links and text carefully for them to be readable. Foreground and background colors should contrast with each other. If you have a dark background, you need to pick a light foreground. If you have a light background color, choose dark colors for your text. The more contrast you have between your foreground

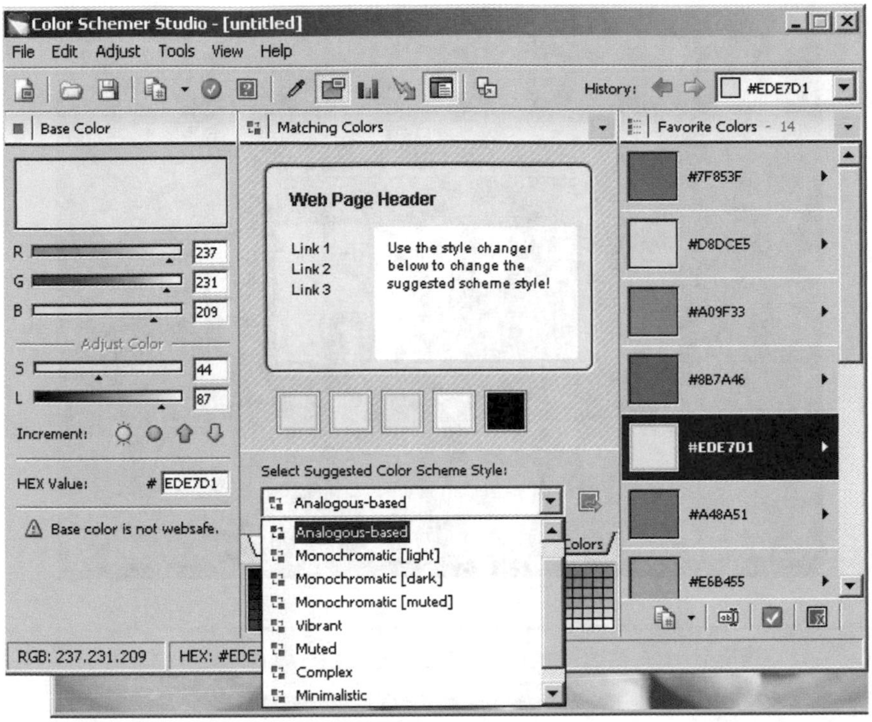

Figure 3.16: COLORSCHEMER STUDIO LETS YOU BUILD ON TOP OF THE COLORS YOU PICKED. EXPERIMENT WITH THE VARIOUS OPTIONS—YOU CAN CREATE NEW SCHEMES USING ANY OF THE COLORS YOU PICKED AS THE NEW BASE COLOR.

and background colors, the easier your users will find it to read your content.

Remember that your ultimate goal is to make a website that's useful. If you choose a foreground color that's too similar to your background color, your users are going to hit that Back button. You've spent a considerable amount of time looking at color, so don't forget to think about this last step.

Links

You should make your links a different color than the rest of your text to help them stand out. You need to think about the color of your links, as well as the colors of the various types of link states: visited links,

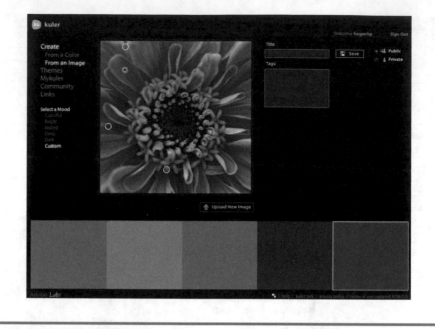

Figure 3.17: USING ADOBE KULER WITH IMAGES

active links, and maybe even hovered links, where the color of the link changes when the user places the mouse pointer on the link.

Your choices for link colors are somewhat constrained when you use an analogous or monochromatic color scheme. A very effective approach to choosing link colors is to use brightness and contrast to differentiate between links your users have seen and links they have yet to see. For example, you can make the links they've visited look more faded out. This helps make new links stand out better—just be sure that you make the contrast obvious enough that your users can tell the difference.

You can see the colors that I'll be using throughout the rest of the tutorial in Figure 3.18, on the facing page. If you're feeling adventurous, you could create your own chart like this and use your own colors. Ultimately, you want to have some way to keep track of the colors you plan to use for each section. You will need to look those colors up when you do your mock-up and then repeat that step when you create your style sheets.

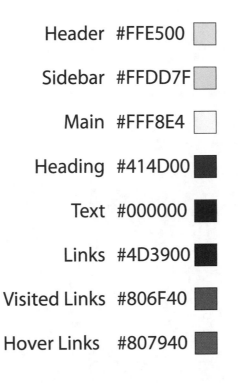

Figure 3.18: I'LL BE USING THESE COLORS FOR THIS BOOK'S EXAMPLES. YOU SHOULD EXPERIMENT AND MAKE YOUR OWN CHOICES.

3.8 Summary

In this chapter, you learned about how color works, how you can use it to evoke emotion, and how to design color schemes for websites. You now have colors you can use for your project, and you could start developing the mock-up now. Before you do that, however, you should learn a bit about typography and fonts. You want to make sure this mock-up looks as nice as reasonably possible before you show it to the stakeholders.

## Chapter 4

Fonts and Typography

You can find tons of huge books devoted to the subject of typography. It's complicated and deep, and people spend their entire lives studying it. Not us, though: we have websites to build and programs to write! So, let's go over the basics of typography and how we can use those basic concepts not only to choose fonts for Foodbox but to improve the flow and readability of our sites.

Typography is much more than the art of picking fonts; it's about making your content readable. Your text is a central part of your application's user interface, so the needs of your UI should influence your decisions about font face, size, and spacing. The role of a traditional typographer is to make the text as easy to read as possible, applying the various rules of typography to the design. If you've made your text unreadable, you've failed as a designer, no matter how nice the rest of the page looks.

4.1 Font Anatomy

It's easier to pick a good, readable font if you understand the basic elements of a font. You can find thousands of fonts out there to choose from, but not all of them are good choices. Some fonts work well for headlines or poster work, while others work better for long text passages.

All characters of a font rest on a *baseline* (see Figure 4.1, on the next page). The height of the lowercase *x* is traditionally used to define a mean line for the font. The distance between the mean line and the baseline is referred to as the *x-height* of the font.

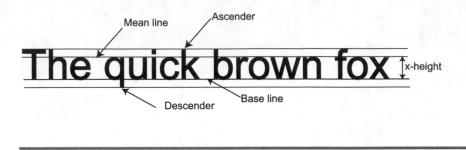

Figure 4.1: THE PARTS OF A FONT

A font has a large x-height if the lowercase *x* is relatively tall when compared to its uppercase *X*. Many designers believe that fonts with large x-heights are easier to read because some letters are easier to distinguish. However, you have to be careful. If you choose a font with an extremely large x-height, the words themselves can become *harder* to read because such a font can resemble text written in all capital letters. It's much easier to read a sentence composed of mixed-case letters THAN A SENTENCE COMPOSED ENTIRELY OF CAPITAL LETTERS.

Lowercase letters of a font, such as *q* and *p*, have *descenders* that drop below the baseline. Some lowercase letters, such as *f* and *d*, have *ascenders* that cross the x-height of the font. Descenders and ascenders can affect the readability of your text because they can interfere or overlap with text on other lines.

4.2 Font Types

We can focus on three types of fonts as web developers: serif fonts, sans-serif fonts, and fixed-width (monospaced) fonts. Each type has advantages and disadvantages that you need to consider as part of your website design. Like everything else in programming and design, these fonts are tools in your toolbox, to be used at the right time for the right job.

Serif Fonts

Serif fonts are easily identified by the tails, or *serifs*, on the letters (see Figure 4.2, on the facing page). Serif characters can have wide strokes at the ends or bottoms but have thinner strokes in the middle or edges.

Figure 4.2: EXAMPLE OF A SERIF FONT

Times New Roman, the default font used in Microsoft Internet Explorer and Microsoft Word, is a good example of a serif font. However, that font was designed for print, and it is a poor choice for use on a computer screen.

One of the chief problems with serif fonts is that the thin strokes in their letters can make them difficult to read on a computer screen, especially if you use a smaller font size. Keep in mind that this runs counter to the rules for printed typography, where a serif font is considered much easier to read.

Serif fonts look great for headings, logos, and other large-print portions of sites. Serif fonts are often associated with elegance and prestige.

Dyslexic users might find it easier to read printed content in serif fonts because of the uniqueness of the characters in the font.

Sans-Serif Fonts

Sans-serif fonts are fonts in which the stroke of the font is constant throughout each character. Literally, they are fonts "without serifs." Arial and Helvetica are well-known examples of this type of font, as is Verdana (see Figure 4.3, on the next page).

Sans-serif fonts are easy to read on the screen, so they make a great choice for your website's main content. You can read sans-serif fonts even at very small sizes.

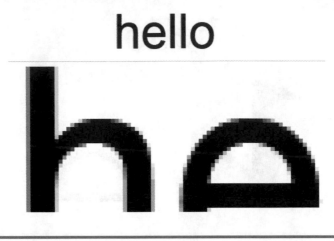

Figure 4.3: EXAMPLE OF A SANS-SERIF FONT

Fixed-Width or Monospaced Fonts

Fixed-width fonts, such as Courier, are fonts in which each character has the same amount of spacing, regardless of how wide the letter typically is. For example, *i* and *w* differ significantly in width in a sans-serif font, but these characters take up the same amount of horizontal space in a fixed-width font. These types of fonts are great when displaying things such as source code or text-based invoices that will be sent in a text-only email.

For example, take a look at the pair of invoices displayed using Myriad Pro, a serif font, and the same invoice using Courier New, a fixed-width font (see Figure 4.4, on the facing page). Notice how the fixed-width font makes the invoice easier to read because each character (including the spaces) has the same spacing and width, so everything lines up properly. Specifically, look at how neatly the columns in the fixed-width invoice line up.

4.3 Dealing with Font Limitations

Standard fonts such as Arial and Times New Roman are used everywhere, so many designers like to use unique fonts in their web designs. The biggest problem with fonts on the Web is that they are not always available on every computer. A lot of programs such as Adobe Illustrator, Adobe Photoshop, and even Microsoft Word come with a ton of

```
Thank you for your order!                    Thank you for your order!

Item        Qty  Price                       Item                Qty    Price
=================================            ======================================
Novelty Flying Disc  1  $5.00                Novelty Flying Disc     1     $5.00
Adhesive Bandages    2  $3.00                Adhesive Bandages       2     $3.00
---------------------------------            --------------------------------------
   Subtotal:      $8.00                          Subtotal:               $8.00
   Tax:           $0.00                                Tax:              $0.00
   Shipping:      $5.00                          Shipping:               $5.00
=================================            ======================================
   Total:         $13.00                          Total:                 $13.00
```

Figure 4.4: AN EMAIL INVOICE FORMATTED WITH MYRIAD PRO (LEFT) AND COURIER NEW (RIGHT)

fonts. You could use any of these fonts in your web design, only to find out that your users don't have those fonts installed.

Web-Safe Fonts

It turns out that web-safe fonts don't truly exist. Microsoft has outlined five fonts—*the Microsoft Web Fonts*—that are available on the widest range of computers (see Figure 4.5, on the next page). If you stick with one of these, you have tighter control over how you present your content, but even then you have no guarantee that your users will have them.

The five Microsoft Web Fonts aren't terrible, but they're not original, and they can be quite boring. They're overused. Many websites use Verdana and Arial as their "standard" fonts because they work almost everywhere.

What it all comes down to is this: you have a basic guarantee that every system will have a serif font, a sans-serif font, and a monospaced font, and the operating system will define which system font is associated with those families by default. However, you have a couple of strategies you can employ to get around these limitations and gain some more control.

Image Replacement

Designers often create an image that contains the text rendered in the font. You see this most often with a company logo or section headings. A lot of designers do their mock-ups in Photoshop or Illustrator, so this is something you're likely to encounter.

Arial
Courier New
Georgia
Times New Roman
Verdana

Figure 4.5: WEB-SAFE FONTS

It's perfectly acceptable to use images of fonts for headings, but it's also important not to abuse this technique just because you want to ensure that your fonts look the same on all browsers. If you just take a Photoshop document and slice it up for use on the Web, you're going to create a whole bunch of additional problems. First, your page will take significantly longer to download because of the size of the images. Second, and more important, your page might no longer be accessible by blind users, who rely on screen readers to speak the on-screen text.[1] These screen readers aren't capable of reading text embedded in an image. For more information on this topic, consult Section 16.1, *What Does Accessibility Mean to You?*, on page 229.

For Foodbox, we'll use a technique known as the *cover-up method*, a type of image replacement where we overlay text on the page with images using CSS. This allows us to create something with style that will still be accessible and will retain the same look across different platforms.

---

1. Using the alt attribute can help some, but it's not useful for large blocks of text. You're better off avoiding images for large blocks of text.

Defining Fallback Fonts with Font Stacks

Another approach that allows you to control the fonts your users see is to define your special font and then define fonts that should be substituted in case your user doesn't have your preferred font installed. A typical CSS style for selecting a font looks like this:

```
body{
    font-family: Helvetica
}
```

This snippet defines the font as Helvetica, a sans-serif font that's common on Mac OS X. The problem is that Microsoft Windows systems don't have this font by default. When a browser reads this style definition on a Windows machine, it will attempt to load up the Helvetica font, which doesn't exist. It will then give up and use the browser's default font, Times New Roman—a serif font.

The difference between these two fonts is huge, not only because of the serif vs. sans-serif issue but also because their basic font sizes are slightly different. Letter widths and heights are slightly larger in Helvetica, so the text on the page might not wrap the same way.

To solve this, you define *fallback fonts* that the browser can use if the first font isn't found. You can define multiple fallback fonts, so it's not uncommon to see a style definition like this one:

```
body{
    font-family: Helvetica, Arial, sans-serif
}
```

This definition instructs the browser to first try Helvetica, then Arial, and then to use the default system sans-serif font if it doesn't find either Helvetica or Arial. This isn't a perfect solution, but it works great for most cases. Many people refer to these as *font stacks*.

Choosing Fallback Fonts

Knowing how to structure your font stack is more important than knowing how to use the font stack itself. Your fallback fonts should be similar to your preferred font. For example, Arial and Verdana are both sans-serif fonts, but Verdana is a bit wider. Geneva would be a better fallback choice.

When building a stack, go from most specific to least specific. Choose your desired font first, then find a suitable replacement that is close enough to make you comfortable. The fonts should be similar in height, width, x-height, descender height, and ascender height—this ensures that your layout isn't thrown off too much when a substitution must be made. Next, specify one of the web-safe fonts that's close in width to your preferred font. Finally, specify one of the default font families provided by CSS (serif, sans-serif, monospaced, cursive, and fantasy). The CSS families defer to the browser, which renders the font like this:

```
p{font-family: Trebuchet, Lucida Sans, Arial, sans-serif;}
h1{font-family:Verdana,Geneva,sans-serif;}
h2{font-family: Baskerville, Times New Roman, Times, serif }
```

The Unit Interactive blog has a great post[2] on font stacks and provides some nice examples.

4.4 Selecting Our Fonts

Selecting effective fonts for our site requires that we first think about our site's content. Our site will contain recipes, so we want to make sure that we provide a font that's easy to read and won't be confusing to our readers. It might not make sense for the entire site to use the same font. We might use a different font for things like the navigation menu, the section and page headings, and other areas. We definitely don't want to create a "font soup," so the best idea would be to keep the maximum number of fonts on a page to two, not counting the site's logo. We will use one font for content and a second font for headings.

Content Font

Most designers find that sans-serif fonts are good choices for content. Although some letters can be more difficult to distinguish individually, the complete words will stand out better on most monitors.

The majority of websites use Arial as the font, with a fallback to Helvetica. Some designers love to use Verdana. It's a wider font, so it tends to fill out space a little better than Arial. However, you should avoid using it for situations where you will need an extremely small font. Verdana gets hard to read if you go below 10px.[3]

Heading Fonts

When it comes to headings, you want to use something that grabs the user's attention. Typically you'll use a larger font size for your headings.

---

2. http://unitinteractive.com/blog/2008/06/26/better-css-font-stacks/
3. Please, please, please don't go below 10px for any font. There's just no reason to go that small. It's awful to read.

@font-face

In the not-so-distant future, you'll be able to link fonts to your pages using @font-face. Unfortunately, support is weak in older browsers. Firefox 3.5 and Safari 4 support @font-face, but previous versions do not. Internet Explorer has supported @font-face for a long time, even on IE 6, but IE requires you to convert fonts to its own proprietary format.

But very soon, you'll be defining your fonts like this:

```
@font-face {
  font-family: "YourFont";
  src: url(/fonts/yourfont.ttf) format("truetype");
}
h1 { font-family: "YourFont", sans-serif }
```

This approach is extremely flexible and easy to implement, except for one catch: most fonts, like photographs, need to be licensed for use like this. They have a copyright, and you have to respect it. Unlike using a font in an image or embedding it in a Flash movie, you're actually distributing the font here, because the client's browser needs to download it.

Thankfully, services like Typekit* are working with font creators and publishers to provide a solution to the licensing issue. Typekit, for example, hosts fonts for you and serves them from its servers, and you simply include a snippet of JavaScript on your page tied to your Typekit account. So, although we're not quite ready to push ahead with this technique, it's something you should keep your eye on, because it will greatly simplify the process.

---

*. http://typekit.com

The quick brown fox

Figure 4.6: MONOTYPE CORSIVA, AN ELEGANT FONT FOR HEADLINES

Some designers prefer to use a bolder variant of the font for headings, while some designers use a different font altogether, which can spice up a content-heavy site.

When choosing a heading font, you should be careful to ensure that your users can read the font easily. It's easy to choose a font that's fancy and elegant, but you should ask yourself if it's going to be easy for your users to identify different sections on your site.

Heading fonts are typically larger than fonts used for the site's content, so you can get away with using a serif font for your headings. You could exploit this to add a touch of elegance to your page.

I'm going to use the Monotype Corsiva font,[4] which you can see in Figure 4.6. It's a good-looking script font for our headings. This is a nonstandard font, but it's used only for headings, so we'll create images of our headings and use image replacement to display them on the page. I'll provide more detail on how to do this later.

4.5 Using the Baseline Grid

Creating a fluid body of text is incredibly important to effective content delivery. Text should flow around images and other elements, columns should line up, and lines shouldn't break in weird places. Most novice web developers let the browser's default settings dictate the way the text flows, but you can get a much cleaner look if you take some time to figure out a few things before you start.

The *baseline grid* is a vertical grid, or several horizontal lines on top of each other, that supports the font characters in a composition. The dis-

---

4. If you have a Microsoft Office product installed, there's a good chance you have this font. If you don't have it on your system, you can purchase it at http://www.microsoft.com/typography/fonts/font.aspx?FMID=1009 or, even better, choose a different font.

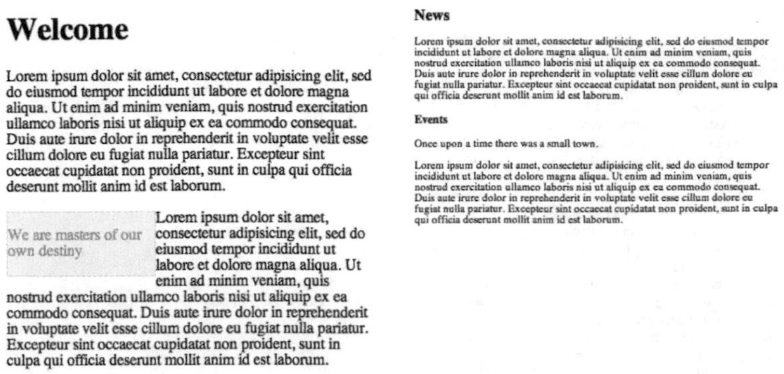

Welcome

Lorem ipsum dolor sit amet, consectetur adipisicing elit, sed do eiusmod tempor incididunt ut labore et dolore magna aliqua. Ut enim ad minim veniam, quis nostrud exercitation ullamco laboris nisi ut aliquip ex ea commodo consequat. Duis aute irure dolor in reprehenderit in voluptate velit esse cillum dolore eu fugiat nulla pariatur. Excepteur sint occaecat cupidatat non proident, sunt in culpa qui officia deserunt mollit anim id est laborum.

We are masters of our own destiny

Lorem ipsum dolor sit amet, consectetur adipisicing elit, sed do eiusmod tempor incididunt ut labore et dolore magna aliqua. Ut enim ad minim veniam, quis nostrud exercitation ullamco laboris nisi ut aliquip ex ea commodo consequat. Duis aute irure dolor in reprehenderit in voluptate velit esse cillum dolore eu fugiat nulla pariatur. Excepteur sint occaecat cupidatat non proident, sunt in culpa qui officia deserunt mollit anim id est laborum.

News

Lorem ipsum dolor sit amet, consectetur adipisicing elit, sed do eiusmod tempor incididunt ut labore et dolore magna aliqua. Ut enim ad minim veniam, quis nostrud exercitation ullamco laboris nisi ut aliquip ex ea commodo consequat. Duis aute irure dolor in reprehenderit in voluptate velit esse cillum dolore eu fugiat nulla pariatur. Excepteur sint occaecat cupidatat non proident, sunt in culpa qui officia deserunt mollit anim id est laborum.

Events

Once upon a time there was a small town.

Lorem ipsum dolor sit amet, consectetur adipisicing elit, sed do eiusmod tempor incididunt ut labore et dolore magna aliqua. Ut enim ad minim veniam, quis nostrud exercitation ullamco laboris nisi ut aliquip ex ea commodo consequat. Duis aute irure dolor in reprehenderit in voluptate velit esse cillum dolore eu fugiat nulla pariatur. Excepteur sint occaecat cupidatat non proident, sunt in culpa qui officia deserunt mollit anim id est laborum.

Figure 4.7: NOTICE HOW THE COLUMNS DON'T LINE UP WHEN YOU DON'T ACCOUNT FOR LINE SPACING.

tance between the horizontal gridlines becomes your unit of measure, and each line on the grid becomes the baseline for your fonts.

The horizontal lines on the baseline grid function like the ruled lines of paper in a notebook. The lines keep the text constrained and evenly spaced throughout the page. To keep the text flowing correctly across columns and around images, you want to make all your images and other assets line up on the horizontal gridlines. The height of each image you use should be evenly divisible by the amount of space between each line on the grid. When everything adheres to the grid, text automatically flows around images, columns of text line up evenly, and everything ends up being much easier to read.

You can see how much elegance the baseline grid can add by comparing a layout that doesn't use it (see Figure 4.7) to one that does (see Figure 4.8, on the next page).

Leading

Leading refers to the amount of vertical space between the lines. It's often called *line spacing* or *line-height* in CSS. White space between lines makes it easier for a reader's eyes to follow the line. This is also the key ingredient to building our grid. The value we choose for our leading is the value we'll use for our vertical spacing. Everything we add to our page will need to be evenly divisible by this number so that everything falls on a gridline.

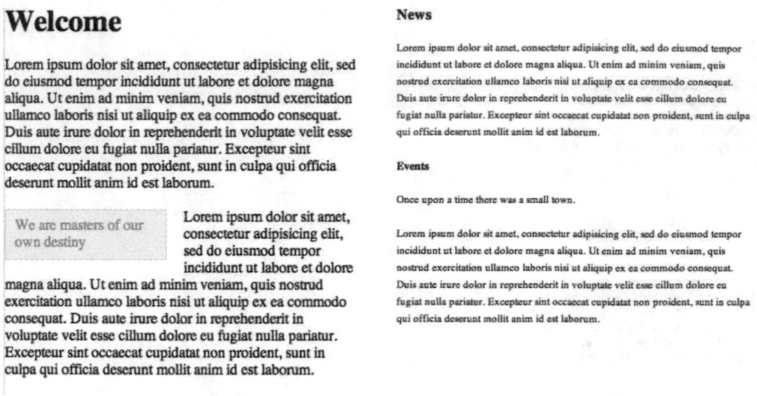

Welcome

Lorem ipsum dolor sit amet, consectetur adipisicing elit, sed do eiusmod tempor incididunt ut labore et dolore magna aliqua. Ut enim ad minim veniam, quis nostrud exercitation ullamco laboris nisi ut aliquip ex ea commodo consequat. Duis aute irure dolor in reprehenderit in voluptate velit esse cillum dolore eu fugiat nulla pariatur. Excepteur sint occaecat cupidatat non proident, sunt in culpa qui officia deserunt mollit anim id est laborum.

We are masters of our own destiny

Lorem ipsum dolor sit amet, consectetur adipisicing elit, sed do eiusmod tempor incididunt ut labore et dolore magna aliqua. Ut enim ad minim veniam, quis nostrud exercitation ullamco laboris nisi ut aliquip ex ea commodo consequat. Duis aute irure dolor in reprehenderit in voluptate velit esse cillum dolore eu fugiat nulla pariatur. Excepteur sint occaecat cupidatat non proident, sunt in culpa qui officia deserunt mollit anim id est laborum.

News

Lorem ipsum dolor sit amet, consectetur adipisicing elit, sed do eiusmod tempor incididunt ut labore et dolore magna aliqua. Ut enim ad minim veniam, quis nostrud exercitation ullamco laboris nisi ut aliquip ex ea commodo consequat. Duis aute irure dolor in reprehenderit in voluptate velit esse cillum dolore eu fugiat nulla pariatur. Excepteur sint occaecat cupidatat non proident, sunt in culpa qui officia deserunt mollit anim id est laborum.

Events

Once upon a time there was a small town.

Lorem ipsum dolor sit amet, consectetur adipisicing elit, sed do eiusmod tempor incididunt ut labore et dolore magna aliqua. Ut enim ad minim veniam, quis nostrud exercitation ullamco laboris nisi ut aliquip ex ea commodo consequat. Duis aute irure dolor in reprehenderit in voluptate velit esse cillum dolore eu fugiat nulla pariatur. Excepteur sint occaecat cupidatat non proident, sunt in culpa qui officia deserunt mollit anim id est laborum.

Figure 4.8: YOU CAN USE THE BASELINE GRID TO MAKE YOUR TEXT LINE UP ACROSS COLUMNS.

Units of Measure

The grid is based on the line-height of your text, which is the distance between baselines of each line of text. If you choose a line-height of 18px, your text should align to a grid that has lines every 18px.

When we define our base font size for the baseline grid, we'll use pixels. This means we'll be using an exact measurement. Some web developers argue that when you use pixel-based font sizes, users can't resize the text. This is only partly true: older browsers don't support resizing text defined as pixels, but most modern browsers allow you to resize the text, as well as the line-height.

We could spend time figuring out the appropriate base font and doing all the math to compute line-heights, margins, and other elements— and we'd still be at the mercy of the browsers because they're going to round values differently anyway. A simple online search will return lots of information about how to do relative font sizing, but even if you find a solution that seems perfect, your image heights and widths are still measured in pixels, so you have to come up with hacks to resize those as well.

Relative fonts used to be hailed as an accessibility feature for the visually impaired because the user could increase the font size using the web browser. However, it made things worse because images didn't

Joe Asks...

Every Article I Read Says That You Should Let People Scale Fonts. Are You Sure You're Giving Good Advice?

I mentioned briefly in the introduction to this book that I was born with congenital cataracts, and I have extremely low vision because of it. I've dealt with small fonts on the Web for a long time, and I've had to use lots of sites created by well-meaning developers who cargo-culted best practices from "accessibility experts" without actually testing them. Low-vision users use assistive devices such as full-screen zoom tools like ZoomText or the ones found in Windows 7 and Mac OS X. When they open a Word document, they use the zoom tools there—they don't resize the fonts on the page. A browser should be no different, especially now that all the major browsers allow full-page zooming.

In 2001, it made sense for developers to jump through hoops to make things work for low-vision users. Hacking images to expand via CSS and JavaScript while providing scalable fonts is pointless now that the browsers have caught up.

resize with the fonts, causing strange page flows and readability problems. Thankfully, there's a better solution now.

Microsoft Word and Adobe Acrobat both let readers zoom in to read the text while preserving the layout, regardless of what unit of measure the author used to render the fonts. This approach is now supported by the major browsers. We'll talk more about accessibility for low-vision users in Section 16.2, *People with Visual Impairments*, on page 236.

Choosing Fonts for Foodbox

You have to start with a base font size to build your grid. For this design, we'll use a 12px font for our body text. It's a good font size, and it's easy to read on the average monitor.[5] You want to provide enough space above and below the line to make it readable and not look cramped. You

---

5. If you find that the majority of your audience is on 24-inch iMacs with the resolution cranked all the way up, that measurement might be a tad too small for them to read. This comes back to knowing your audience.

also want to ensure that you don't take up too much space between lines of text. When choosing a line-height, choose a number that's evenly divisible. Let's use a line-height of 18px because that will give us a nice wide buffer. A good rule of thumb to follow is to take the base font size you define and multiply it by 1.25 or 1.5. If you have a 12px font and a line-height of 18px, you can express that as 12/18 for your font size. This notation is popular among typographers who want to state the font size and the line-height.

So far, we've decided on a body-text size of 12px with a line-height of 18px. To make the grid work, you must adhere to the 18px grid size for everything you do. That means that all top and bottom margins must be in multiples of 18px (or add up to 18px, such as 9px and 9px). Any time you add vertical space, you must make sure that you add it in multiples of 18px so that your page elements will line up with the grid. When you crop a photograph, you'll need to make your image height some multiple of 18 or add padding using CSS to make it line up.

For subheadings, we can increase our font size to 18px, the height of the line itself. That would look pretty nice, but we'd also need to make sure that we leave another 18px space below each subheading.

For our headings, we'll double the base font, making them 24px in size. At this point, we've exceeded the line-height of 18px, so we will need to double the line-height for our headings to 36px to ensure that things stay aligned.

We'll revisit the baseline grid when we start thinking about our item placement. Our margins, borders, padding, image heights, and other elements need to adhere to the baseline grid, or our design falls apart.

Here's a summary of the fonts we've chosen:

Section	Font	Size	Line Height
Headings	Monotype Corsiva	24px	36px
Sidebar headings	Monotype Corsiva	18px	18px
Subheading	Arial	14px	18px
Body	Arial	12px	18px

You should feel free to experiment with these settings I chose. Don't just follow what I used—be creative! For example, you might try making some adjustments to the font sizes to see how that affects the look and feel of the layout.

4.6 Summary

Typography is an important part of good web design. Failing to think about the fonts you'll use and how they impact readability will make things more difficult for people to get anything out of your content. Defining a grid system to base your layout on will improve both the readability and the aesthetic appeal of your site.

With our font sizes and styles in place, we can move on to building the digital mock-up of the site. Our next task is to work on the logo for Foodbox.

Part II

Adding Graphics

## Chapter 5

Designing the Foodbox Logo

Your original sketches included a logo for Foodbox. You will often have an existing logo that you need to re-create or tweak. Your client might also have contracted with a third party to create a logo that you will need to incorporate into the site. In the case of Foodbox, it is up to you to create the logo from existing artwork because the original site doesn't use the logo, and there's just no suitable digital version available. As a guide, you can use the sketch in Figure 2.4, on page 19.

5.1 Setting Up a Working Folder

It pays to be organized in your projects. If you've ever used Ruby on Rails, you know that a major advantage of that framework is its standard directory structure. Unfortunately, there's no such standard available to us, but most web designers have their own way of keeping track of things. For this project, we'll use a simple directory structure with places for our style sheets and our images.

Create a new folder called Foodbox. Within that folder, create three additional folders: images, stylesheets, and originals.

The originals folder will hold all your work files, such as your Illustrator and Photoshop documents, as well as any stock or other photography given to you by a client. The images folder will hold the images that you'll use directly in the web page you create. The stylesheets folder will hold the CSS styles you will create once you build the site.

Joe Asks...

Must I Have Adobe Illustrator?

Of course not. On the other hand, Illustrator is a great tool to learn if you're looking at doing design work. It's used by print and web designers all over the world, so learning a little about it can only help you. Adobe makes 30-day trial versions available on its website, which should be more than enough to get you through this chapter. If you want an alternative to Illustrator, I recommend Inkscape.* The exercises in this chapter use Illustrator; if you use a different vector-graphics tool, you'll have to translate the steps described to that environment.

---

*. http://www.inkscape.org/

5.2 The Foodbox Logo

When you're doing logo work, it's important to use a tool that supports vector-based graphics. That way, you can scale your logo to any size and use it not only on a website but in print media as well. The industry standard for this is Adobe Illustrator, and we'll use that program to re-create this logo.

The Foodbox logo consists of four squares and the word *Foodbox*. The finished logo should look like Figure 5.1, on the facing page. You can re-create this logo in only a few steps.

Open Illustrator, and create a new document. Dimensions don't really matter here because we'll scale it later, when we integrate it with our Photoshop document. We'll use Illustrator only to create a logo here, so I won't go into great detail about how everything works. However, I urge you to investigate Illustrator further if you plan on doing more graphics work, because it's a wonderful tool.

Let's start with the four boxes. We need to draw a two-by-two array of boxes with rounded corners. We can do this in a handful of steps by drawing one box using specific dimensions and then using Illustrator to replicate that box for us:

1. Select the Rounded Rectangle tool from Illustrator's tool palette by clicking and holding the Rectangle tool. This will make the other

Figure 5.1: OUR FINISHED LOGO

shape choices fly out from the menu. Then choose the rounded rectangle.

2. On the Options toolbar, change the fill to #FCEE21, a yellow color, and choose black for the stroke.

3. Now, double-click the canvas. A dialog box appears, asking you to enter the dimensions of the square. Enter 100pt for both the height and the width. Use 12pt for the corner radius, and click OK. You've just drawn a single square by defining its exact dimensions.

4. Now, double-click the Selection tool on the tool palette. This opens the Move or Copy dialog box.

5. We want to copy the box, and we want to ensure that we have a nice, even space between the two boxes after the copy. The box we just made is 100 points wide. Enter 110 in the horizontal box, and click Copy. This creates a copy of the box 110 points away from

---

Joe Asks...

Whoa! Where Did These Colors Come From?

I used variations of the colors in our Color palette. I adjusted the saturation slightly to make the colors in the squares show up better, and I did some test prints to make sure that the logo looked similar when printed.

---

the start of the first box, which means we now have two boxes placed 10 points apart.

6. We'll use that same Copy command to create the other two boxes, this time adjusting vertically rather than horizontally. Select both boxes by drawing a box around them with the Selection tool, and then double-click the Selection tool to open the Move or Copy dialog box again. This time, set the horizontal value to 0 and the vertical value to 110. Click Copy, and you have your four squares, evenly spaced.

Next, we need to apply a colored fill to each box:

1. Press [F6] to display the Color palette.

2. Select each square with the Direct Selection tool, and then double-click the color-fill square on the Color palette to choose the color.

3. Clockwise from the top left, the box colors should be yellow (#FCEE21), green (#C2EE21), orange (#FCBA21), and beige (#FCEEB5).

Now it's time to add some text. To make the logo look balanced, we want to make sure that the word *Foodbox* is as tall as our boxes. To do this, we'll use *guides*.

Most drawing tools provide guides that you can place on your composition to help you align items or help you define where items in your composition should be placed. The concept of guidelines is nothing new to anyone who's done design work before. We'll use guides to align our text quickly and easily:

1. Ensure that the rulers are showing by pressing [Ctrl]+[R].

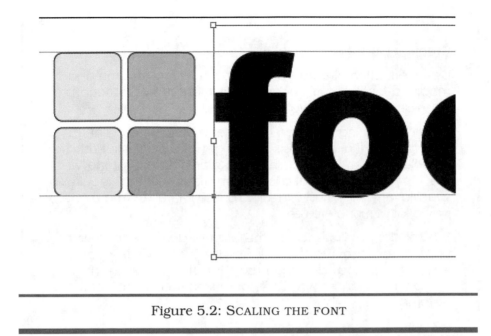

Figure 5.2: SCALING THE FONT

2. Create a guide that touches the top of the boxes. Place the mouse pointer anywhere on the horizontal ruler at the top of the image. To create a new guide, press and hold the mouse button, and then and drag it down toward the boxes. Position the guide so it touches the top of the boxes, and then release the mouse button to place the guide.

3. Place another guide along the bottom of the boxes. You can now use these guides to place the text.

You should have two guides placed like the horizontal lines above and below the boxes, as shown in Figure 5.2.

Now we need to add the text to our logo:

- Select the Text tool.

- Use the Options panel to choose Arial Black for the font style and 72pt for the font size.

- Click the canvas, and type *foodbox*. Don't worry if you didn't place it between the guides—we're going to move it now.

- Choose the Selection tool from the tool palette. The section you just typed will now have resizing handles that you'll use to scale up text so it's the same size as the boxes. Hold down the Shift key,

---

Creating Outlines

Designers often use Illustrator's Create Outlines command to modify a font once it's been applied, but the command provides an additional advantage, as well.

When I am doing a design for a client, I ask if the client has a logo already. If a logo exists, I try to get a copy of it in Illustrator or EPS format so I can scale it and manipulate it for the website. Occasionally, I'll get a logo from a designer that requires a specific font that I must either find online for free or (more often) pay a lot of money to use.

The solution to this is to ask the original designer to create a copy of the logo. I take that logo, use Create Outlines on any text in the image, and then use that. This preserves the way the font looks, and it's portable across platforms and operating systems.

---

and drag the upper-right resizing handle on the text area until the top of the *f* in *foodbox* touches the guide you placed. Check to make sure that the bottom of the *f* also touches the guide. If it doesn't touch, keep resizing and repositioning until you get it. Don't worry about any other letters that drop below the guide; we'll get those next.

If you look carefully, you'll notice that a few of the letters drop below the guide. Let's fix that by slightly modifying the text shapes:

1. Select the text layer with the Selection tool.

2. Select Text > Create Outlines. This command turns the text object into vector shapes. You can't change the text anymore, but you can use any of Illustrator's drawing or manipulation tools on these shapes.

3. Choose the Direct Selection tool from the palette, and draw a box around the lower half of the *o*. Now press the up arrow key four or five times, until the bottom of the *o* touches the guide.

4. Do this with the rest of the letters that cross the bottom guide.

Finally, click the Select tool, and press Ctrl+A to select everything. Hold down the Shift key, and use the resize handles to resize the logo so it is constrained within the *bounding box*, which is the solid black rectangle on the background of the canvas.

Save this document as foodbox_logo.ai, and put it in the originals folder in your project folder. We'll need to import this into our Photoshop project later, so when you save, make sure you select the option to create a PDF-compatible file. If you miss this step, Photoshop won't be able to import the file.

Keep in mind that we used a vector-based drawing tool, so we can use this logo for anything from coffee mugs to huge billboards. We can resize the logo as required, without impacting its image quality.

5.3 What If We Need to Create Our Own Logo?

In this example, we had a drawing we could follow, and we were essentially learning to use Illustrator to re-create that drawing. But what kinds of things would you need to think about if you were developing a logo for your product or business?

Think about the most successful logos today. People all over the world recognize Coca-Cola's logo. The Nike swoosh is pretty noticeable, too. However, these two logos are completely different in the way they advertise the products they represent.

It turns out that you can approach designing a logo much as you approach designing a website.

People process images faster than they process sentences or tag lines, and you want your logo to take advantage of that where you can. People look at the Coca-Cola logo, and they don't need to read the words; they immediately recognize the logo and associate it with the company's product. This is your ultimate goal with your logo—you want your logo to represent you and only you.

Instant recognition is achieved only through the logo's constant and consistent use. If you're always changing your logo, it's harder to gain that brand recognition you're looking for. A logo represents you. People remember a logo, and having an inappropriate one will sink things pretty quickly. The logo of a law office will be very different from the logo of a waterslide park.

If your logo will contain words, be sure the words are readable. Use clear typefaces that are readable at very large and very small sizes.

Keep the color choices simple and safe. Use what you learned about evoking emotion to your advantage with your logo.[1]

Unlike a web page, your logo might appear often in print, so test colors on a printer from time to time to make sure that they look acceptable. When you work on the Web, use the RBG color mode. When you're designing anything that might end up being printed, you need to work in the CMYK color mode. You can save your CMYK-based images to RGB mode for use on the Web, but going the other way is extremely difficult when it comes to matching colors.

Finally, be sure to test your logo without color. For example, does it work when printed in black and white?

5.4 Summary

Vector-based tools such as Illustrator make it easy to build scalable and versatile logos. The next time you need to design a logo, try some of the techniques we explored in this chapter, such as duplication and font manipulation. Remember to be creative. In fact, feel free to play with the logo we created here. Make some variations. Use different shapes, different fonts, different sizes, or different placement, or try to apply some of the advice on logo design and create your own completely different logo for Foodbox.

Now it's time to tackle the next step of the process: building a color mock-up.

---

1. Also, be aware of any cultural problems with your color choices. Certain colors are offensive to certain people, so be sure you do some research.

## Chapter 6

Design Mock-up: The Structure

With our sketch and color choices in hand, we'll use Adobe Photoshop to mock up the front page of the Foodbox site. In this chapter, we'll rough out the structure of the page and set up the header and footer. Along the way, you'll become familiar with some of the layout options available in Photoshop, which will help you keep your design aligned to the grid we defined previously.

6.1 A Bit About Layers

Layers are awesome. No other word I might use can describe how great they are. Layers allow you to create and manage a composition by letting you develop your graphics in pieces. Each layer acts like a separate document. You can cut and paste, copy, select, delete, and even apply effects to individual layers. Layers are also transparent, so you can use them to build up your composition in pieces. You can see how you might combine layers in a site mock-up in Figure 6.1, on page 81.

It's common for a designer to take a photograph and then place some text on top of that photograph in a separate layer. This way, the text isn't combined with the photograph, and the designer can even change it later, provided that the original Photoshop document is still available.

When you export an image from Illustrator or Photoshop to a JPEG, GIF, PNG, or other document, Photoshop combines, or *flattens*, your layers. If you lose or delete the original document, you must start over from scratch because you won't be able to recover the individual layers. Many logos, buttons, and other graphical elements have to be recreated all the time for this reason.

Joe Asks. . .

Must I Use Photoshop?

No, you don't have to, but you should, for the same reasons I outlined in the *Joe Asks. . .* on page 72. Photoshop is the industry standard for working with photographs and raster graphics. Although it is technically possible to use less expensive or open source alternatives to complete this task, I will use Photoshop in this book's examples.

Of course, I don't recommend that you rush out and buy the Adobe Creative Suite just to work with this book. Adobe provides 30-day trials that should give you enough time to follow the examples in this book and decide if this is really something you want to do. Once you've gone through the exercises with Photoshop, it should be easy for you to do something similar in another program.

It's also worth noting that you don't necessarily need the most recent version of Photoshop to complete this book. The examples in this book should work with any recent version.

If you're still not convinced, grab a copy of GIMP* or Gimp-Shop,† a modified version of GIMP that has been altered to work more like Photoshop, and try to follow along with the examples in this book.

---

*. http://www.gimp.org/downloads/
†. http://www.gimpshop.com/download.shtml

We'll be using layers extensively in both Illustrator and Photoshop; you'll need to save your original files for each element as you go.

6.2 The Basic Structure

Start by dividing your basic sketch for the home page into four rectangular regions: a block for the heading, another for the footer, and then two more for the content columns (see Figure 6.2, on the facing page). The key here is thinking in rectangles when it comes to a website's structure. In fact, you should look for the rectangles in the websites you visit every day.

Figure 6.1: A COMPOSITION MADE UP OF LAYERS

Figure 6.2: SECTIONS HIGHLIGHTED WITH A COLOR OVERLAY

Screen Size

When you build a web page, you have no idea what screen size to use in our website. The best approach you can take is to target the average reen size first. At the time of writing, the majority of users on the Web use a resolution of 1024 by 768, and a significant percentage use even higher screen resolutions.[1]

These statistics can be misleading, though. Even if a user has a wide-screen monitor set to a high resolution, the user might not have the browser maximized; it could be sitting side-by-side with some other applications. People can also use cell phones, PDAs, iPods, and even the Nintendo Wii to browse the Web. Your site must be at least readable on almost any display size.

Create a new document in Photoshop called foodbox_mockup that is 900px wide and 756px high, with a resolution of 72 dpi. Set the color mode to RGB, and set the background to white. I have chosen these dimensions because we're shooting for a target screen size of 1024 by 768, and we need to make our page narrower than that to account for the browser's scroll bars and to give ourselves a little breathing room on the edges. We're going to build a *fixed-width* layout.

Once you create your new document, save it as foodbox_mockup.psd in the originals folder in your project folder.

Fixed-Width Layouts

In fixed-width layouts, the page size stays the same, regardless of the size of the browser window. Such layouts are easier to design and implement than flexible, or *liquid*, layouts. Liquid layouts require a lot more testing and often a lot more code to ensure that content is readable in every instance. If you neglect to take proper care with a liquid layout, rows of text could end up being extremely long as they stretch across the page or too narrow—in either case, your site would be hard to read. A fixed-width layout is easy to implement in a short amount of time.

However, different types of sites demand different types of layouts. Sites that deal with lots of information might require a fluid site. A web-based application that runs a business and displays a lot of data might not

---

1. According to http://www.w3schools.com/browsers/browsers_display.asp at the time of writing, 54% of users have monitors with the resolution set to 1024 by 768, and 26% of users have their monitors set to even higher resolutions.

The Fold

The page dimensions I used will cause some of the page to be displayed *below the fold*, which means that some users with smaller monitors will have to scroll down to see the page. The term *fold* comes from the print world and refers to the area of a newspaper that you would see on the newsstand before you had a chance to unfold the paper. In theory, you want to display as much of your site's important information above the fold as possible. However, that theory doesn't hold completely true anymore. Although people don't enjoy having to scroll horizontally to see more content, most users are used to scrolling downward. If you can structure your page so that it's evident to your users that they need to scroll down for more content, they certainly will.

work well on a constrained layout. You need to evaluate your situation and design a layout to fit your specific needs, rather than following a trend or reusing the same template for every site you build.

Setting Up the Grid

We covered some details of working on a grid when we discussed basic typography in Section 4.5, *Using the Baseline Grid*, on page 62. It so happens that we can make Photoshop show us a grid on top of our canvas, and we can use that grid to line up our elements, including text. The default grid settings won't work for what we want to do, so we'll need to make a couple of minor adjustments.

Begin by changing the units for the rulers topx using Edit > Preferences > Units and Rulers. Next, set the value for Gridlines Every to 18px with one subdivision using Edit > Preferences > Guides, Slices, and Count. This displays a grid that will serve as your guide throughout the upcoming chapters. The distance between the gridlines is 18px, which is the same size as your line-height for your fonts. While you're in the grid settings, set the color of the gridlines to something obnoxious, such as a bright lime green or another color that is completely different from any color you plan to use in your composition. This will make the grid stand out more once you start adding more elements.

In a default Photoshop workspace, the grid and rulers are not enabled. Toggle the rulers on by pressing [Ctrl]+[R], and toggle the grid on with [Ctrl]+['].

Defining Regions with Guides

When you designed the logo, you learned how to use guides to help you line up the text of the logo with the four boxes. You'll find it helpful to divide this composition into its various sections using guides so that you can easily draw and line up elements.

We'll use the Rectangle Shape tool to draw the various sections of our page, as outlined by our sketch. We'll start with the header and footer. In this exercise, you will make the header and footer the same color, but you should feel free to experiment.

We'll define our header and footer heights first. Our header should be tall enough to show our logo clearly. The footer doesn't need to be as high because it will show a copyright statement and the terms of service for the site. When we define the vertical heights for these regions, we should think about the baseline grid again. We decided on a unit of 18px for our grid, so the height of our header and footer should divide evenly by 18. Let's try values of 108px high for the header and 54px for the footer.

To place the guide for the header, place the mouse pointer anywhere along the horizontal ruler at the top of your composition. Click and drag downward to the 108px mark of the ruler on the side. Release the mouse button to place the guide. Place another guide at 702px for the footer.

The sidebar should be wide enough to include the recipe search form and the tag cloud. Try making the sidebar 306px wide. You can always adjust it later. Place the mouse pointer anywhere along the vertical ruler on the left side of the composition. Click and drag to the right until you reach the 306px mark on the ruler along the top. Release the mouse button to place that guide.

We now have all four regions defined by guides, as shown in Figure 6.3, on the facing page. We can now fill them in with rectangular shapes. Notice that the borders of all four sections fall on gridlines. We've now defined all four regions; we'll spruce up this layout soon.

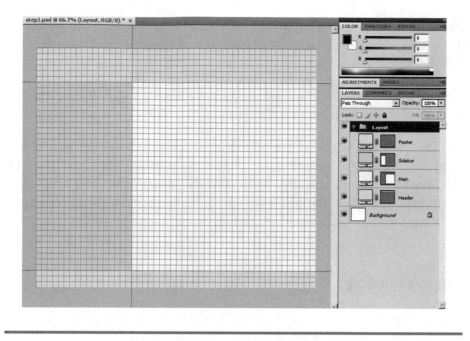

Figure 6.3: OUR FOUR REGIONS

Drawing the Boxes

Now we'll follow the guides and draw rectangles over each region. First, select the Rectangle tool by pressing $\boxed{U}$. While you're at it, make sure that the Shape Layers option is selected.

In the Options panel, click the color square, and enter ffe500 for the color. Click OK. Draw a rectangle across the top of the screen so it touches the guide you placed at the 108px mark. To do this, place your mouse pointer at the upper-left edge of the canvas. Next, click and hold the mouse button down while dragging right and downward until you reach the right edge of the screen.

Now create the footer. Press $\boxed{Shift}$+$\boxed{Ctrl}$+$\boxed{N}$ to create a new layer; it's always a good idea to create each item on your composition in its own layer because you can move it around more easily later. When you create the layer, Photoshop asks you to name it. This will make it easy for you to find that layer again. Draw another rectangle at the bottom of the screen. This time, start at the guide you placed at the 702px mark.

Next, draw the sidebar. Again, create a new layer for the sidebar, and label it appropriately. Change the color to FFD67F, and draw the box on the left side of the screen. The sidebar rectangle should fit nicely in the guides you drew. Start at 0 across, 108 down, and go to 300 across, 702 down.

Finally, fill in the remaining whitespace with another shape layer, and then change the color to FFF7DF.

We have defined our four regions defined; now we can start thinking about the other things that reside on our home page. Our sketch shows the Foodbox logo in the top of the screen, and we already have that ready to go. We need to make a few other elements, so let's keep going—right after we save our work, of course.

6.3 Placing the Logo

One reason Photoshop works so well for creating web page mockups is its ability to work together with other programs. We have a logo we drew in Illustrator, and we can now take that image and import it directly into our mockup as a vector object. When we import the vector logo into our composition, we'll need to resize it to make it fit where we want it. We can use guides to define where the logo should go.

Make sure the rulers and grid are still showing, and create two horizontal guides. The first guide will cross the left ruler at 18px and should overlap the first horizontal gridline. The second guide should be placed at the 90px mark, right on that horizontal gridline. This will give us 18px above and below the logo. Create a vertical guide by clicking and dragging from the left ruler and stopping at 18px on the horizontal ruler. That will give us a nice box in which to place the logo.

Select File > Place, locate your logo file, and click OK. Drag the logo to the top-left corner of the screen so that its top-left corner comes to the intersection of the two guides. You'll use the resize handles to adjust the image. Hold down the Shift key, and grab the lower-right resize handle. Drag diagonally up and left until the bottom-right corner touches the guide defined at 90px. Now press Enter to place the file.

When you place an Illustrator document into a Photoshop document, the object is placed as a *smart object*. Editing this smart object opens Illustrator, and changes you make there are automatically reflected in your Photoshop document when you save them.

Figure 6.4: OUR LOGO IN OUR DOCUMENT

6.4 Organizing Our Composition with Layer Groups

We have tons of layers in our project at this point. It can get tricky to find everything we need, but we can use of a feature in Photoshop called *layer groups* to simplify managing things. A layer group is a folder on the Layers palette that you can use to organize your layers.

Create a new layer group called *Layout* by clicking the Layer Group button on the Layers palette. Rename the group by right-clicking and choosing Rename.

Now, within the Layers palette, drag the header, sidebar, main, and footer layers into this group.

You can collapse layer groups to help you focus on the layers you want to work on. You can also turn them on and off or even duplicate the entire group. You can also use this feature to isolate things easily. We'll use layer groups throughout the next few chapters to keep our composition organized.

6.5 Adding a Reflection to Our Logo

Steve remembers that one of the stakeholders wanted to have a reflection under the logo. Many sites use this technique, commonly referred to as the *wet-floor effect*, where text appears to be resting on a surface that reflects the text or logo. We can apply that effect quickly using layer groups and masks:

1. First, create a new layer group called *Logo*. Drag the Foodbox logo layer into this layer group. The reflection of the Foodbox logo is going to be a separate layer, so we want to keep these two layers together.

2. In the Layers palette, right-click the layer containing the Foodbox logo, and choose the Duplicate Layer option. Name the layer *Foodbox Logo Reflection.*

3. Ensure that the reflection layer is selected in the Layers palette. Select the Marquee tool, right-click the image, and choose the Free Transform option to bring up the resizing handles. Click and drag the handle in the middle at the top of the image, and drag it downward, past the bottom. This inverts the selected area and creates the reflection. You should be careful to bring the reflection straight down and make it exactly as high as the original layer; use the gridlines to guide you. You can hold down the [Shift] key to help you make a straight transformation.[2]

   Press the [Enter] key to accept the changes in the transformation. You can press the [Esc] key to cancel the transformation and start over again if you need to do so.

4. We can make the reflection fade out in a few different ways, but the simplest method is to use Photoshop's layer masks feature. Select the layer you just transformed, and choose the Add Layer Mask button at the bottom of the *Layers* palette. Masks let you hide parts of an image or composition. The contents of any layer covered by a layer mask will be hidden.

5. If we use a gradient instead of a solid color, we can quickly make a mask that will fade out the area beneath the mask. Select the Gradient tool from the tool palette. The Gradient tool might not be visible; remember that it shares the same tool palette location as the Paint Bucket tool. If the Paint Bucket tool is visible, simply click and hold while hovering over the Paint Bucket tool to make its menu fly out and expose the Gradient tool.

   The Gradient tool's options will change at the top of the Photoshop window. Select a gradient that goes from white to black; you should see a preset for this listed when you select the gradient.

6. With the Gradient tool configured and the layer with the mask selected, hold down the [Shift] key while drawing a line straight down, starting at 72px on the left ruler and ending at 108px.

---

2. You can use the Flip Vertical transformation option if you don't want to do this manually and then just move the flipped version directly below the original.

Figure 6.5: REFLECTING THE LOGO

The black part of the gradient will act as the mask, giving you the desired fade effect. You might have to try this a few times to get it to look exactly the way you want.

6.6 The Footer

The footer also needs some text. Like the original site, the footer needs to contain the copyright notice and links to the terms of service and privacy policy.

Select the Text tool, and choose a 10px black Arial font to place this information in the footer. If you want to create the appearance of a hyperlink, use separate text layers for the terms of service and privacy policy pieces so you can give them a separate color. You should use the color you chose for hyperlinks when you built your color scheme.

Don't spend too much time mocking up the text here. It doesn't need to be perfectly centered. You're going to replace this with actual text markup in the content document. The goal here is to create the desired effect so that you can get feedback on it.

6.7 Wrapping Up

In this chapter, you learned how to do quite a bit with Photoshop. You learned how to import other images, work with layers, and use guides to align elements. Now it's time to fill the structure with our content.

## Chapter 7

Design Mock-up: The Content

In the previous chapter, you accomplished two important goals: you divided your document up into the four regions, and you set up the header and the footer. Now we'll fill out the content in the sidebar and main content areas. You'll also mock up a search box and a tag cloud for the sidebar. In the main content area, you'll mock up a banner image, create a text blurb, and place the elements you've created.

7.1 Creating the Search Box

Our sketch put the search area at the top of the sidebar with a large heading and the search box directly underneath it (see Figure 7.1, on the next page). Let's use what we know about the baseline grid again and position everything along the gridlines here. Before you go any further, create a new layer group called *search area* to contain all the objects we create in this section.

As before, we'll use guides to help us position elements. Create a new horizontal guide that crosses 126px on the left ruler. This will help us position the heading. If you're getting tired of counting gridlines, you can add a guide by specifying its position and orientation. Select View > New Guide, and enter the appropriate information. You could create a second guide across 162px to define the heading region, but it's not essential to do this because the heading's ascenders will touch the guide at 126px. Because the font will be 24px high, we need to account for the extra line-height. Instead of a line-height of 18px for our headings, we need to up that value to 36px.

Press [T] to select the Font tool, and choose 24-point Monotype Corsiva for the font (or substitute any serif font you like if you don't have this

Figure 7.1: THE COMPLETED SEARCH AREA

font). Set the font color to 4B541C, the dark-green color we selected for our headings in our color scheme. Click the canvas right below the guide you defined and enter this text: *Search Recipes*. Use the Move tool to reposition the text so that it fits in the guides.

Now you'll draw the search box using a combination of the shape tool and some layer effects. To prepare, place a few guides to define the region for the search box. Our existing horizontal guide that crosses 162px will mark the top of the search box. Place two vertical guides that cross the top ruler at 270px and 288px, respectively. This will define the space for the search box and the search button. Each of these guides lands on a vertical gridline.

Create a new layer, and name it *search box*. Now select the Rectangle Shape tool, set the fill color to ffffff, and then draw a rectangle within the guides you defined for the search box. Right-click the search box layer's thumbnail, and choose Blending Options. Select Stroke from the left menu, and ensure that the Stroke option is selected. Make sure the size is set to 1 and the fill color is set to 000000.

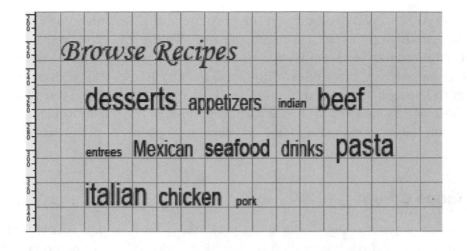

Figure 7.2: OUR COMPLETED TAG CLOUD

7.2 The Browse Recipes Tag Cloud

Our application uses tags to categorize the recipes. Users can tag recipes to make it easier to find things in a large collection. A lot of popular sites use a feature called a *tag cloud* to display the most popular tags in the system. The tag cloud uses several different font sizes to display which tags have the most items associated with them. For example, if we had three times as many recipes associated with the dessert tag than any other category, it might be several times larger in the tag cloud than any other tags. We'll build something that looks like Figure 7.2. Tag clouds usually have five to six different font sizes, but we can implement our mock-up with only three sizes: a large font, a medium font, and a small font.

Start with the header, using the same font and color you used for the search box header. Fit the header between horizontal guides you place at 216px and 252px. Create a new layer, select the Type tool (press ⊤), and be sure your color is set to 4B541C, which is the same greenish color we used for the search box header. Enter the text *Browse Recipes*, and then use the Move tool to drag the text block between the guides. Finally, make sure this text is even with the search heading. Be sure to use the guides and rulers! If you're having trouble getting things to line up just right, try using the arrow keys on your keyboard to nudge the text a tiny bit.

Now you can place the tags on the page using the Text tool. For example, choose a font size of 18pt, choose Arial for the font type, and select Bold as the style. Set the color to 54431C, and place *Desserts* on the canvas between the guides you placed. Next, place several other words in this area using a separate text block for each word. When you place these words, be sure to choose various font sizes and use multiple lines to simulate a working tag cloud, as shown in Figure 7.2, on the previous page.

7.3 Scope Creep

You know what really stinks about projects? Scope creep. It seems that every project I've ever worked on has been affected by scope creep in one way or another. Sometimes it's an unhappy customer, and other times it's an overzealous sales manager who wants to wow the client.

Sadly, it's a fact of life. No project has requirements written in stone. As a developer, you learn to embrace changes. So, to make you feel completely comfortable as a developer, I'm going to add an element not shown in the sketch: a second tag cloud.

The Popular Ingredients Tag Cloud

Each recipe in Foodbox has ingredients, so let's make another tag cloud that lists the most popular ingredients. This time I'd like you to give it a try on your own.

When you make the tag cloud, you should follow the same techniques you used to make the previous tag cloud. Use the grid and guides to place the header and the various items. Some examples of ingredients might include *Oregano*, *garlic*, *black beans*, *apples*, *bananas*, *cheese*, and *lettuce*.

Three lines of tags for the ingredients should be enough to fill out the sidebar. With that out of the way, let's finish up by filling in the middle region of the layout.

7.4 Mocking Up a Tasty Masthead

Photographs can help a website come alive. You can do a lot with colors, fonts, and gradients, but nothing beats a good *high-quality* photograph for adding that extra punch. The reason I stress the quality is because a poor-quality photo on a website will stick out like a sore thumb.

Photographers Are Your Friends

If you are considering doing some website work for money, you should consider hiring a photographer to take pictures for you. There are a lot of benefits to this. For one, you can get exactly what you want without having to take the time to learn it yourself.

Professional photographers might be expensive, but they're often worth it. They do this for a living, so they know all the tricks of the trade.

If you can't afford a professional, you might consider contacting a local photography club to see whether there's any interest there. People in a photography club are hobbyists, but they are often quite good, as well. Be sure to offer compensation, though. If you're getting paid, they should, too.

Whether you decide to hire a professional or a hobbyist, you should keep in mind that expertise is important. Would you hire a professional programmer or someone still in college looking to build a portfolio? You might get amazing results from either, but the professional is far more likely to deliver the quality you need and expect.

Photography is tricky business. It takes lots of practice to take good pictures. I know, because I've tried for a long time to get pictures to come out just right, and I'm nowhere close. I've had some clients hand me pictures taken with a digital point-and-shoot camera and ask me to use them on their website. The pictures are often crooked, too dark, or have awful lighting. You can use Photoshop to fix some of these issues, but a better approach is to start with a good picture.

So, where do we get good photographs for a website? If your budget doesn't allow for a photographer, visit iStockphoto[1] or another photo-sharing website. You can even find public domain or liberally licensed photographs at Flickr.[2]

For example, I found a nice image of pasta[3] at iStockphoto. I like the picture because it's clear and has even lighting. The image is too big

---

1. http://www.istockphoto.com
2. http://www.flickr.com
3. http://www.istockphoto.com/stock-photo-3762141-italian-meatballs.php

Figure 7.3: OUR PROGRESS SO FAR

for our page, but we can crop a nice, tight, rectangular area from the image after we get it into Photoshop.

You don't have to pay to use an image in your mock-ups. All the images from iStockphoto are visibly watermarked, unless you've purchased them.[4] Navigate to the image's URL and then right-click the image to bring up your browser's context menu. Select Copy Image to place the image on your clipboard.

When we place this image into Photoshop, we will resize it to make it taller and wider. This is fine for a mock-up, but you should never, ever do this for a real application. If you had your own photograph, you'd use a high-quality version that would be much larger; however, we won't pay for this image until our stakeholders approve the selection.

Let's place the banner on the page so it looks like Figure 7.3.

Create a new layer group called *Main Content*. Within that group, create a new layer (Ctrl+Shift+N) called *Pasta Photo*. Paste your image and use the Move tool to place the upper-left corner of the image at 306px across and 108px down. This is right where the middle region starts.

---

4. If you decide to use the image later, you can purchase it and replace the image in your Photoshop mock-up because it's on its own layer.

It's Not Free Just Because It's There!

Many people believe that if an image is on the Web or if it's available on Google Images, then they can use it on their own website. Nothing could be further from the truth. The fact is, unless you see it explicitly spelled out otherwise, the image is copyrighted by the photographer or the organization that posted the image.

Obtain permission for any photographs you want to use. If possible, get written permission or buy your photos through a service that specializes in stock photography.

Your previous guides for the banner and sidebar touch at this point. With the Marquee tool selected (M), right-click the newly pasted image, and choose the Free Transform option. While holding down Shift, drag the bottom-right corner of the image diagonally downward and left until the right edge of the image touches the edge of your composition. Press Enter to apply the transformation.

Now, use the Marquee tool to select the rectangular region where your image will eventually reside. Start from the upper-left corner where your guides meet. Your selection area will snap to the guidelines you created. With the Move tool (V), use the arrow keys to move the selection down until you're somewhere in the middle of the pasta image. Make sure the region of the image you want to keep is within the selection area, and choose Select > Inverse (Ctrl+Shift+I). Press the Delete key to remove everything except for the area you wanted to keep.

Finally, switch to the Move tool again (V), and use the arrow keys to move the image back up between the guides for the banner.

7.5 Main Content

We have no idea what we want to say on our home page, other than *Get Cookin'*, but we know we want to say something. We could just make something up, but then someone would probably pick apart our attempt at writing content. Instead, we'll borrow a page from traditional print mock-ups and use *Lorem Ipsum*. Lorem Ipsum is just dummy text that has been a print-industry standard for more than 500 years.

At first glance, it looks like real text, so it's great for filling in space when you don't have real content. Visit http://lipsum.org and generate a paragraph of text. This is standard dummy text, so it's also useful for making people concentrate on the design of the site, rather than the content. This works because everyone will know right away that the text on the page is meaningless.

Let's get some text on this page! Grab the Text tool, change the text color to 4B541C, and set the font to 36px Monotype Corsiva. Now place the *Get Cookin'* text on the page. Move the newly created headline into position at 324px on the top ruler and 288px on the left ruler. This is the same gridline that rests atop your second row of tags in the first tag cloud.

Body Text

Create a new layer called *Body Text*, and select the Text tool. Use guides at 324px and 486px on the left ruler to define the top and bottom boundaries of the text block we're going to use. Place a vertical guide at 612px to define the width of the text block. Using the Text tool, draw a rectangle to fill in the box created by your guides. Next, place the Lorem Ipsum dummy text into the text area, select the text you just pasted, and change the leading[5] to 18px, the font size to 12pt, the font color to 000000 (black), and the font face to Arial. The text now lines up with the gridlines.

7.6 Simulating the Browser

So far, we've built a decent mock-up of the page, but it isn't a good approximation of what it will look like in the web browser. We have designed a mock-up with fixed dimensions, but the Web is fluid. We should see what our site will look like on a monitor that has a wider width.[6]

Select Image > Resize Canvas, then change the width from 900px to 1200px. With the default settings, Photoshop will add the extra pixels evenly to the left and right of your image.

---

5. You might recall that *leading* is the vertical space between lines (see Chapter 4, *Fonts and Typography*, on page 53).

6. This is a huge problem for people accustomed to working with paper. Paper has boundaries, but the Web does not. You should always think about how to design without edges.

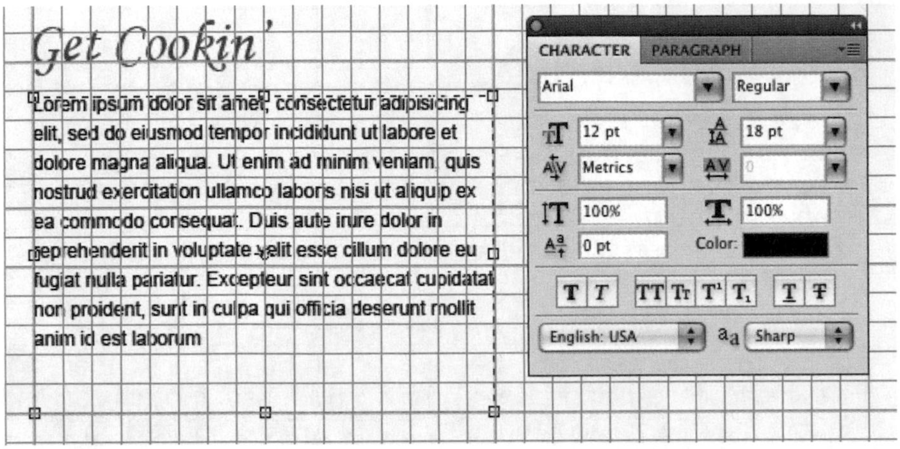

Figure 7.4: SETTING THE TEXT LEADING TO LINE UP WITH GRIDLINES

When we started this design, we decided to use a fixed-width design that makes the implementation a lot simpler. However, this mock-up does show a lot of whitespace on the left and right of the page. One technique we can use to give the appearance of a fuller page is to center the logo and the rest of the site in the browser window, as we had originally planned, and then stretch the background color of the header to fit the entire width of the window. This will help give us the appearance of a full-screen site, but we won't have to spend a lot of time doing the more advanced coding required to build a liquid design.

Choose the Move tool (V), and right-click the header. Next, choose the header layer from the pop-up menu. This is a great way to select a layer without having to search through all the layers in the Layers palette. Choose the Marquee tool, right-click the header, and choose Free Transform to activate the resize handles for the layer. Drag the left- and right-resize handles to the edges of the canvas, and then press Enter to commit the transformation.

By expanding the canvas, you can get an idea of how the page will eventually float in the middle of the screen. You used Photoshop's shape tools to define the site's regions, so it's easy to reshape them without diminishing their quality.

> **Hybrid Layouts**
> _____
>
> In recent years, especially as wide-screen monitors have become popular, designers have been looking at ways to make designs that take these new dimensions into account. The *hybrid layout*—a layout that is mostly fixed-width but has regions that expand the entire width of the screen—is a popular choice.
>
> Often, the header will expand to fill the full width of the screen, but the main content stays centered, as in our design. Other times the footer expands as well, creating an effect that fills out the screen while constraining the content so it's organized and readable.

7.7 Summary

We created quite a few elements in this chapter, and we learned how to simulate content in our document. We still have a few elements that we must create before we can move on to transforming this mock-up into code. Let's get that wrapped up next.

## Chapter 8

Putting the Finishing Touches on the Mock-Up

We have a few elements that we need to create for Foodbox. We need a search icon that will act as the button for the search form, and we need to make the sign-up button that will reside in the main part of the site.

Now, you could certainly go out and find a magnifying glass icon for your search, and you could use a button generator. However—as when coding—you get better results if you roll your own solution that's customized to what you're building. Mismatched icons can ruin a design, and the time you spend searching for an icon could have been used to make your own in just a few minutes.

These graphical elements could be created on the same canvas that contains the rest of the mock-up, but to keep that file organized, we'll use new files for each of these elements.

8.1 Creating the Search Icon

You can create a search icon using either Photoshop or Illustrator. If you need to create icons of various sizes that need to be scalable, you should use Illustrator. As you learned when you created your logo, a vector graphic scales nicely without distortion. However, in this case, you need a simple search icon for your search button. It has to be a fixed size, which means you can accomplish that quickly by using Photoshop.

Create a new Photoshop document called *Search Icon*. Give it a height and width of 18 pixels. Set the background contents to transparent, and set the resolution to 72 dpi.

Creating the Icon's Background

Hold down Ctrl+Spacebar, and click the mouse to zoom in. Each time you click, you'll go in another zoom level. Keep zooming until you reach 1200%. At this point, you can see the checkerboard pattern on the canvas that indicates that you're working on a transparent background.

Rename the current Layer 1 to *Background*. Then, select the Rounded Rectangle tool from the tool palette. Set the radius of the tool to 2px. The *px* is important. If you leave that off, it will pick a default unit of measure, like inches. Ensure that the mode for this tool is set to Fill Pixels and that the Anti-Alias option is selected. The rectangle's color doesn't matter because we'll change it in the next step.

Snapping to Pixels

We've used Snap to Grid to help us constrain our shapes, but now we'll make more complicated shapes with rounded corners. Snap to Grid can help us ensure that each edge of the rounded corner will look exactly the same. To make the shapes you draw snap to pixels, click the drop-down arrow to the right of the shape selector buttons on the options toolbar, and select the Snap to Pixels checkbox. When developing mock-ups or creating buttons, I recommend always using this option.

Now, place the cursor on the top-left corner of the canvas. Click and drag diagonally down and right, filling the canvas with the rounded rectangle. Line up the cursor with the bottom-right of the canvas, and then release the mouse button to create the shape.

Right-click the layer thumbnail, and choose Blending Options. Select the Gradient Fill option, and double-click the Gradient style to edit the gradient. Choose the same green you used for your headings as the color for the right side of the gradient. Set the left side of the gradient to 000000 (black). When you apply the gradient, you should have a gradient that transitions from green to black, as shown in Figure 8.1, on the facing page.

Creating the Magnifying Glass

Now it's time to draw the magnifying glass. Photoshop has some nice shape tools, but we're going to draw the magnifying glass itself using

Figure 8.1: A CIRCULAR SELECTION WITH THE MARQUEE TOOL

an old Photoshop technique: we're going to create it using the Marquee selection tool.

Create a new layer called *Magnifying Glass*. Select the Elliptical Marquee tool from the tool palette. Hold down the [Shift] key, and create a circle that fits neatly inside the icon area. You should have something that resembles Figure 8.1. Select Edit > Stroke, and then set the width to 2px give a white color.

Select the line-drawing tool, and set the weight to 2px. Draw a diagonal line at the lower left of the magnifying glass to create the handle, as shown in Figure 8.2, on the following page.

We now want to create a "glassy" effect. We could use the Marquee tool to select the area within the circle, but that's too much work. We can use the Magic Wand tool instead. Select the Magic Wand tool from the tool palette, and click anywhere inside the circle. The area within the circle is now selected.

Create a new layer called *Glass*. Set the foreground color to FFFFFF (white), and select the Gradient Fill tool. On the Options toolbar, double-click the gradient, and select Foreground to Transparent from

Figure 8.2: THE MAGNIFYING GLASS WITH A HANDLE

the gradient presets. With the new settings applied, use the tool to draw a straight line from the top of the magnifying glass to the bottom. As with many other transformation and selection tools, you can hold down the Shift key while dragging to force a straight line.

Your finished icon should resemble the one in Figure 8.3, on the next page. Save the Photoshop file as search_button.psd in the originals folder with your other Photoshop documents.

Placing the Search Icon

Switch back to your mock-up document, and choose File > Place. Select the search_button.psd file you just created, and position it right next to the search form. Save your document when you have things the way you like them. You can see the finished search area in Figure 8.4, on the facing page.

Figure 8.3: THE COMPLETED ICON

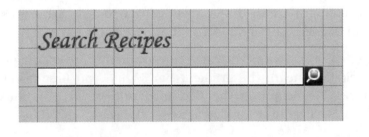

Figure 8.4: THE COMPLETED SEARCH REGION

8.2 Creating the Sign-up and Login Buttons

Our sketch shows two large buttons on the right side of the page. To create these buttons in the space we've left for them in our mock-up, we'll use some of the same techniques we used in Section 8.1, *Creating the Search Icon*, on page 101. Begin by creating a new document with a transparent background called *button*. Set the width and height to be 216px wide by 72px high; this will fit nicely into the space we have left.

Select the Rounded Rectangle tool from the tool palette, and then set the corner radius to 10px, which will give you nice rounded corner to the button.

Create a new layer from the Layers palette or via Shift+Ctrl+N, and label it as *button background*. We'll draw the button on the new layer.

Draw the button using the rounded rectangle that you configured. Do this by clicking and dragging from the top-left corner of the canvas to the bottom-right corner. If you set a foreground to a color other than white, you can see what you're drawing more clearly. It won't matter what color you choose because it's going to be changed in the next step.

Next, right-click the layer containing your button, and choose Blending Options. This will bring up the Layer Style dialog box. Select the Gradient Overlay tool to bring up the options for the gradient. Double-click the gradient image in the editor to display the Gradient Editor. I've labeled the color bucket as 1 and the transition point as 2 (see Figure 8.5, on the facing page).

You need to design a gradient that gives the button some definition. The key to getting this gradient right is to make sure you control how sharp the color changes are in the gradient. The Gradient Editor displays a long band of colors that represents the current gradient.

You specify the colors that make up the gradient by selecting one of the color buckets beneath the gradient bar. When you first bring up the gradient bar, the default gradient contains only two colors, but you can add colors by clicking the space between the color buckets.

Our button's gradient will contain only two colors, but we'll need three color buckets to make the transition. Set both the left and right color buckets to FFEABF, and then click between the color buckets in the space below the bar to add a third color bucket. Set the color of this bucket to FFAE00. If you're wondering, these colors are variations of the orange used in the sidebar.

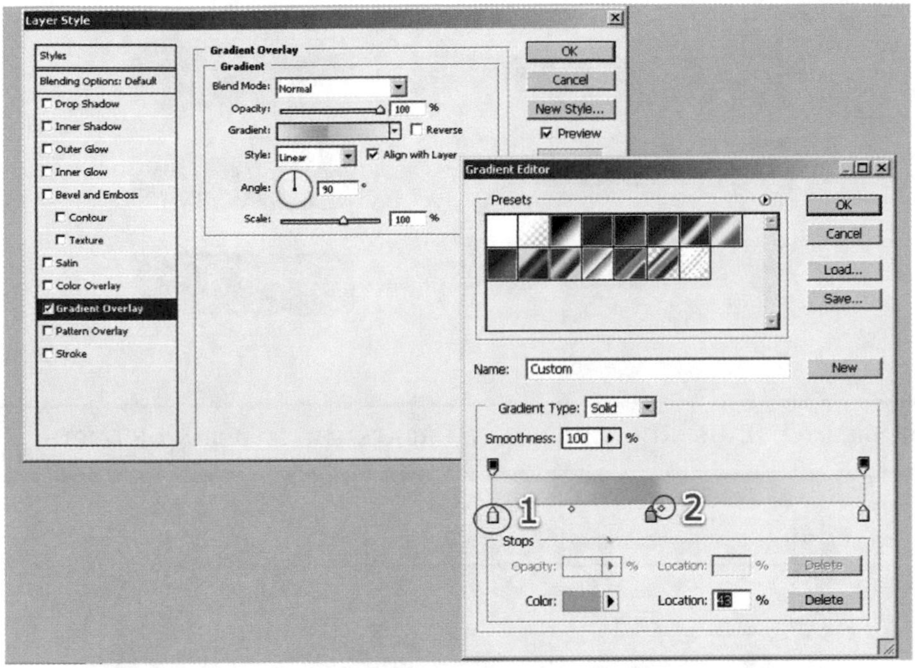

Figure 8.5: GRADIENT OPTIONS

Notice the round dots that exist along the gradient band in the editor. By moving these points closer toward a color, you can increase or decrease the blend. For this button, we'll create a hard transition between the colors by dragging the right dot to the left as close to the middle color as we can. This creates a nice horizontal line through the button, giving it a bit of dimension. You can see the specific settings I used in Figure 8.5. Click OK in the Gradient Editor once you design your gradient. Feel free to experiment with the Gradient Editor; you can see other examples of its effects in Figure 8.6, on the following page.

You can help the button stand out a little more by adding a *stroke*, which is an outline around the button. Select Stroke from the list of layer effects, and then choose a stroke width of 1px. Use a dark color such as black to make the button stand out more, or use a lighter color to make the stroke less noticeable. You can lower the opacity to around 45% to soften the stroke. Be sure to add the stroke to the inside the button so the stroke doesn't add to the width and height of the button.

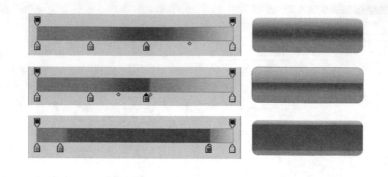

Figure 8.6: USING GRADIENTS TO CREATE THE ILLUSION OF DEPTH

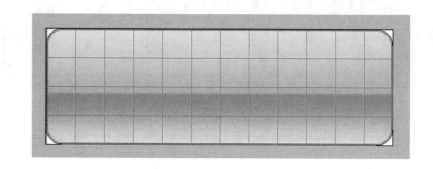

Figure 8.7: THE FINISHED BUTTON

Save your button as button.psd in the originals folder of your project. You'll need it later to create the login button.

Adding Text

Choose the Text tool, and add this text to the button: *Sign Up*. Experiment with the colors using what you now know about color theory. I recommend a dark color for the text on this button. Regardless, be sure to choose text that sharply contrasts the background of the button. You might also want to change the layer effects for the text to give it a bit of a bevel.

Save the file as signup_button.psd.

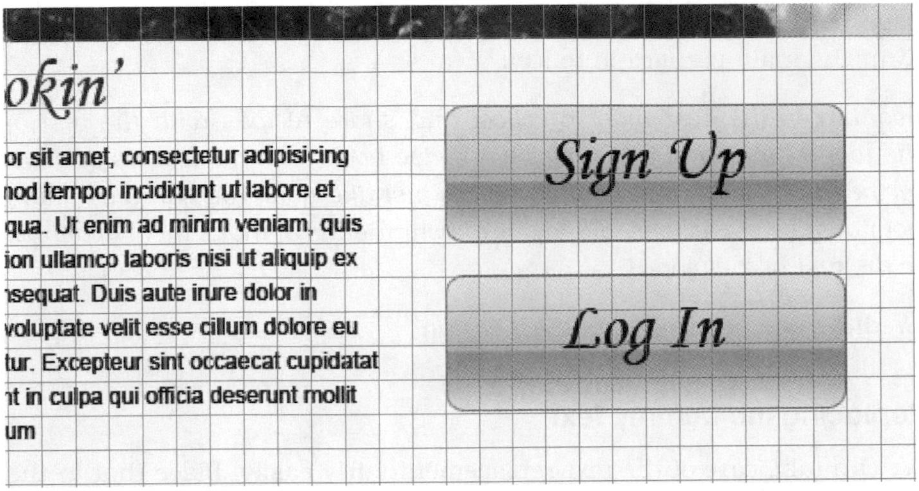

Figure 8.8: BOTH BUTTONS IN PLACE

Adding the Sign Up Button

Switch back to the mock-up file, and place the Sign Up button on the page using the same technique you used to place the logo. Position it into the spot you left for the Sign Up button.

Now save the mock-up again.

Creating the Log In button

Reopen signup_button.psd, and change the text to *Log In*. Select the Move tool, and nudge the text to make sure it's centered. After you add and position the text layer, save the file as login_button.psd and place it in the mock-up below the Sign Up button.

You can see both buttons in place in Figure 8.8.

8.3 You've Got Content!

You've just been informed by Steve that the stakeholders have finally decided on what they want to say on the main page. Everyone loves how the site is shaping up, but the stakeholders noticed that you have a whole bunch of blank space on the page. They've decided that they like the idea of featuring the most recently added recipes on the home page, as the original site had. They have also have decided on what they want the main paragraph to say:

Foodbox is the best way to collect and share recipes with the rest of the world. You can build your own recipe book from thousands of great recipes from renowned chefs or users just like you. You can also share your own secret recipes with a few of your friends or make them available to the rest of the world!

Create an account today and get cookin'!

Replacing the Dummy Text

We can take care of the text replacement fairly easily. Place that in the main text region, replacing the dummy text. You'll notice that it's a bit shorter than the previous block of text you had there, so you need to adjust things a bit. Select the text you just pasted, and increase the font size to 14px. You still have a little more room than you had before, but now you need a little more room to add the recipes the stakeholders asked you for!

Adding the Latest Recipes Section

We don't necessarily have to fill up the whole area at the bottom of the page, but we can certainly add a heading and a couple text blocks for recipes. Create a new 16px heading called *Latest Recipes* using the Monotype Corsiva font you used for the other headings. Place this heading beneath the introductory text, but be sure to leave some space between the new header and the existing content. Don't forget that you could duplicate the Get Cookin' layer and then change the position and text to quickly create this new heading. Then you could skip setting the color, font, and size. It's all about working smarter.

Beneath the headline you just added, create a few fake recipes. Use 14px Arial for your font this time. Nudge the recipes over a bit, as you did with the entries in the tag clouds; 18 pixels, or one block on the grid, should be just enough to make it look nice. Put each recipe title on its own line, and be sure to leave a line space between each one, using the gridlines as a guide.

Underneath the recipe, put a simple description of the recipe using a 12px Arial font. Indent the text over another 18px. You can see the results in Figure 8.9, on the facing page.

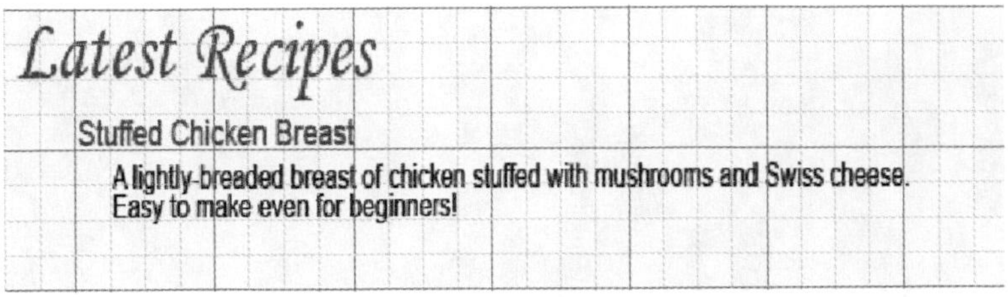

Figure 8.9: THE LATEST RECIPES SECTION

Figure 8.10: OUR FINISHED MOCK-UP

8.4 Summary

You're now at a point where you can comfortably start building the site. In this chapter, you learned how to work with layer groups, how to work with text, and how to apply some layer effects and masks. The techniques you learned in this chapter will become extremely valuable to you as you develop more sites, because you'll be able to provide your clients with vibrant, attractive mock-ups. Best of all, you'll have assets you can eventually extract from these mock-ups when it comes time to produce the final page.

Part III

Building the Site

## Chapter 9

Building the Home Page with HTML

You've spent a lot of time working on the design of this site, but now you have to transform your mock-up into a functional web page. You'll do this in several stages. You'll begin by deciding how to structure the document that will contain your content. Next, you build the HTML document's skeleton, defining the various regions on the page using simple, well-structured markup. Then you will apply some basic styling to create a layout for the content using Cascading Style Sheets (CSS). You'll also apply colors, font styles, and images.

We'll build the HTML document in this chapter, and then we'll spend the next three chapters working with CSS to apply the design elements to the document.

A web page isn't a fixed canvas like your Photoshop document, so you might not be able to translate it exactly. Unlike a printed brochure or a poster, a web page doesn't have a fixed size. A web browser's viewing area will change depending on the screen size or the window size set by your user. For example, your user might view the site through a small window or through one that fills the entire width and height of the screen. You will almost always need to make some adjustments along the way. When you're done, the real page won't look *exactly* the same as the mock-up, but it'll look so close that most people won't even be able to tell the difference. It's important not to get hung up on making sure that every single pixel is exactly in the right spot.

\\// **Joe Asks. . .**
>ᴗ<
‿   **I Already Know HTML. Why Do I Have to Read This?**

You might be familiar with HTML and the basic concepts of how to get a page to render in a browser, but that's not enough to build a web page. Think about how long it took you to get good at writing code. You had to learn more than just syntax; you also had to learn why things work the way they do. If you don't understand how HTML works, it will be difficult for you to get style sheets to work properly, and it will be even harder for you to implement a solid design that renders well in multiple browsers. This chapter starts you on the path to *understanding* HTML instead of merely knowing it. You want to progress from being able to write it by hand to knowing how to generate it properly using server-side tools.

9.1 Working with Web Standards

Separation of concerns is something that experienced developers think about all the time. When you're developing a web application that has models, controllers, and views, it's considered good practice to separate your display logic from your business logic. Web designers understand this concept pretty well, too. A website designed with web standards in mind will have its content separated from the design and the behavior.

When you hear someone talking about designing with *web standards*, that person is referring to using standardized best practices and philosophies. Standards bodies such as the World Wide Web Consortium (W3C) set many of these standards. Others standards are simply best practices set by pioneers of the web-design community.

A website or web page that is in compliance with web standards has the following attributes:

- The content and structure is marked up using valid HTML or XHTML. This includes using a proper *doctype* and *character set*.
- The presentation is rendered using valid CSS. This means that CSS governs the site's layout, font colors, font styles, page colors, and other non-content-related presentation aspects.

- The web page should be accessible to everyone, regardless of web browser, platform, or disability.
- The site meets basic usability guidelines for navigation, links, and structure.
- Behavior is separated from the content and its presentation. JavaScript that works on all platforms is used, and it degrades gracefully for platforms, devices, and users who can't use it.

This list sounds reasonable, but how do you implement something like this? You start by building a *valid* HTML document that contains your content and defines your structure. If you've ever composed simple HTML, this will be a piece of cake for you. But don't worry: even if you've never dabbled in HTML before, you'll pick up the lessons in this chapter quickly.

9.2 The Home-Page Structure

Try to visualize your pages as regions of content, as opposed to rows and columns, and you'll find it much easier to develop pages that not only conform to standards but are also much more flexible—you want to be able to switch out your style sheets and completely change the layout of the page.

For Foodbox, we want all the content for our sidebar to be in its own region, and we want all the content for our main area to be in its own region. We're going to do the same thing we did when we created our mock-up—divide the page up into sections.

You can divide your mock-up into four basic regions:

- header
- sidebar
- main
- footer

These four regions are easy to identify. However, you can build a flexible structure that you can manipulate easily if you further divide the page into subsections. The key to accomplishing this is to look for logical groupings of content.

For example, let's express the mock-up's regions in outline form:

- Page
    - Header
    - Middle
        * Sidebar
            · Search Recipes
            · Browse Recipes
            · Popular Ingredients
        * Main
    - Footer

In this example, we have an overall region called page. We divide this region up into a header region, a middle region, and a footer region. The outer, or parent, region, acts as a point of reference that we can use for positioning, and we can also control the overall page width by changing the width of the outer region.

The sidebar and main regions are wrapped in another region called middle. Like the outer page region, this middle region acts as a reference point, but it also serves another important purpose: it provides flexibility. We might not want a sidebar region for some of our pages; for example, we might want a full-width main region for displaying the content instead. On those pages, we could omit the sidebar and middle regions and place the content right in the main region, using CSS to resize it.

This structure is fairly common. It's the structure for your standard two-column layout with a header and a footer, one of the most common website types. The neat thing about standards-based design is that you can reuse this skeleton for another project if you want to, because your style sheets will define your column widths, colors, and other visual elements.[1]

9.3 Semantic Markup

Semantic markup makes sure your document is structured so that it can be interpreted by machines, devices, or people. For example, Google's web crawler uses tags such as h1 and href attributes on links to determine the importance of web pages and their content.

---

1. This approach works great for *skinning* a website; you could use this technique to let your users have their own themes. Visit http://www.csszengarden.com to see a great example of a single document rendered in multiple ways.

Joe Asks...

Can't We Just Slice and Dice Our Mock-Up?

In the old days of web development—and by "old" I mean those medieval times of 2004—it was common practice for developers to take a Photoshop document and use tools like Fireworks or ImageReady to slice the image up and generate HTML. This approach gives you a quick-and-dirty way to make a web page, but it also has some serious problems.

For example, it almost always involves using HTML tables for layout. This was *the* way that every web designer built web pages before CSS became a viable alternative. Among the many problems with this approach was that it made life more difficult for users who browse with screen readers.

Also, this approach doesn't separate the content from the design, so you can't easily make multiple presentations of your content available, such as a version of your site for printing and another version customized for display on mobile devices.

Finally, and most important, using tables for layout means that you will duplicate all the table HTML code on every page of your site. Every time someone requests a page, that data must be transferred to the end user. On a small-scale site, this just means your pages might take longer to get to the end user. If you run a site that gets lots of hits, you might start to see it in your monthly bills from your ISP. When you host a website, you have to pay for all the traffic that you serve, so if you have a lot of traffic, it's in your best interest to reduce file sizes wherever you can.

Designing with CSS and web standards allows you to define the look and feel of a website using files that end users download only once but share across all the pages you serve them. This improves performance and saves you money.

You need to use HTML tags for their intended purpose so that they describe the content they contain properly. Your page will have headings, paragraphs, lists, and other elements. HTML has lots of tags that are designed to mark up content. Headings, for example, should use syntax something like <h1>About Us</h1>. An HTML parser will see this tag and know it's the most important headline on the page.

It would be completely inappropriate then to do something like <font size="+2">About Us</font>. Unfortunately, many developers do precisely this because they don't like the fact that, by default, the h1 tag places a margin above and a line break below this tag's content when it is rendered.[2]

You can use CSS to solve the visual issues quite easily once you understand how everything works. For example, you might use CSS to change the way all headings look, or you might use it to modify the appearance of a single heading on a single page. Best of all, one CSS file can be applied to many pages, so instead of setting every heading on 100 pages, you can add a couple of lines to your style sheet.

9.4 The Home-Page Skeleton

Open your favorite text editor,[3] and create a new file. Immediately save this new blank file as index.html. The index.html page will be the home page for the site. Web servers will serve up the index page whenever a request comes in for a path and a page is not specified.

The Doctype

Each HTML page must have a doctype to help a validation tool ensure you're serving properly coded markup. It's extremely important to make sure you have a valid page before you apply style sheets or JavaScript. Invalid markup can cause styles to be applied incorrectly or cause JavaScript code to fail horribly. Your web browser relies on a well-formed document to apply styles and behaviors properly, so failing to close a tag might trip up a user's browser.

More important, doctypes force certain browsers to interpret a page differently. For example, Internet Explorer 6 has a *quirks* mode that is extremely forgiving to invalid markup, but you can spend a lot of time

---

2. Some WYSIWYG HTML editors write code like this too, so it's not just novices.
3. I recommend Notepad++ for Windows and TextMate for Mac.

Default Page Names

Web servers have a concept called *default pages*. A default page is rendered whenever a page is not specified for a directory. Web servers serve files from a directory structure. You have pages within folders, and the universal resource locator (URL) contains the path to the folder and file the user requests. For example, if you requested the http://www.foo.com/products/superwidget/about.html URL, the web server at http://www.foo.com would look in the products/superwidget folder for a file called about.html.

If you requested the http://www.foo.com/products/superwidget URL, then you've requested an incomplete resource, so the web server tries to figure out what you meant. First, it looks to see what actually exists at that location on the server. If it finds a folder there, it looks at a list of default filenames and then checks to see whether any of those filenames exist within that folder. Common default filenames include index.html, index.htm, and default.htm.

If the server can't find a default file, it might return a directory listing, or it might return an error message if an administrator configured the server to not allow directory listings. Many webmasters believe that disabling directory browsing adds a level of security to their sites; however, I don't think you gain much security by doing that. If you don't want people to see something, don't publish it to the Web.

When you link to a resource that has a default page, you should either include the filename in the URL or use a trailing slash after the directory name. This *courtesy URL* tells the server that you are in fact requesting a directory from the server, and you expect the server to return the default file. Courtesy URLs work best on the home page of a site.

For maximum performance and to avoid confusion, you should always link directly to the complete resource. Links to the Foodbox home, for example, should always end with index.html. This way, the server can just serve that file and then get on with handling the next request.

scratching your head trying to make your page work in other browsers that are more strict about what they will render. However, you can use a doctype declaration that forces IE 6 into *standards* mode, which isn't perfect, but it'll get us by.

You can choose from a few different doctypes. The doctype you use dictates what tags you can use in your document, as well as the validation rules that will be used to check your markup. The two most frequently used doctypes are *XHTML 1.0 Transitional* and *HTML 4.01 Strict*.

XHTML 1.0 Transitional

For a long time, XHTML Transitional was considered *the* way to build pages for the Web. A primary reason for its use was that it forced web browsers into standards mode. That's not much of an issue today, but XHTML continues to have some advantages over regular HTML. XHTML markup is more strict, which forces developers to think more about a page's structure. It also requires that you use lowercase letters when defining tags and attributes, which can be helpful when parsing documents. Finally, it requires every tag to have a closing tag.

Unfortunately several browser support issues undercut the benefits of using XHTML, including its extensibility. Internet Explorer does not understand how to handle XHTML unless it's served as HTML using the text/html content type instead of the more appropriate application/xhtml+xml. Serving XHTML as HTML forces browsers to deal with tag soup; the browser expects HTML tags, but it gets XHTML instead, so it spends time reworking the document.[4] You lose a lot of the benefits of XHTML that your users see, and these browser issues can in fact introduce some new problems into your page. For example, self-closing div and span tags, which are perfectly valid in XHTML, get their trailing slash removed by browsers when served as text/html, which leaves them unclosed, affecting all elements that follow.[5]

These issues have prompted some designers and developers to switch back to using regular HTML again, in the form of HTML 4.01 Strict[6] or the HTML 5 specification.

---

4. http://xhtml.com/en/xhtml/serving-xhtml-as-html/
5. http://www.webdevout.net/articles/beware-of-xhtml#myths has some great examples of how the content type affects the output of a page written in XHTML.
6. http://mezzoblue.com/archives/2009/04/20/switched/

HTML 4.01 Strict

We're using HTML 4.01 Strict in this book's examples. With HTML 4.01 Strict, elements must still adhere to a hierarchy, but case doesn't matter, some tags don't need to be closed, and self-closing tags don't exist. It's important to remember that these are only language issues, and they don't make HTML's syntax any worse or better than XHTML's syntax. As long as you make sure you validate your documents, you'll have no trouble with browser compatibility, user experience, accessibility, CSS, or JavaScript.

We'll use HTML 4.01 Strict in these examples, but I'll make sure to stress well-formed, valid, semantic markup. This will keep a future transition to XHTML 1.0 Strict or HTML 5 simple. Whichever doctype you choose to use in your work, you should realize that you almost always serve both doctypes to browsers as HTML, so the only *real* difference between the two doctypes is syntactical. Don't let yourself get caught up in a holy war.

Adding the Doctype

Place this doctype declaration in your document. Everything else in your document goes after the doctype.

`homepage_html/index.html`

```
<!DOCTYPE HTML PUBLIC "-//W3C//DTD HTML 4.01//EN"
  "http://www.w3.org/TR/html4/strict.dtd">
```

Don't bother typing it in yourself, though. Most web page editors have a template you can use, or you can go to your favorite search engine and search for *HTML 4.01 Strict doctype* to find an example.

The HTML Tag

A web page is a hierarchy of elements, much like an XML document. The html element is the root element of the document. All other elements in the document will reside within that element. Almost all elements in a web page have an opening tag and a closing tag. You can think of the opening and closing tags as scope markers, similar to curly braces in Java.

Add the html tag to your document immediately after the doctype, and be sure to add the closing tag. This is a good habit to get into when you do web-page development. Add the element's tag, immediately add the closing tag, and then reposition the cursor between the opening and closing tags. Forgetting an element's closing tag results in invalid

> **Joe Asks. . .**
>
> ### Is XHTML Dead?
>
> The W3C's recent decision to stop work on the next version of XHTML to focus more resources on HTML 5* has not killed off XHTML 1.0. but it does show that HTML 5 is the way to go when it comes to web markup.
>
> The main reason many programmers and standards advocates prefer XHTML over HTML is its strict syntax. All tags must have closing tags, all tags and attributes must be in lowercase, attribute values must be quoted, and stand-alone elements like br, img, meta, and hr need a trailing slash. With the exception of the self-closing elements, all these are perfectly legal with HTML 4.01 Strict, and you can use every one of these coding practices with HTML 5.
>
> XHTML isn't going to be worked on anymore, so it's dead in the same way that COBOL is dead—it works, and it's not going away any time soon. You shouldn't rush out and convert all your sites to HTML 4.01 Strict or HTML 5, but you should consider all your options when you start work on a new site.
>
> ---
>
> *. http://www.w3.org/News/2009#item119

markup, which in turn causes browsers to apply your styles in strange ways. Invalid markup also causes other web developers to break out in a rash of expletives or, worse, punches. You should do your best to avoid this.

`homepage_html/index.html`

```
<html lang="en">

</html>
```

Attributes

Each tag supports various attributes that you can specify within the tag's declaration. Attributes help describe the tag in more detail. The html tag we used has an attribute that describes the language we use in this document.

> ### Self-closing Tags
>
> If you're used to XML, you might be familiar with the idea of self-closing tags, or tags that have a trailing slash when there's no closing tag. The HTML 4.01 Strict doctype doesn't support these, but the XHTML 1.0 Strict and Transitional doctypes do, and so does the HTML 5 doctype.

The Head and Body

You can always find two elements within the scope of the html element: head and body. The head element contains all the metadata about the page, including the page's title that appears in the bookmark link and in the browser's title bar, as well as links to load JavaScript files, style sheet files, and other assets. The body element contains the visible contents of the web page.

Add the head tag and its associated closing tag to your document, immediately below the html tag you just defined:

homepage_html/index.html

```
<head>

</head>
```

It's a good idea to indent your tags, just as you would indent code within an if..else statement. Doing this will help you later, when your document gets bigger.

Add these two lines to the head element:

homepage_html/index.html

```
<meta http-equiv="Content-Type" content="text/html; charset=utf-8">
<title>Foodbox</title>
```

Tags Without Closing Tags

Some tags in HTML don't have any scope because they don't wrap any content or perform any transformation on content. Many of these tags can be considered content themselves.

Examples of this include the img tag, which inserts an image into the document; the br tag, which adds a soft line break; and the hr tag, which creates a horizontal rule.

\\/
:><
‿   **Joe Asks. . .**

Aren't You Supposed to Set the Content and Encoding in the HTTP Headers?

You are absolutely supposed to set the headers correctly, but some browsers use the value of the meta tag anyway, as do the validators. Using the meta tag in the page's source can only help you describe your content better. Other developers can use the value in the meta tag to see your intentions when they follow your work.

Finally, and most important, using the meta tag lets you develop and validate HTML that's not served by a server. You can open an HTML file on your hard drive, and it will render with the correct encoding.

When you do serve the file from a server, make certain that the value for the Content-Type header matches what you specified with the meta tag.

The meta tag is an example of a content element. This tag lets us describe our document with metadata. In this case, we use a meta tag to tell the browser or interpreter what character set our content will use. Sometimes you might paste in content from another source, and this content might contain symbols, curly quotes, or other characters that can't be viewed in all browsers or on all computers. Specifying a certain character set causes HTML validators to alert us when we use content like this.

We can use meta tags to provide more information to browsers, search engines, and other consumers of our page. We'll do a lot more with these tags in Chapter 18, *Search Engine Optimization*, on page 257.

The Page Title

The title tag is important. The text you place within that element will be displayed in the title bar of the web browser. It's also used as the default text when a person bookmarks the page, and it shows up in the search results for most search engines. In this case, the name of the site is good enough, but subsequent pages should have additional text in that element, such as *About This Site | Foodbox* or *Top Recipes |*

Block and Inline Elements

Almost all elements that reside within the body tags of your page are either block or inline elements. Understanding the difference between these types of elements can save you a lot of time when you're ready to style your pages with CSS.

By default, block elements begin on a new line. Examples of block elements include div, h1, h2, h3, p, ul, li, table, and form.

Inline elements, on the other hand, are rendered on the same line as other elements by default. Examples of inline elements include a, b, i, span, em, strong, label, select, input, textarea, u, and br.

You want to remember this point: block elements can contain other block elements or inline elements. Inline elements can contain only text and other inline elements; they cannot contain block elements.*

---

*. They might render in a browser, but your page won't be valid, and you will have a lot of trouble applying styles or working with JavaScript later.

Foodbox. The title displays in a site's bookmark and in the title bar, so we want to place the site name in all the headings. However, it might get truncated, so we also want a specific part of the title to show up first. For example, *Latest Recipes | Food...* looks better to users and search engines than *Foodbox | Latest Rec...* does.

The head section of the page will contain more elements as you move closer to the finished product, but you can begin building the visible part of the page right now. It makes no sense to do much search engine optimization or scripting at this stage.

The Body: The Main Event

All of the visible content of your page resides within the body tag.

Add the body and closing tags to our document, leaving some space between the tags so we have some room to work. At this point, we've built a standard HTML 4.0 Strict template (see Figure 9.1, on the following page).

You learned how to break down the elements of the page into sections in Section 9.2, *The Home-Page Structure*, on page 117. Now you have homepage_html/index.html

```
<!DOCTYPE HTML PUBLIC "-//W3C//DTD HTML 4.01//EN"
  "http://www.w3.org/TR/html4/strict.dtd">

<html lang="en">

  <head>

    <meta http-equiv="Content-Type" content="text/html; charset=utf-8">
    <title>Foodbox</title>
  </head>

  <body>

  </body>
</html>
```

homepage_html/index.html

Figure 9.1: An example of a default HTML template

to mark those sections up with code. To do that, use the div tag to *divide* the page into sections. div tags are invisible elements, so they don't take up any visible space on the page when it's rendered. They do have some special properties, though. For one thing, they are block elements, which means they begin on a new line. You can find a more detailed explanation of block elements in the sidebar on the preceding page.

The Page Wrapper

We can constrain all the content in the page we're creating to our desired width of 900px by creating a top-level region. We will place all the other regions of the page, such as sidebar, header, and footer, in this new region. Later, you can use this outer region as a point of reference for all other elements. Good coders document their code, and HTML permits comments, so add this code immediately after the opening body tag:

homepage_html/index.html

```
<div id="page"> <!-- start of the page wrapper -->

</div> <!-- end of the page wrapper -->
```

You must give the browser some way to identify the regions of your page so it can apply styles and behaviors. Note that the id attribute is unique to the document. This means you can't have more than one page id on a single page. If you do, your page won't validate, and it will likely start doing strange things when you apply styles.

The HTML comments in that code might prove a big help later, when the document gets longer and harder to read.

The Four Content Regions

You can use div elements to stub out the header, footer, sidebar, and main regions of the page:

`homepage_html/index.html`

```
    <div id="header"> <!-- start of header -->

    </div> <!-- end of header -->
    <div id="middle"> <!-- container for the sidebar and main region -->
      <div id="sidebar"> <!-- the sidebar -->

      </div> <!-- end of the sidebar -->

      <div id="main"> <!-- start of main content -->

      </div> <!-- end of main content -->
    </div> <!-- end of middle container -->
    <div id="footer"> <!-- start of the footer -->

    </div> <!-- end of the footer -->
  </div> <!-- end of the page wrapper -->

  </body>
</html>
```

This example includes an extra div called middle. Whenever you have two regions that you'll eventually want to display side-by-side, you should wrap those two regions with another region. It doesn't add that much extra markup to the document, and it makes your design more flexible. For example, if you need to eliminate the sidebar on another page of the site, you could omit the two inner regions and style the outer region. Here we wrap the sidebar and main regions the same way we wrapped the entire page.

We've put the structure in place, so let's add the content.

Alternative Text

The alt attribute for images gives you an easy way to improve the usability and accessibility of your site. Alternative text is displayed when images can't be displayed. Users who are blind rely on alternative text to describe the images to them, so it's a good idea to make your descriptions *descriptive* rather than vague! "A blue car" isn't as strong as "A vintage 1957 blue Chevrolet in front of the downtown mall."

Alternative text also comes in handy for text-based browsers and mobile-phone users with low-bandwidth connections. Another reason to make sure you always include good alternative text descriptions for your images is that search engines use them. Search engines can't read your images either, and your alternative text descriptions become extremely important at that point. I'll cover this issue further in Section 16.2, *Alternative Text Attributes*, on page 231.

9.5 The Header

The content for the header region consists of only the Foodbox logo, which we'll include with the img tag. This tag has a src attribute that specifies the path to the image. This path works like the href attribute of the a tag; it can be a URL or a relative path to a file. We'll discuss URLs in detail in Section 9.6, *The Recipes Tag Cloud*, on page 133.

When placing an image on a web page, it's always a good idea to specify the height and width of the image. We don't have the image right now, so we'll let that go for the moment; however, we definitely want to come back later and add this. For now, specify the image source and an alt attribute for the text. This alternate text gets displayed if the image can't be loaded; it's also extremely helpful for your users who use screen-reading software.

Place your cursor within the region defined by div id="header", and insert the following code:

homepage_html/index.html

```
<img src="images/banner.png" alt="Foodbox">
```

Now save your work. You're done with the header region for now, and you can move on to the next region.

9.6 The Sidebar

The sidebar region contains quite a bit of content. It has a search area, a tag cloud for recipes, and a tag cloud for ingredients. We will wrap the various sections in their own containers to make positioning easier when we get to that stage. Let's start by mocking up the HTML form.

The Search Form

HTML forms are simple. The hardest part about working with them is tying them into your back-end system. The Foodbox site's simple search form has only two elements: the keyword field and the submit button. A harder problem to solve is that HTML forms need to submit their results to a URL. To create the form, we need to know the URL that the form needs to send its data to, as well as what the server-side code expects the form field to be called, so it can pull out the data.

Fortunately, this is as simple as glancing at the code for the existing Foodbox site because it has the information you need:

```
<form method="get" action="/recipes/">
  <input type="text" name="keywords">
  <input type="submit" value="search">
</form>
```

This code tells us that the form uses a GET request to send data to the recipes URL. It also tells us that we need to call the form keywords. That gets us moving, but we need to clean up some problems with this code.

First, the input tags don't have closing tags. This could be because they were forgotten, or it could be because the version of HTML used originally did not require these tags to have closers. Our doctype does, though, so we need to take care of that. The input tag is self-closing, so that's an easy fix.

Second, the form and the two input tags all should have an id attribute. This will help with the eventual styling we want to do. Finally, we plan to have an image of a magnifying glass instead of a button.

Aside from the form itself, the search section needs a heading called *Search Results*.

<u>**Headings**</u>

Placing text content on the page is as simple as typing the text into the appropriate region. However, you want to consider how that text should be rendered.

HTML provides several tags designed for marking up text. In fact, HTML includes six different tags for marking up headlines: h1, h2, h3, h4, h5, and h6. The lower a headline's number, the more important it is.

Every web page should have at least one main headline that uses the h1 tag. Search engines use that and other headlines as part of their method for determining how important content is. We'll reserve our main headline for the main content region and use the h2 tag for the section headings.

Add this code to the sidebar region to build the search section:

`homepage_html/index.html`

```html
<div id="search">
  <h2 id="search_header">Search Recipes</h2>
  <form id="search_form" method="get" action="/recipes/">
    <div>
      <input type="text" id="search_keywords" name="keywords">
      <input type="image" alt="Search" src="images/search.png">
    </div>
  </form>
</div>
```

Let's walk through this code. The search section of the sidebar region is wrapped in its own region with its own ID; this gives you extra flexibility when you add your styles to your document. The search form somewhat resembles the original version of the form from the old site, and it gets an ID that will be useful for styling elements and adding JavaScript behavior.

We have placed a div tag around the input fields of the form to make validation happy. When using HTML 4.01 Strict, input tags have to be placed within a div or within a block-level element such as a headline or paragraph.

The most significant change you'll notice is that the form no longer has a submit button; we've replaced it with an *image button*.

\\/ Joe Asks...

Can I Use a Link Instead of a Submit Button to Submit a Form?

You can, but it's a bad idea. Links are meant to retrieve information, while buttons are meant to send information. Going against this standard is difficult and creates some unnecessary usability issues.

You must use JavaScript to use a link to submit a form. You make the link call a JavaScript function that submits the form. I won't show you how to do this because I don't want to encourage this practice. It's *a bad idea*. For one, it leaves users without JavaScript out in the cold.

People claim to have reasons for doing this all the time, but it boils down to the developer trying to achieve a certain visual effect. An image button goes a long way toward making a form look much more appealing. Another appropriate alternative would be to use CSS to transform the button into something that looks like a link.

An image button works like a regular submit button. When the user clicks the image button, the form's data is sent to the URL specified by the form. The difference is that, with an image button, you get to substitute the normal, boring, OS-specific submit button with any image you choose.[7]

The Recipes Tag Cloud

You typically implement tag clouds on the server, where you have some mechanism that queries your database for the most popular tags ranked by their frequency of use. You then take those results and render the HTML code to display the tags. A common approach is to use CSS styles to control the appearance of the tags and link them to the frequency. This is a book about design, so I will leave the server-side

---

7. Many form fields, such as checkboxes, radio buttons, drop-down select boxes, text areas, and buttons inherit their style from your users' graphical interface. There's no way around this, so when you're designing a website, be sure to test it with different operating systems to see how it will look.

implementation up to you. Instead, we'll concentrate on mocking up the tag cloud so you can see how to apply the styles.

As I already mentioned, tags in the cloud get styled differently based on how popular they are. If a tag has many associated recipes, we want to make it appear quite a bit larger than the others. Less-important tags should appear smaller. To keep this simple, let's keep the number of levels in the tag cloud to five. We'll use level one for the most-used tags and level five for the least-used tags.

Each of the entries in the tag cloud is a link to a page displaying recipes for that tag, but how do you apply the style? We need to reuse the styles that will be associated with the cloud; this is a good indication that we want to use the class attribute. Like an id attribute, a class attribute can be applied to every element in an HTML document.

You define a link by using the a, or *anchor* tag. You can links to other documents on the same server, other servers, or even spots on the same page. To make a link, you define an anchor tag and use the href attribute to specify the URL you want the link to point to. The text between the opening and closing tags becomes the hyperlink. Let's drill down on some of the various types of hyperlinks.

Absolute Links

An absolute link contains the full path to the resource, including the protocol, the server name, and the location of the resource on the server:

```
<a href="http://www.google.com/">Google</a>
```

Relative Links

A relative link relates to the current path. To create links to documents within your own site, you can use relative paths to reference a resource in a folder within the same directory as the current file:

```
<a href="about/index.html">About Us</a>
```

You can also reference a resource in a directory above the current file:

```
<a href="../index.html">Back to the home page</a>
```

Relative links can also be relative to the site's root:

```
<a href="/index.html">Back to the home page</a>
```

If you think that this resembles file traversal on a Linux-based filesystem, you are correct.

Anchors

You can also create links to parts of the page. You can define a named anchor using the a tag like this:

```
<a name="ingredients"></a>
<h1>Ingredients</h1>
....
]]>
```

You can then create a link on the same page that "jumps" to that part of the page when clicked:

```
<a href="#ingredients">Ingredients</a>
    ]]>
```

You can append the anchor to any absolute or relative URL, directing your users to a particular part of the page:

```
<a href="http://www.yourfoodbox.com/recipes/55#ingredients">Ingredients</a>
```

Anchors are extremely useful on long pages with lots of content. You can use them to build a table of contents (TOC) for your page, enabling users to jump down the page to the topic they want to see. You can also place a *Return to the Table of Contents* link at the end of each section so the reader can return to your TOC without scrolling.

You could mock up this tag cloud by putting the URLs on each link you make, but that's time-consuming, and you will eventually replace these links with code that will generate these links for you. For now, you can create links that don't do anything when you click them. You can use the pound (#) character instead of a string that points to a file or a web address. This is a great way to see how links will look without having to make the links work if someone clicks them. Think of it as *stubbing out* your links.

The next step is to create a section in the sidebar region for the first tag cloud:

homepage_html/index.html

```
<div id="browse_recipes">
  <h2 id="browse_recipes_header">Browse Recipes</h2>
  <a class="level_1" href="#">desserts</a>
  <a class="level_4" href="#">appetizers</a>
  <a class="level_5" href="#">indian</a>
  <a class="level_2" href="#">beef</a>
  <a class="level_5" href="#">entrees</a>
  <a class="level_4" href="#">mexican</a>
  <a class="level_3" href="#">seafood</a>
  <a class="level_4" href="#">drinks</a>
```

```
  <a class="level_2" href="#">pasta</a>
  <a class="level_1" href="#">italian</a>
  <a class="level_2" href="#">chicken</a>
  <a class="level_4" href="#">pork</a>
</div> <!-- end browse_recipes -->
```

Each hyperlink has a class assigned to it, and we'll assign a different font size to those classes when we build the style sheet. We will also wrap this section with a div tag and render its heading with the h2 tag, as we did in the search section.

The Ingredients Tag Cloud

The structure of the second tag cloud will be identical to the one in Section 9.6, *The Recipes Tag Cloud*, on page 133. You need to change the ID, the heading, and the tag contents. Don't feel bad about copying the same block of HTML from the previous tag cloud and altering its contents. You're not writing code here, you're marking up content. The normal rules about not repeating yourself don't apply. Get it done as fast as you can. Marking up content with semantically correct structure isn't glamorous work. People care how it looks, not how it works.

When you finish with the new section, it will probably look something like this:

homepage_html/index.html

```
<div id="popular_ingredients">
  <h2 id="popular_ingredients_header">Popular Ingredients</h2>
  <a class="level_2" href="#">oregano</a>
  <a class="level_4" href="#">garlic</a>
  <a class="level_3" href="#">black beans</a>
  <a class="level_3" href="#">apples</a>
  <a class="level_3" href="#">bananas</a>
  <a class="level_5" href="#">cheese</a>
  <a class="level_3" href="#">lettuce</a>
  <a class="level_1" href="#">chicken</a>
</div> <!-- end popular_ingredients -->
```

As with the recipes cloud, you have your heading and links inside their own region.

This wraps up the sidebar region. At this point, you should save your work and take a look at your page in a web browser to see how it looks so far.

⚡ Joe Asks...

What Does the Pound Sign Do?

The pound sign (#) refers to a location within an HTML document. It makes it possible for you to create links that point to a specific section within a document. For example, a link to <a href="index.html#news">News</a> loads up the index page and jumps directly to the section of the page that has the anchor defined with <a name="news">News</a>.

In the case of our tag clouds, we used only a single pound sign for the URL, which the browser will interpret as "jump to the top of the page." Basically, nothing will happen.

On a side note, you might occasionally see the pound sign used as a placeholder when JavaScript code is attached to the link using the onclick attribute:

```
<a href="#" onclick="showAddUserForm(); return false;">
    Add New User</a>
```

This is a popular solution, but you should avoid doing this at all costs. Users without JavaScript enabled will be unable to use the link because it will jump them to the top of the page. Instead, you should use a true link that accomplishes the same functionality. In the case of an "add user" form, the link could point to a separate page that allows the user to add the user. Then you could use unobtrusive JavaScript to attach the behavior for the click event.

9.7 The Main Content

Our main region consists of a large horizontal image, a column of text, the Sign Up and Log In buttons, and the Latest Recipes section. Three of these elements are images that we'll have to extract from our mockup. We haven't extracted those yet, so we can stub those out, as we did with the image button for the search form.

Pasta Image

Let's add a reference to the pasta image using the img tag, as we did for the banner. Place this code within the <main>...</main> tags:

homepage_html/index.html

```
<img id="main_image" src="images/pasta.jpg"
    alt="Pasta and marinara sauce">
```

Again, we assume here that you'll eventually have an images folder within the folder that contains this page, as well as a pasta.jpg file inside that folder. Until you do that, the browser will display the text specified by the alt attribute.

Alternate Text

All image elements in your site need to have some alternate text that displays if the image can't be loaded for some reason, such as the user is using a screen reader or a text-based browser. The alt attribute lets you specify that text. When using this attribute, it's important to be descriptive. You'll pass validation if you put only *image* in each tag, but that isn't helpful to your users. Be sure to describe the content contained in the picture.

Text Content

The text-content area has the Get Cookin' text heading and the paragraphs of placeholder text beneath it. We will use CSS to replace the header with an image (as we do for other headers), and we will wrap the text content inside <p> tags. As we do with sidebar elements such as the search and tag clouds, we place the header and paragraphs in their own regions:

`homepage_html/index.html`

```
<div id="main_text">

  <h1 id="get_cooking">Get Cookin...</h1>
  <p>Foodbox is the best way to collect and share recipes
        with the rest of the world. You can build your own
        recipe book from thousands of great recipes from
        renowned chefs or users just like you.  You can also
        share your own secret recipes with a few of your friends
        or make them available to the rest of the world!</p>

  <p>Create an account today and get cookin!</p>
</div><!-- end main_text -->
```

Note that two separate paragraphs exist here. In the mock-up, the Create an account... section is separate from the rest of the body copy. You might be tempted to use a <br /> tag to force a line break, but you need to think about what the content represents. You have two separate paragraphs here, so you should mark them up as such in your document.

> ## Joe Asks…
>
> ### Why Are We Embedding Images for the Buttons Instead of Styling Them with CSS, As We Plan to Do with Section Headings?
>
> We're reserving image replacement to preserve how our type looks. The Log In and Sign Up buttons we made do more than replace text—they behave more like controls on the interface. That said, feel free to use CSS. If you prefer that approach, you can replace the headings using the same method we'll use in Chapter 12, *Replacing the Section Headings Using the Cover-up Method*, on page 191.

The Sign Up and Log In Buttons

You use the img tag to place the buttons the user will use to sign up or log in with. You should treat this area as another region of your document, creating a new div with an appropriate ID and adding an image for the button.

You want this button to be clickable, but it won't submit any data, so you don't need to use a form. Instead, you will make an image out of a hyperlink. Do you remember how the a tag works? Anything between the opening and closing tags becomes the hyperlink. It so happens that if you wrap an img tag with an a tag, you get a clickable image. Add two img tags and wrap them with links, one for the Sign Up button and one for the Log In button:

`homepage_html/index.html`

```
<div id="signup_login">
  <a href="/signup/">
      <img src="images/btn_signup.png" alt="Sign up">
    </a>
  <a href="/login/">
      <img src="images/btn_login.png" alt="Log in">
    </a>
</div><!-- end signup_login -->
```

Note that each of these image tags has its alt attribute specified to match the text on the buttons. This will help blind and screen-reader users locate the buttons more easily. These images also have a border around them to denote that they are clickable. This border doesn't look good, so we'll eventually use CSS to remove it.

The Latest Recipes Section

Now you need to mock up a couple recipes for the Latest Recipes section, as you did for the tag clouds. Eventually, you will write some code to grab the latest *n* recipes from the database and then to loop through and display them. You don't need to go through that process now because you're building this document to get feedback on the design.

The styling for this section is slightly more complex than for the other sections. The recipe title is a normal heading, but the paragraph that contains the description has a slight indentation. To make this easy, we can give the description paragraph tags a class attribute. The class attribute makes it easy to apply a style to a group of elements or its children. When we eventually apply the style, we'll specify that only paragraphs that are children of the div element with the ID of latest_recipes will be indented:

`homepage_html/index.html`

```
<div id="latest_recipes">

  <h2 id="latest_recipes_header">Latest Recipes</h2>

  <div id="latest_recipe_1" class="latest_recipe">
    <h3><a href="#">Stuffed Chicken Breast</a></h3>
    <p>A lightly breaded breast of chicken stuffed with mushrooms
          and Swiss cheese. Easy to make even for beginners.</p>
  </div>

  <div id="latest_recipe_2" class="latest_recipe">
    <h3><a href="#">Chocolate Pancakes</a></h3>
    <p>This complete-from-scratch classic pancakes recipe is sure
       to please even the pickiest eater, especially chocolate
       lovers.</p>
  </div>

</div>
```

Each one of these recipes has the class attribute set to latest_recipe. Unlike id attributes, a class attribute can be repeated as many times as you want. You have to think ahead about the design and how you plan to apply the style sheets to your document when you code up your content.

Having the digital mock-up available to you makes it a bit easier to do this, because you can see how some areas might share style elements.

9.8 The Footer

The footer region of the page contains the copyright notice and hyperlinks to the privacy policy and the terms of service. On the original site, the copyright notice was rendered with a special character that doesn't show up correctly in some web browsers. It's possible for these special characters to sneak into web pages, especially if the developer uses a visual editor such as Dreamweaver or FrontPage and pastes in content from Microsoft Word.

Special characters such as the copyright symbol, left and right curly quotes, and many others must be specified using *entity codes*.

Within the footer region, enter the following text:

```
homepage_html/index.html
<div id="footer"> <!-- start of the footer -->

  <p id="copyright">Copyright &copy; 2010 Foodbox,
                    LLC, all rights reserved.</p>
  <p id="privacy_and_terms">
    <a href="terms.html">Terms of Service</a> |
    <a href="privacy.html">Privacy Policy</a>
  </p>
</div> <!-- end of the footer -->
```

© is an example of an entity code. When the browser encounters the entity code, it renders the appropriate character. This ensures that the copyright symbol is rendered accurately in the various browsers and fonts that a user might have.

In this example, I gave the paragraph tags a unique ID instead of defining new div tags. The paragraph tags are already block elements; these elements take only one line of text apiece, so it doesn't make sense to add the extra markup for the div tags.

In your quest to create a flexible content document, you should try to avoid adding any superfluous elements.

Entity Codes

You've seen how you can use entity codes to render the copyright symbol, but you can use them for other things, as well.

The browser ignores spaces greater than one character, but sometimes you might need to have an extra space in the middle of a paragraph. Use the   entity code or a *non-breaking blank space* to force the browser to display a blank character.

People you work with who are familiar with print, such as a company's PR department, might not like the normal quotes provided in HTML. They might ask you to use *curly* quotes instead. You can achieve this using " and ".

You can do a web search for *HTML entity codes* to see many examples of these codes. Every special character has an entity code, including those pesky accented letters in foreign languages.

At this point, you have a completed page that should look a lot like this:

`homepage_html/index.html`

```
<!DOCTYPE HTML PUBLIC "-//W3C//DTD HTML 4.01//EN"
  "http://www.w3.org/TR/html4/strict.dtd">

<html lang="en">

  <head>

    <meta http-equiv="Content-Type" content="text/html; charset=utf-8">
    <title>Foodbox</title>
  </head>

  <body>
    <div id="page"> <!-- start of the page wrapper -->


      <div id="header"> <!-- start of header -->

        <img src="images/banner.png" alt="Foodbox">
      </div> <!-- end of header -->
      <div id="middle"> <!-- container for the sidebar and main region -->
        <div id="sidebar"> <!-- the sidebar -->
```

```
    <div id="search">
      <h2 id="search_header">Search Recipes</h2>
      <form id="search_form" method="get" action="/recipes/">
        <div>
          <input type="text" id="search_keywords" name="keywords">
          <input type="image" alt="Search" src="images/search.png">
        </div>
      </form>
    </div>

    <div id="browse_recipes">
      <h2 id="browse_recipes_header">Browse Recipes</h2>
      <a class="level_1" href="#">desserts</a>
      <a class="level_4" href="#">appetizers</a>
      <a class="level_5" href="#">indian</a>
      <a class="level_2" href="#">beef</a>
      <a class="level_5" href="#">entrees</a>
      <a class="level_4" href="#">mexican</a>
      <a class="level_3" href="#">seafood</a>
      <a class="level_4" href="#">drinks</a>
      <a class="level_2" href="#">pasta</a>
      <a class="level_1" href="#">italian</a>
      <a class="level_2" href="#">chicken</a>
      <a class="level_4" href="#">pork</a>
    </div> <!-- end browse_recipes -->

    <div id="popular_ingredients">
      <h2 id="popular_ingredients_header">Popular Ingredients</h2>
      <a class="level_2" href="#">oregano</a>
      <a class="level_4" href="#">garlic</a>
      <a class="level_3" href="#">black beans</a>
      <a class="level_3" href="#">apples</a>
      <a class="level_3" href="#">bananas</a>
      <a class="level_5" href="#">cheese</a>
      <a class="level_3" href="#">lettuce</a>
      <a class="level_1" href="#">chicken</a>
    </div> <!-- end popular_ingredients -->
  </div> <!-- end of the sidebar -->

<div id="main"> <!-- start of main content -->

  <img id="main_image" src="images/pasta.jpg"
      alt="Pasta and marinara sauce">

  <div id="main_text">

    <h1 id="get_cooking">Get Cookin...</h1>
    <p>Foodbox is the best way to collect and share recipes
            with the rest of the world. You can build your own
            recipe book from thousands of great recipes from
            renowned chefs or users just like you.  You can also
```

```
                                    share your own secret recipes with a few of your friends
                                    or make them available to the rest of the world!</p>

                        <p>Create an account today and get cookin!</p>
                    </div><!-- end main_text -->
                    <div id="signup_login">
                        <a href="/signup/">
                            <img src="images/btn_signup.png" alt="Sign up">
                        </a>
                        <a href="/login/">
                            <img src="images/btn_login.png" alt="Log in">
                        </a>
                    </div><!-- end signup_login -->
                    <div id="latest_recipes">

                        <h2 id="latest_recipes_header">Latest Recipes</h2>

                        <div id="latest_recipe_1" class="latest_recipe">
                            <h3><a href="#">Stuffed Chicken Breast</a></h3>
                            <p>A lightly breaded breast of chicken stuffed with mushrooms
                                    and Swiss cheese. Easy to make even for beginners.</p>
                        </div>

                        <div id="latest_recipe_2" class="latest_recipe">
                            <h3><a href="#">Chocolate Pancakes</a></h3>
                            <p>This complete-from-scratch classic pancakes recipe is sure
                                to please even the pickiest eater, especially chocolate
                                lovers.</p>
                        </div>

                    </div>

                </div> <!-- end of main content -->
            </div> <!-- end of middle container -->
            <div id="footer"> <!-- start of the footer -->

                <p id="copyright">Copyright &copy; 2010 Foodbox,
                                    LLC, all rights reserved.</p>
                <p id="privacy_and_terms">
                    <a href="terms.html">Terms of Service</a> |
                    <a href="privacy.html">Privacy Policy</a>
                </p>
            </div> <!-- end of the footer -->
        </div> <!-- end of the page wrapper -->

    </body>
</html>
```

9.9 Validating Your Markup

One of the reasons you're doing all this hand-rolled HTML is so that you can have a valid document. The W3C, the standards body that defines the specifications for HTML, XHTML, and CSS, provides an online validation tool that you can use to check any page by either providing a URL or by pasting in your source code.

Some text editors that support HTML editing make the process of validating your local file quite easy, but I prefer using the Firefox web browser and the Web Developer Toolbar. This combination runs on all platforms, so it's always available to me.

Setting Up Firefox for Web-Page Development

Firefox is a popular web browser, but it's also a great tool for website development. You can extend Firefox with plug-ins or *extensions* that add new features to the browser. We can use Firefox and a couple of extensions to help us develop and test websites and web applications.

If you don't already have the latest version of Firefox installed, visit the Firefox website[8] and download the installation program. Install the browser and launch it.

The Web Developer Toolbar

The Web Developer Toolbar transforms the Firefox browser into a powerful development environment for web-application developers and web designers. The tool makes it easy to validate your pages against the W3C page validation service, and it also features a live CSS editor that we'll use in the next chapter.[9]

Install the Web Developer Toolbar by pointing Firefox to https://addons. mozilla.org/firefox/60/, selecting the Add to Firefox link on the page, and then clicking the Install button in the security dialog box that appears.

You need to restart the Firefox browser after you install all the extensions. When Firefox restarts, you can find your new Web Developer Toolbar immediately beneath the bookmark's toolbar.

---

8. http://www.getfirefox.com/
9. Application developers might be interested in the ability for the Web Developer Toolbar to clear session cookies and inspect headers.

Joe Asks. . .

Why Develop with Firefox When Most People Use Internet Explorer?

If you design and develop with Firefox, you'll find that you spend much less time in the development process than you would if you used Internet Explorer. This is because Firefox is a bit pickier about how it renders pages, whereas IE lets you break some rules that will eventually cause you nightmares when it comes time to build your style sheets. You still need to test your stuff against Internet Explorer, but the idea is to build for Firefox and then tweak for IE using some special IE features such as conditional comments to include IE-specific styles. You'll spend much less time making the site work across platforms if you follow this approach.

Internet Explorer gets more standards-compatible with every release, and it's always important to test on as many browsers and platforms as you can. However, Firefox remains the best way to develop pages because it features good support for web standards, and it includes powerful plug-ins designed to help you work better.

Firefox for Linux

Linux users should consult their distribution's documentation. You could build Firefox from source, but there's a good chance that you have a Firefox package available via your distribution's package management system. For example, Ubuntu users can install Firefox with this instruction:

```
sudo apt-get install mozilla-firefox
```

> ### Firebug
>
> The Firebug* extension makes debugging and inspecting HTML, CSS, and JavaScript much easier. We won't be using it in this book, but you will find it an invaluable tool. Firebug will show you all the CSS style definitions, widths and heights, and other attributes of elements. It's essentially a debugger for web developers.
>
> Firebug Lite[†] is a cross-browser version that can help you get out of trouble when you're working with Internet Explorer.
>
> ---
>
> *.   http://getfirebug.com/
> †.   http://getfirebug.com/lite.html

Validating Your Document

Validation doesn't take too long, and if you've made no coding errors, you'll get a friendly message telling you that your page is valid. If you get a message that says you have errors, the validation report will show you the problem spots in your code. In the event that this happens to you, you should work on the errors one at a time, starting from the top. A single error at the top of your document can trigger ten more. Fix the first problem and revalidate.

The validator will even catch situations where you've used some symbols inappropriately, such as the ampersand character. Many application developers use the querystring to pass parameters back to the server, as shown here:

http://www.example.com/search?first_name=homer&last_name=simpson

Although that URL will work, it won't be considered valid if the validator sees it in your code. To pass validation, you must encode all ampersands within the source as &. This isn't usually a problem if you use a modern web framework, but you'll still see this issue pop up occasionally.

9.10   HTML 5

HTML 5 is still in draft form at the time of writing. Of course, that hasn't stopped people from adopting it already. It's not widely supported on every browser yet, but it's fully backward-compatible. In fact, the HTML

5 doctype even forces Internet Explorer 6 into standards mode. This compatibility makes it easy to use CSS to build presentable websites. The HTML5 Gallery[10] lists websites that have already made the move.

What makes HTML 5 so interesting is that it places even more emphasis on marking up content. In this chapter, we use div elements to mark up our heading, sidebar, main content, and footer. If we were using HTML 5, our markup might look like this:

homepage_html/index_html5.html

```
<!DOCTYPE html>

<html lang="en-US">
  <head>
    <meta http-equiv="content-type" content="text/html;charset=utf-8" />
    <title>Foodbox</title>
  </head>

  <body>
    <section id="page">

      <header id="header">
        <img src="images/banner.png" alt="Foodbox">
      </header>
      <section id="middle">
        <aside id="sidebar">

          <section id="search">
            <h2 id="search_header">Search Recipes</h2>
            <form id="search_form" method="get" action="/recipes/">
              <div>
                <input type="text" id="search_keywords" name="keywords">
                <input type="image" alt="Search" src="images/search.png">
              </div>
            </form>
          </section>

          <section id="browse_recipes">
            <h2 id="browse_recipes_header">Browse Recipes</h2>
            <a class="level_1" href="#">desserts</a>
            <a class="level_4" href="#">appetizers</a>
            <a class="level_5" href="#">indian</a>
            <a class="level_2" href="#">beef</a>
            <a class="level_5" href="#">entrees</a>
            <a class="level_4" href="#">mexican</a>
            <a class="level_3" href="#">seafood</a>
            <a class="level_4" href="#">drinks</a>
```

---

10. http://html5gallery.com/

```
        <a class="level_2" href="#">pasta</a>
        <a class="level_1" href="#">italian</a>
        <a class="level_2" href="#">chicken</a>
        <a class="level_4" href="#">pork</a>
      </section>

      <section id="popular_ingredients">
        <h2 id="popular_ingredients_header">Popular Ingredients</h2>
        <a class="level_2" href="#">oregano</a>
        <a class="level_4" href="#">garlic</a>
        <a class="level_3" href="#">black beans</a>
        <a class="level_3" href="#">apples</a>
        <a class="level_3" href="#">bananas</a>
        <a class="level_5" href="#">cheese</a>
        <a class="level_3" href="#">lettuce</a>
        <a class="level_1" href="#">chicken</a>
      </section>
    </aside>

    <section id="main">
      <img id="main_image" src="images/pasta.jpg"
          alt="Pasta and marinara sauce">

      <article id="main_text">
        <h1 id="get_cooking">Get Cookin...</h1>
        <p>Foodbox is the best way to collect and share recipes
              with the rest of the world. You can build your own
              recipe book from thousands of great recipes from
              renowned chefs or users just like you.  You can also
              share your own secret recipes with a few of your friends
              or make them available to the rest of the world!</p>

        <p>Create an account today and get cookin!</p>
      </article>

      <section id="signup_login">
        <a href="/signup/">
              <img src="images/btn_signup.png" alt="Sign up">
            </a>
        <a href="/login/">
              <img src="images/btn_login.png" alt="Log in">
            </a>
      </section>

      <section id="latest_recipes">
        <h2 id="latest_recipes_header">Latest Recipes</h2>
        <article id="latest_recipe_1" class="latest_recipe">
          <h3><a href="#">Stuffed Chicken Breast</a></h3>
          <p>A lightly breaded breast of chicken stuffed with mushrooms
                and Swiss cheese. Easy to make even for beginners.</p>
        </article>
```

```
                    <article id="latest_recipe_2" class="latest_recipe">
                      <h3><a href="#">Chocolate Pancakes</a></h3>
                      <p>This complete-from-scratch classic pancakes recipe is sure
                          to please even the pickiest eater, especially chocolate
                          lovers.</p>
                    </article>
                  </section>
                </section>
              </section>

              <footer id="footer">
                <p id="copyright">Copyright &copy; 2010 Foodbox,
                                    LLC, all rights reserved.</p>
                <p id="privacy_and_terms">
                  <a href="terms.html">Terms of Service</a> |
                  <a href="privacy.html">Privacy Policy</a>
                </p>
              </footer>
            </section>

        </body>
      </html>
```

This code is much more descriptive than what you see in HTML 4.01 Strict. However, HTML 5 remains a moving target, which is why I chose to focus on HTML 4.01 Strict in this book. If you feel adventurous, you might try implementing the rest of the exercises in this book using the HTML 5 template.[11]

9.11 Summary

In this chapter, you learned how to build a structured content document that's valid and ready to be styled. You can use the structure you used here in future projects because it contains only content and structural elements. The main thing you should take away from this chapter is that your document should be structured in a way that is flexible but also semantically marked up and *valid*. We separated each logical element group with markup, and then we allowed the available markup tags in HTML to handle the rest of the content. Now it's time to transform this document using CSS.

---

11. Older browsers won't recognize the new elements like aside yet, so they can't be styled, but you can use Javascript's document.createElement(); method to make browsers recognize the new elements. Just remember that this requires that your users have Javascript enabled.

## Chapter 10

Creating Assets from Our Mock-Up

We have our skeleton for the home page in place; next, we need to get the logo and other images ready for use on the Web. We can use pieces from our mock-up in our final web page. In this chapter, you'll learn about the various graphic file formats you can use in a website. You'll also learn how to slice up your Photoshop document and export sections to individual files that you can then reference in your HTML document or your style sheets.

10.1 Graphics Optimization

Before you start exporting images, you should familiarize yourself with some of the important issues relevant to using graphics on the Web, such as file size, file types, and image optimization. Many of the available graphics tools will do this optimization for you, but to make good choices that best suit your situation, you should understand the how and why of optimization.

Graphics optimization is the process of reducing the file size of images used on web pages, while preserving the quality and clarity of those images. This process provides a few key benefits:

Smaller images are friendlier to your end users.

People will be able to download the web page faster if you've optimized your images. Your website will appear faster to them, and they will be less frustrated than if they had to wait thirty seconds for all your huge, unoptimized images to appear.

Smaller images are more bandwidth-friendly. Web hosts usually limit how much data your website can serve per month. If your images are smaller, you won't hit your quota as fast. Some providers will even charge fees when you exceed your limit. Commercial organizations that host their own websites also pay a bandwidth fee. It might seem trivial, but the savings will add up if you get a significant amount of unique visitors to your site.

Smaller images take up less space. Sure, we've all heard the argument that disk space is cheap, but disk space is even cheaper if you don't have to buy as many disks to store all your huge images. Amazon's S3 service charges for both the space used by your files and your bandwidth. It's in your best interests to keep the image sizes small so you pay less for storage and data transfer.

Download Times

Even though many people have fast Internet connections, you still need to think about download times for your assets. A 100KB JPEG might appear small, but add in five of them, the 122KB Prototype JavaScript library, several CSS files, and several other assets, and it can take a few seconds or more for those images to download. Users tend to be incredibly impatient, and you want to do everything you can to make your pages load as quickly as possible.

You can use various methods to calculate the total size of a page. Adding up the file size of your page, scripts, style sheets, and images using a calculator is one way. Another, more accurate way is to let an outside service do it for you. Visit http://www.websiteoptimization.com/services/analyze/, and enter the address of your site to see a detailed report.[1]

---

1. This method requires that you have your page or application available to the outside world. If this isn't an option, then you'll need to do a manual calculation of the sizes or use an editor such as Dreamweaver, which can give you a report of the page size and estimated download times.

10.2 Dealing with Different Graphics Formats

Optimizing images can be difficult because you need to consider the type of image you're working on. For example, photographs need to be optimized differently than charts or logos.

When you work in a web browser, you work primarily with three graphics formats: GIFs, PNGs, and JPEGs. We'll be using each of these formats in our site.

GIFs

GIF, short for *Graphics Interchange Format*, is a graphics format that uses a palette of up to 256 distinct colors from the 24-bit RGB color space. You don't use it for photographs because of this limited-color space, but it's great for logos. The GIF format also supports animations.

Historically, GIFs have often been used for logos and buttons because they support transparency, which means you can place a GIF on the page and see the background through parts of the logo. However, developers are increasingly adopting PNGs because of that format's superior transparency support.

Optimizing GIFs

GIF images allow a maximum of only 256 colors in the image. You optimize GIFs by reducing the number of colors that will be stored in the file. If you have only 16 colors total in your logo, you tell your graphics software to limit the output to 16 colors. Reducing the colors reduces the file size, but you might end up making the image look terrible. The more complex the image, the more colors you'll need to store. Photoshop lets you preview the image as you optimize it, so you'll have an idea of how it will look under each setting.

When you reduce the number of colors in a GIF, you need to do it by a factor of two; 16, 32, 64, 128, and 256 are acceptable values for the number of colors. You won't notice any real size savings if you use other values, and going below 16 colors can cause some problems for you. The image might not render at all in some rare situations, so don't bother going that lower than that.

Photoshop's Save for Web & Devices feature allows us to control the colors used in a GIF, as shown in Figure 10.1, on the next page.

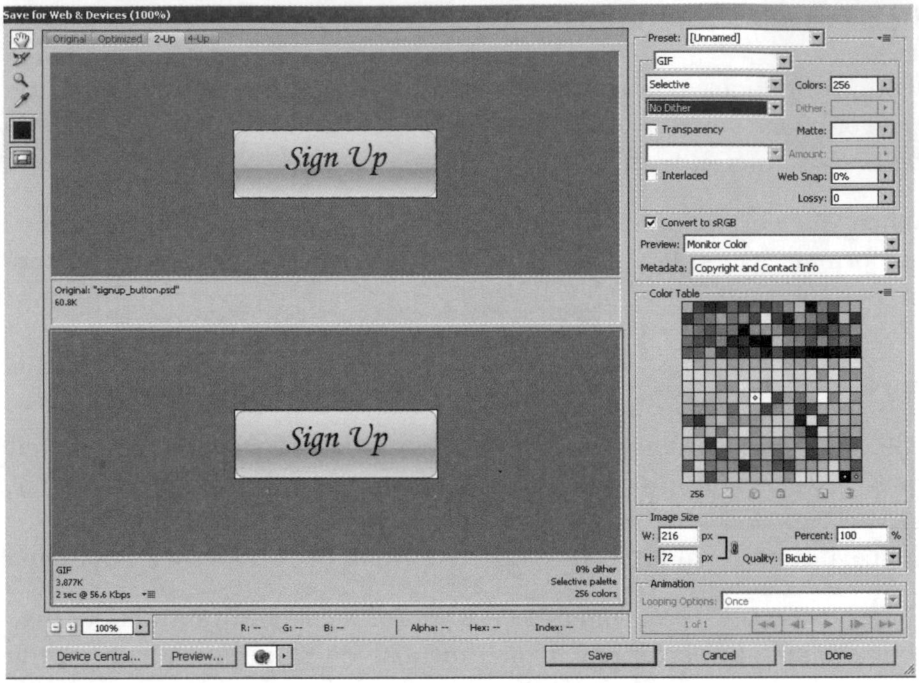

Figure 10.1: THE SAVE FOR WEB & DEVICES OPTION IN PHOTOSHOP HAS SEVERAL PRESETS FOR GIFs THAT AUTOMATICALLY PICK THE COLORS NECESSARY IN YOUR IMAGE.

PNGs

PNG, short for *Portable Network Graphics*, is a bitmap image format that uses lossless compression and was designed to replace the GIF format. It supports only RGB colors, and it's designed for use on the Web. It also supports transparency quite well. Unfortunately, this transparency is supported only in newer browsers, but don't be afraid to use it because the image quality can be amazing.

PNG Optimization

When you optimize a PNG, you select a bit depth of the image. The more complicated the image, the larger the file size. However, unlike JPEGs, PNG files use a lossless compression, so PNG is a nice format for logos and other nonphotographic artwork, especially logos, icons, and buttons with shading, shadows, or glossy detailing.

> ### Don't Recompress a JPEG!
>
> You should avoid recompressing a JPEG whenever possible. If you've compressed the original image by 20% and still haven't gotten the file size you wanted, don't compress the new image further; instead, compress the original file again. It's important to keep your original files uncompressed, so you can go back and re-create them.

Be sure to watch your file sizes when using PNGs; a 24-bit PNG with transparency can be quite large.

JPEGs

JPEG is a compression format for photographic images. It's widely supported, but it uses a lossy compression, so artifacts can be created if you compress too much or recompress multiple times.

JPEGs do not support transparency at all, and you should use them only for photographs. Logos, screenshots, and gradients are definitely not appropriate uses for JPEGs.

Optimizing JPEGs

To optimize a JPEG, you simply compress the image to make it smaller. Compression can reduce the file size dramatically, but can also reduce the image quality. You need to strike a balance between file size and quality when optimizing JPEG images.

JPEGs are compressed when you save the file. For example, in Photoshop you save the file as a JPEG and choose the compression level, as shown in Figure 10.2, on the following page. All graphics programs work the same way when compressing JPEGs; they ask you to specify the compression level in terms of the quality of the image. More compression means less quality.

If your image is still too big after you've optimized it, your only other option is to reduce the height and width of the image to make the file size smaller.

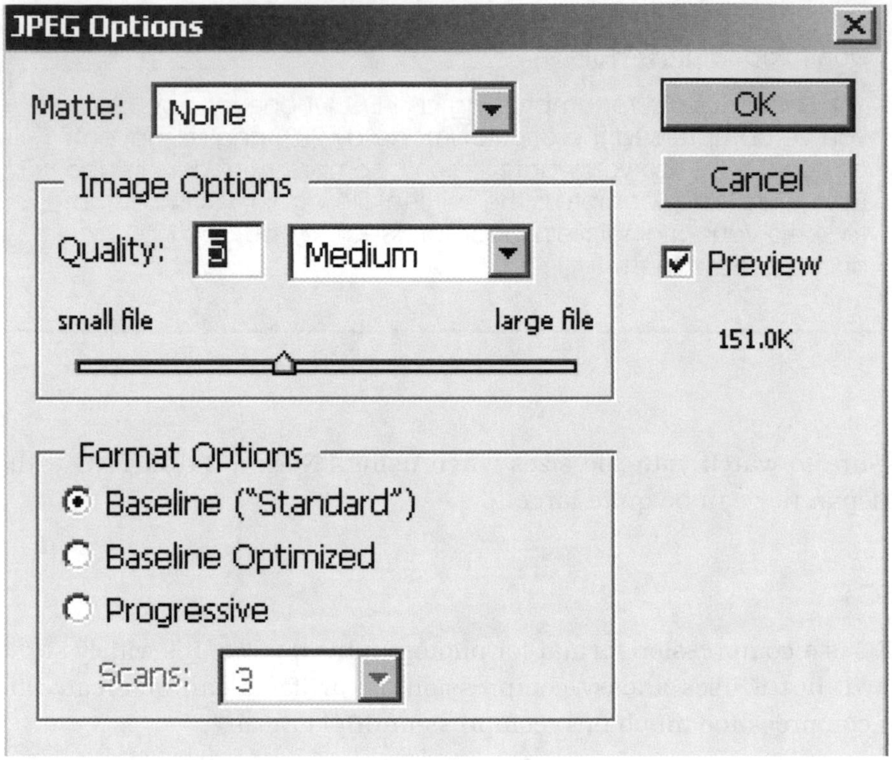

Figure 10.2: COMPRESSING A JPEG

Digital Cameras

Some consumer-oriented digital cameras store their photos as JPEGs. If your camera saves images in this format, you will definitely want to check with your manufacturer to find out how much these images are compressed. If possible, your original images should be uncompressed. Some cameras have an option to change how the image is stored. I recommend storing your images in the RAW format and using Photoshop to convert them to JPEGs. Consult your manual for more information.

If you get your photos from photographers, ask them to provide you with RAW or digital negative (DNG) files—and be sure to ask for this *before* the photographer takes the pictures!

10.3 Slicing Up Our Document

Open your mock-up file. We're going to grab some images from this file using the Slice and Slice Select tools, and Photoshop will do all the graphics optimization for us, as long as we give it a little direction. We don't want to transform the entire mock-up into a web page automatically; rather, we want a few images that we can use from our style sheets.

Double-Checking the Mock-Up

We need to make sure that all our elements are within the gridlines. We'll use the gridlines as guides to create slices, and we don't want to accidentally slice off part of a word or image. Zoom in to about 300%, and then hold down the Spacebar to activate the Hand tool. Click and drag with the mouse pointer to pan around the canvas and make sure that your logo, headings, and images are all contained within gridlines. You don't want the edges of your fonts or images to overlap any gridlines. You can see an example of what you want to avoid in Figure 10.3, on the next page.

If you do find something that crosses a gridline, select the Move tool and right-click (Windows) or Command-click (Mac) the section of the canvas that overlaps the line. This brings up a context menu that shows the layers underneath the cursor. Select the layer for the offending element, and then use the arrow keys to nudge it in small increments until the image is where it needs to be.

10.4 Creating Slices

We're going to create several slices from this document. We will eventually save the slices as different file formats, but the slicing process is the same. Let's start by turning the Foodbox logo into a slice.

Select the Slice tool from the tool palette,[2] and then use the Slice tool to draw a box around the Foodbox logo using the gridlines that surround the logo. The upper left should be at 72px across and 18px down, and it should end at 558px across and 108px down. Make sure that the Snap to Grid option is enabled to make this process go more quickly.

---

2. In previous versions of Photoshop, the Slice tool had its own menu item; however, in Photoshop CS4, it's located beneath the Crop tool.

Figure 10.3: AN ELEMENT NOT QUITE WITHIN THE GRIDLINES

Slices from Guides

You can skip all this slicing by hand if you remain diligent about placing guides when you do your mock-up. When you select the Slice tool, you have the option to press the Slices from Guides button. If you do this, you will create additional slices that you'll have to ignore later, and you'll also have to make sure that you've placed your guides appropriately. You could end up splitting images in half unintentionally.

Depending on the number of slices you need to make, this method might save you time, even if you have to make some manual adjustments afterward.

This is the approach many of the plug-ins for GIMP use to slice images.

Now select the Slice Select tool, which you find underneath the Slice tool on the palette (click and hold to expand the section of the palette to reveal it) and double-click the logo slice. Set its name to *banner*. The name you set here is used as the filename for the slice when you export the file. You should name each slice you plan to export. If you don't, Photoshop will name the slice for you, and you'll find it much harder to keep things organized later.[3]

Slicing Up the Rest of the Image

Create slices for the rest of the elements using the same technique you used for the banner; don't forget to name each slice as you create it. When you finish, you should have slices for the following elements:

- The Search Recipes header (search_recipes)
- The search button (search)
- The Browse Recipes header (browse_recipes)
- The Popular Ingredients header (popular_ingredients)
- The pasta image (pasta)
- The Get Cookin' header (get_cookin)
- The Latest Recipes header (latest_recipes)
- The Log In button (btn_login)
- The Sign Up button (btn_signup)

When slicing, make sure you always slice to the gridlines. If any part of the image crosses a gridline, go to the next gridline. The slices we create should be evenly divisible by our line-height of 18px so that they don't throw off our baseline grid.[4] You can see how the slices should work out in Figure 10.4, on the following page.

To make things easier when we do the CSS image replacement for the sidebar headings, make the slices all the same height and width, approximately 180 by 36. Make both the Get Cookin' and Latest Recipes images 198px by 54px.

---

3. Naming the slice as you create it also helps you identify slices you create vs. ones that Photoshop creates for you. In the event you have a slice that overlaps or you select a slice you didn't mean to export, you can tell from the filenames which slices are good and which ones you can discard.

4. You can make your slices any size you want, but be prepared to add the right amount of margin and padding to the image element using CSS so that you still adhere to the grid.

Figure 10.4: YOUR DOCUMENT WITH ALL SLICES CREATED

You can verify the dimensions of a slice by looking at the slice info displayed when you set the slice name. For example, select the Slice Select tool and double-click the Get Cookin' slice. The X and Y coordinates denote the starting point of the slice. The height and width are relative to that starting coordinate. The Get Cookin' slice should be at 378 X and 252 Y. The width should be 162px, and the height should be 54px.

Save your document. The slice settings you made are saved along with the document, so you don't have to create the slices the next time you want to work with the document.

10.5 Extracting the Banner as a Transparent PNG

You can export the logo as any file format you want, but we'll use a PNG for this site. The PNG is lossless and can support many colors. Our logo has the faded reflection, which introduces a little more complexity than a standard GIF, while a JPEG might compress the logo too much and cause it to look distorted.

Figure 10.5: TRANSPARENT LAYERS BEHIND THE FOODBOX LOGO

We don't need to make this image transparent—it could just sit on top of the yellow background, and nobody would know the difference when they look at the page. But we need an excuse for you to learn how to make transparent PNGs, so you can use them when you do need one.[5] When you created this file, you set the background to white. For Photoshop to export a transparent PNG, you must get rid of all the layers below it. This means you have to convert the background layer to an actual layer. Find the background layer in your Layers palette, and double-click it to bring up the Layer Properties box. Name it *background_layer*, and click the OK button.

Hiding Layers

To export the banner as a transparent PNG, you need to hide any other layers below the banner. Hide the background layer, and the yellow header layer by clicking the eye symbol next to each layer. Photoshop displays a checkered pattern to indicate a transparent area. Your banner should look something like Figure 10.5.

Saving the Slice

Photoshop uses the Save for Web & Devices menu item rather than the normal Save as command to create web-optimized images. Select that command, and you'll be presented with a preview of your document, sliced up nicely.

---

5. You can read that as "when the client wants one."

Figure 10.6: EXPORTING THE FOODBOX LOGO

Select the slice for the logo. Whenever you select a slice, the properties pane on the right side updates to display the properties for that particular slice. Each slice can have different output settings, so you can export PNGs, JPEGs, and GIFs, each with their own settings.

Set the type to PNG-24, and make sure that the Transparency option is selected. When you select the Transparency option, the background behind the logo changes from white into the same checkerboard pattern you saw in the canvas, as shown in Figure 10.6.

Click the Save button to bring up the Save Optimized As dialog box. Set the Save In location to your Foodbox project folder. Photoshop will automatically create an images folder for you. Leave the filename alone, but change the type to Images only, and change the Slices option to Selected Slices. The filename will be generated automatically from the slice name you specify.

Verify that the banner.png file exists in the images folder within your working folder, and get ready to export everything else.

10.6 Exporting the Rest of the Elements

Unhide the background layer and the heading layer, and then choose the Save for Web & Devices option again. Select the pasta image slice, and set its file type to JPEG. Move the quality slider to 80. The higher the quality, the larger the file size, so you have to strike a good balance here to make it look good.

Select the Log In Button slice, and choose PNG 8. This time, don't select the transparency option. Do the same with the Sign Up Button slice and the search icon. We don't need the extra information a 24-bit PNG would provide because these icons have few colors and will work perfectly.

The header images should work fine as GIFs.[6] Select the Get Cookin' slice, hold down the [Shift] key, and click the other headings. With all the slices selected, you can simply change the type to GIF, and the setting will apply to all the slices.

Hold down the Shift key, and click the pasta image, the search button, Log In button, and Sign Up button slices. Click the Save button to save all the selected slices to your images folder. Use the same settings in the Save Optimized As dialog box, and the images will export to the right location.

Once you export the images, save your Photoshop document. Photoshop persists the slice and settings information in this document, so you can tweak and export graphics with ease.

10.7 Summary

In this chapter, you learned how various types of images work in a web page, as well as how to make those graphics by slicing up the mock-up you used to plan your design. Using slices in Photoshop to manage your image optimization makes it ridiculously easy to change the appearance of your site at a later date. Simply change the underlying mock-up and reexport the slices to create another site.

Now it's time to beautify our website with visual styles.

---

6. We use GIFs here instead of PNGs only for the purpose of illustrating this exercise; you could also use 8-bit PNGs for these.

## Chapter 11

Defining Your Layout with CSS

We've come a long way with our redesign implementation, and we're nearing the finish line. It's now time to tackle one of the more conceptually difficult parts of web design: positioning elements with CSS. The implementation itself isn't complicated, but understanding how it works is often much more difficult than understanding what colors go together. This chapter aims to guide you through the various twists and turns of CSS so that you can learn how to take your flat content document and transform it into something that closely resembles the mock-up you did.

11.1 Browsers Are Awful

If it weren't for web browsers, or rather their competing manufacturers, CSS-based web design would be easy. Unfortunately, we live in a world in which open source and commercial-software developers constantly fight about how standards should be implemented. We've touched on this concept a few times before, but Internet Explorer and Firefox don't render things the same way. Supporting a web design that works on two browsers is bad enough, but you can't forget about Apple's Safari browser, the various Opera-based browsers, or Google's Chrome. Each browser has its own advantages and flaws, and it's your job as a web programmer to understand those strengths and weaknesses, so you can present a useful and attractive site to your audience.

You can hack around the problems by using various CSS rules that trip up a given browser's CSS interpreters so that certain rules are ignored by certain browsers, but that's a dangerous approach. Many of these hacks rely on bugs in the browsers, and bugs eventually get fixed, even

> **Don't Just Copy Code!**
>
> Please don't just copy code you find on the Web! You can find many neat CSS tricks out there, but many of them rely on browser hacks or make other assumptions you might not be familiar with. I believe you shouldn't use anything in your software that you don't understand. Before you use some CSS in your site, know what it does and how it works, as you would with any other code in your application.

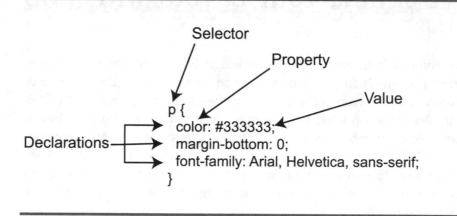

Figure 11.1: THE COMPONENTS OF A CSS RULE

by Microsoft. Developers got used to Internet Explorer 6 and its quirks. They built pages relying on various CSS hacks to force their page to display the way they wanted. That browser hadn't been updated in about five years; however, many developers found themselves scrambling to fix their pages when Microsoft released Internet Explorer 7. You don't want to end up like those developers; you want to write code that will continue to render into the future.

11.2 The Basics of CSS

Cascading Style Sheets (CSS) is a language used to describe the presentation of an HTML document. Most people who dabble in the Web start by using CSS to change the appearance of text on a page.

They quickly discover that they can set a style rule for all paragraphs in a site, instead of specifying a rule for each paragraph in hundreds of pages.

That's just the tip of the iceberg. You can use CSS to add color and images to your document, or even to change the entire structure and layout. In this chapter, you'll learn how to define the layout of Foodbox by applying style rules to the various regions you defined previously.

A CSS rule is composed of *selectors* and *declarations*, as shown in Figure 11.1, on the preceding page. Let's explore a CSS rule in more detail.

Selectors

The selector is the part of the rule that specifies what element or elements the rule should apply to. A selector can be a reference to an HTML tag, an ID, or a class.

Types of Selectors

A selector that refers to an HTML tag consists of the tag itself without the angle brackets. In this example, all the h1 tags will be blue:

```
h1{
  color:#009;
}
```

p, h1, and body are all examples of selectors that refer to HTML tags.

Selectors that reference an ID in the HTML document always start with a hash mark. This code defines the width of the element on the page with the ID of page:

```
#page{
  width:900px;
}
```

#page, #header, and #footer all refer to IDs.

Finally, selectors that reference a class start with a period:

```
.box{
  border:1px solid #000;
}
```

.box, .important, and .newsitem all apply the rule to elements with the specified class.

Declarations: Properties and Values

A declaration defines the style you apply to the selector. Each declaration sets a value to a CSS property, so if you want to set the text color of all h1 elements to red, you set the color property to #F00, the shorthand hex notation for red. You can see the rule in action in this snippet:

```
h1{
  color:#F00;
}
```

In a declaration, the property and value are separated by a colon, and each property-value pair is separated by a semicolon.[1] If you have multiple declarations in a single rule, you can place them all on their own lines, like this:

```
h1{
  font-size:24px;
  font-weight:bolder;
  color:#f00;
}
```

Or, you can cram the entire thing on one line, like this:

```
h1{font-size:24px;font-weight:bolder;color:#f00;}
```

The one-line version of the rule might be hard on the eyes, but removing the line breaks and extra spaces is one way to reduce bandwidth, which can help reduce load times. You probably want to keep a nicely formatted version of the style sheet while you develop, but you could easily set up something in your site-deployment process to strip out all the spaces and breaks before you upload it to the server. You could also apply this strategy to HTML because it's not sensitive to spaces and line breaks, either.

That Cascading Part

You don't have to declare all the rules that apply to an element in a single rule. You can spread out declarations over various files or continuously add to a CSS rule using inline styles or page-level styles:

```
/* Set the line height */
p{line-height:18px;}

/* set the color */
p{color:#003;}
```

---

1. You can omit the last semicolon in a CSS rule, but you shouldn't because you might forget about it later if you add more declarations to the rule.

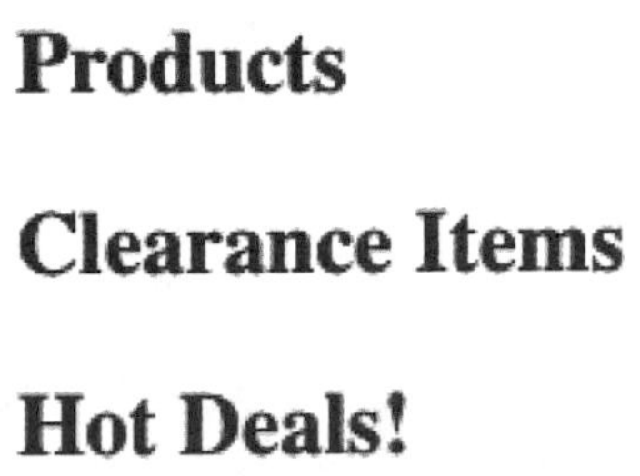

Products

Clearance Items

Hot Deals!

Figure 11.2: We used an ID selector to override other rules to make the heading red.

This feature allows you to separate your styles functionally. You can have one CSS file control the layout of the page and another that specifies fonts and colors.

However, CSS styles applied to elements can sometimes conflict with each other. CSS has its own method for determining the order of precedence, called the *cascade*. Style sheets can come from three different sources: the author (that's you), the user (users can apply their own styles to override yours), and the browser's defaults. The cascade assigns a weight to each style rule, depending on the rule's origin. To keep it simple, we'll cover only conflicts within style sheets you create, and we won't worry too much about what users do to customize their browser.

Rules in the author style sheets have more weight than browser or user style sheets, but rules within author style sheets can collide as well. Understanding how the cascade works can help you avoid collisions in your styles and override styles safely in appropriate situations.

ID Selectors

Selectors with IDs are more specific than other selectors. For example, if you define all h2 tags to be blue but you want a specific one to be red, you might consider applying an ID to that heading using the ID in the selector:

`css_layout/examples/01_selectors.html`

```
<h2>Products</h2>
<h2>Clearance Items</h2>
<h2 id="special_promotion">Hot Deals!</h2>
```

Products

Clearance Items

Hot Deals!

Figure 11.3: THE CSS CLASS SELECTOR CHANGED THE SECOND ITEM GREEN BUT COULD NOT OVERRIDE THE THIRD ITEM, BECAUSE CLASS SELECTORS DON'T OVERRIDE ID SELECTORS.

`css_layout/examples/01_selectors.html`

```
h2{color:#00F;}
#special_promotion{color:#F00;}
```

In this example, the Products and Clearance Items headings will be blue, and the Hot Deals! heading will be red, as shown in Figure 11.2, on the preceding page. Under normal circumstances, IDs always take precedence over other style definitions.[2]

Class Selectors

Class selectors are more specific than regular HTML selectors, but not as specific as an ID. We can use the promo class on our headings, as in the following example:

`css_layout/examples/02_selectors.html`

```
<h2>Products</h2>
<h2 class="promo">Clearance Items</h2>
<h2 class="promo" id="special_promotion">Hot Deals!</h2>
```

And we can define the styles for these headings:

`css_layout/examples/02_selectors.html`

```
h2{color:#00F;}
#special_promotion{color:#F00;}
.promo{color:#0F0;}
```

---

2. A better approach would be to use a class instead because IDs must be unique to a page.

This time we have a blue Products heading, a green Clearance Items heading, and the Hot Deals! heading remains red, as shown in Figure 11.3, on the preceding page. The class overrides the rules for the h2 tag, but the rule attached to the ID selector still wins out.

Order Matters

When no precedence can be determined, the cascade picks the most recently defined style. This is the part that lets you override styles on a per-page or per-element basis, and it's one of the most useful features of CSS. A style sheet can be split across multiple files, and the browser will apply the rules to elements as it finds them. As long as you're careful and you understand how the cascade works, you can take advantage of the flexibility.

For example, let's say that the styles for our headings look like this:

`css_layout/examples/03_selectors_page_style.html`

```
h2{color:#00F;}
#special_promotion{color:#F00;}
.promo{color:#0F0;}
```

Then, you add a new style at the page level:

`css_layout/examples/03_selectors_page_style.html`

```
#special_promotion{color:#FF0;}
```

The rule at the page level takes precedence over the rule in the style sheet *because it's defined again*. The Hot Deals! heading is yellow instead of red (see Figure 11.4, on the following page).

It's important to understand that an entire CSS rule is *not* overridden when there's a collision. Only the individual declarations that conflict are affected.

We will redefine rules many times in this chapter, but we'll do it mostly to combine rules together; the goal will be to separate layout from design, rather than to override rules.

The Importance of !important

Sometimes you need to change how the cascade works so that you can get a rule to apply as you see fit. CSS provides the !important keyword to force the cascade to apply the rule regardless of precedence. For example, take a look at Section 11.2, *Class Selectors*, on the preceding page. Our rule tied to the promo class couldn't override the rule attached to the special_promotions ID because ID selectors always win. However, we

Products

Clearance Items

Hot Deals!

Figure 11.4: WE DECLARED THE COLOR FOR THE HOT DEALS HEADING TWICE. THE DECLARATION THAT OCCURS LAST IS USED BY THE BROWSER.

can force the promo rule to apply by appending !important to each declaration we want to force to the top of the precedence order:

`css_layout/examples/04_selectors_important.html`

```
h2{color:#00F;}
#special_promotion{color:#F00;}
.promo{color:#0F0 !important;}
```

This time, the Hot Deals! heading is green, as shown in Figure 11.5, on the facing page.

11.3 How Browsers Use CSS

Now that you know how to define styles, you should know how this whole styling process works from the point of view of the web browser. When you request a web page, the browser parses the HTML and begins rendering the output. If it encounters a style or a style sheet reference, the browser applies those rules during the rendering process. Style sheets can be referenced in three ways.

Inline Styles

HTML elements all have a style attribute that allows you to define CSS properties as part of an element's declaration:

```
<h1 style="color:#f00;font-size:18px;">Welcome</h1>
```

This method is often used by application developers when they design helper functions and tag libraries. Although this is a nice feature, it's

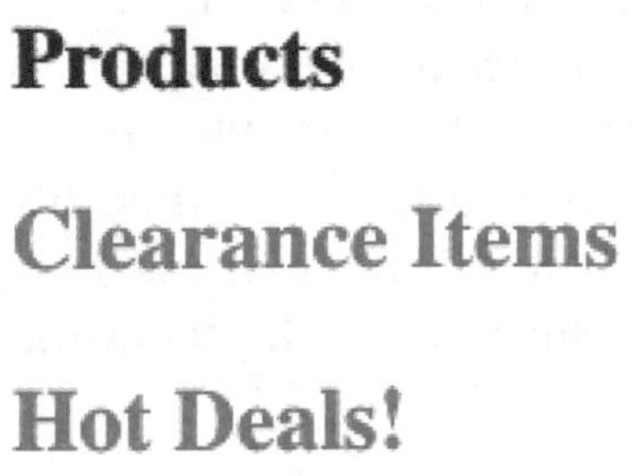

Products

Clearance Items

Hot Deals!

Figure 11.5: USING THE !IMPORTANT KEYWORD CAN OVERRIDE PREVI-
OUSLY DEFINED RULES.

one of the worst ways to apply styles to a document. Imagine seeing
this in a document:

```
<h3>Services</h3>
<ul>
  <li style="color:#300;">Computer repair</li>
  <li style="color:#300;">Small business networking support</li>
  <li style="color:#300;">Computer hardware sales</li>
  <li style="color:#300;">Web development</li>
</ul>
```

You use the same style declaration repeatedly, increasing the amount
of code in the HTML document. By doing it this way, you lose the ability
to reuse this style information. If you had to make this list available on
multiple pages, you'd have to repeat these definitions even more. If the
client decided she wanted to use blue instead of red, you'd have a lot of
changes to implement. It also mixes content with design, which we're
trying to avoid.

This technique is not all bad, though. Sometimes you might have a
specific element on a specific page that requires just a bit of tweaking,
and you don't want to bother with putting it in the global style sheet.
You know how this method works, so you should reserve it for those
special cases. That said, it's too easy to abuse this technique. Server-
side programmers like to do things like this:

```
<?php
  echo '<p style="font-size:18px;color=' . $color . ';">' . $description + '</p>';
?>
```

This might seem like a great approach at first, but this makes it ridiculously hard to change colors and fonts later because it's easier to change style sheets than it is to change server-side code. Please, for the love of all that is good and right, avoid abusing CSS like this. It's bad. In fact, it's Comic Sans bad. It has such a lure, too, because it's easy to code. Instead, you should use a class, as in the following snippet:

```php
<?php
  echo '<p class="description">' . $description + '</p>';
?>
```

You can then define the description class elsewhere and decide how it should look without having to change your server-side code.

The Style Tag

HTML also has a style tag that you can use to define an entire style sheet within the header of your document:

```
<style>
  body{
    font-family: Arial, Helvetica, sans-serif;
    font-size:12px;
    line-height: 18px;
  }

  h1{font-size:18px; line-height:36px;}
  h2{font-size:16px;}
  h3{font-size:14px;}

  #page{
    width:900px;
  }


</style>
```

This method is extremely useful in those cases where you want to have a page with its own style elements that don't belong in the sidebar style sheet. The problem here is the same one you encountered with inline styles: you are mixing content with presentation, and you lose the ability to share these styles with another page in your site.

This is also an excellent method to use when first implementing some CSS rules on a template, because you don't have to create any additional files. The CSS code you use in the style element can be cut and

---

Joe Asks...

What's the Deal with the Three-Digit Color Codes? I Thought Hex Codes Were Six Digits

CSS provides a shorthand syntax for color codes if the digits in each pair are the same. For example, the color red is represented as #ff0000. This code translates to "red all on, no greens, and no blues." Because F, 0, and 0 are repeated, you can shorten this to #F00. Simply put, this is another way to help reduce the character count in a document.

---

pasted into a separate CSS file when you are ready to build additional pages.

External CSS Files

Using the link tag, you can attach a style sheet to your HTML document just as you'd attach an external JavaScript file. Your user's browser will download the external file and apply it to your page. Subsequent requests to the same file should be cached by the user's browser. If you use the same file across multiple pages, you can improve your user's experience significantly because you have to send only the content of your page and not the extra CSS code.

This is generally the best method for working with style sheets, and it's the method we'll use throughout the rest of the exercises in this book. The other methods are perfect solutions for those one-off style changes you have to make occasionally.

11.4 Creating and Linking a New CSS Style Sheet

Open your text editor, and create a new blank document. Save the document into the stylesheets folder as layout.css. You'll use this file to define all the CSS rules that define the layout and alignment of the site. Later we'll place fonts and color rules in another file.

Close that text file. We're not going to use the text file to edit the styles at this time. Instead, we'll use the Web Developer Toolbar in Firefox.

Open your home page's HTML document, and add the following code within the <head>...</head> section:

```
<link rel="stylesheet" href="stylesheets/layout.css"
    type="text/css" media="screen" charset="utf-8" />
```

This is an example of a link to an external style sheet. Here, we use a relative link to the layout.css file in the stylesheets folder. Like the img tag, the link to the style sheet can be relative to the document, relative to the site root (/), or an absolute link to a style sheet somewhere on another server.

Style sheets can be locked to a specific type of display. For example, you can specify that a style sheet should be used only when the document is displayed on a screen or that it should be used only when the page is printed. This makes it easier for you to design presentations for printers or mobile devices. That said, you shouldn't trust the media type alone. Web browsers are responsible for interpreting this, and some browsers don't, especially screen readers and some mobile devices. You should always test your site.

11.5 Defining the Basic Structure, Header, and Footer

Open the index.html file in Firefox. At this point, the page is plain, but it's also readable and usable. This is what your page would look like in a text-based browser or another device that doesn't support style sheets. Let's make some changes to this document using the Edit CSS feature of the Web Developer Toolbar, so we can see the changes in real time.

Open the CSS Editor in Firefox by pressing Ctrl+Shift+E or by choosing CSS > Edit CSS on the Web Developer Toolbar. The Edit CSS pane appears, usually at the bottom of the window. Change the position of the window so that it sits to the left of your document by clicking the Position button to the right of the Edit CSS tab on the editor window.

If this document had any styles defined either within the head tags or defined in separate style sheets, they'd show up in the editor, and you could modify them. However, we're starting with a blank canvas.

Browser Defaults

Each browser has its own way of displaying pages. Some browsers use different margins, line spacing, font sizes, and even colors when displaying pages. This can complicate things when we start defining line-heights and other elements, but we can get around that by defining a

> ### Save Often!
>
> You know that you should save often, but when working in the CSS editor in Firefox, you need to be especially diligent about saving your work. Navigating to another page or reloading the page you're on can reset the styles in the editor to the original versions, whereupon you lose all your work. Although it's nice to be able to see your CSS changes in real time, you might be more comfortable switching to your favorite text editor.

CSS rule that zeroes out the defaults for all the major elements. Place this rule into the CSS Editor, and watch as all the spacing between lines disappears:

`css_layout/layout.css`

```
body, p, h1, h2, h3, h4, h5, h6, ul, li, form{
  margin:0;
  padding:0;
  line-height:18px;
}

p, h2, h3, h4, h5, h6{
  margin-bottom:18px;
}
```

The first rule removes the margins (the space around elements) and the padding (the space within elements) from the elements listed. It also applies a default line-height of 18px, which overrides whatever default line-height the browsers might use by default.

The second rule resets the bottom margins on paragraphs and headings to 18px. This helps everything line up on our grid exactly as we want it.

Sharing Rules

Selectors can be grouped so that you can share rules. Though not always necessary, this is a great way to reduce the amount of code you write in the CSS document. Consider these three rules:

```
p{
  line-height:18px;
}

h2{
  line-height:18px;
}
```

> \/ / Joe Asks...
>
> ### Can I Use One of the Existing CSS Reset Style Sheets on the Web?
>
> Sure you could, but I don't recommend using one without modifying it first. Remember the sidebar on page 166? Take a look at Eric Meyer's popular reset style sheet.* This is handy, but you have to remember that it's intended to be general, and it resets a ton of elements that you might never use on your page. It's often easier to reset the elements yourself if you write the styles.
>
> ---
>
> *. http://meyerweb.com/eric/tools/css/reset/

```
h3{
  line-height:18px;
}
```

You can separate selectors in a rule by commas, which enables you to apply one rule to multiple elements:

```
p, h2, h3{
  line-height:18px;
}
```

Less code means fewer characters that you need to transmit over the wire. Although this looks like a great way to keep your code small, keep in mind that this approach might make it more difficult to keep your document organized.

The Box Model

Every block element in HTML is basically a box, and the width and height of the box consist of the dimensions of the element itself, plus any padding, borders, and margins. If you declare a box with a width of 50px, but you add 2px of padding on each side, a 1 pixel border on each side, and then define left and right margins of 5px each, the width of the element would be (50 + 2 + 2 + 1 + 1 + 5 + 5), or 66px. That calculation becomes important if you have to put this new box into an existing space that's only 50px wide.

Different Box Models

Once again, browser inconsistency causes problems for the web developer. For many years, Internet Explorer used a different algorithm to interpret the width of a box. It considered the border and padding to be *part of the content width*. That means the content area that we declared as 50px gets *reduced* to 44px (50 - 2 - 2 -1 -1). You can imagine the problems this can create.

Internet Explorer 6 and 7 both use the standard algorithm to compute the box widths, but only if the browser renders pages in standards mode. Unfortunately, the default rendering mode is quirks mode, which uses the older algorithm. You can consider quirks mode to be a sort of backward-compatibility mode. I will continue to consider it a complete pain in the neck.

Fortunately for us, making IE work in standards mode is a matter of choosing the right doctype and character encoding, and we've already taken care of that in our HTML template, so we should not see any issues with our element widths.

Centering the Content

When we defined the layout in Photoshop, we originally said that the width of the page itself would be 900px wide. Now we know that the width of a web page is the width of the web browser, but we won't develop a liquid layout here that expands and contracts with the width of the window. We'll use CSS to define the width of the page itself.

Our index.html page has a div tag with an ID of page that encapsulates the header, footer, and middle regions. We'll apply the width to this tag, along with a few other properties:

`css_layout/layout.css`

```
#page{
  display:block;
  width:900px;
  margin: 0px auto;
}
```

This rule defines the width of the element to be 900px, and it defines margins on the element as 0px on the top and bottom and figures out the left and right margins automatically.

The verbose definition for margins would look something like this:

```
margin-top:0;
margin-right:auto;
margin-bottom:0;
margin-left: auto;
```

However, we can use a shorthand syntax for margins that looks like this:

```
margin:0px 5px 5px 0px
```

This line defines margins for the top, right, bottom, and left sides of the element. That might look tricky at first, but you could compare it to the arrangement of hours on a clock. You have 12 at the top, 3 on the right, 6 on the bottom, and 9 on the left.

You can compress this code even more if you use the same syntax we used in our example, and you can define margins on all four sides to be the same using margin:0. You'll see this shorthand a lot because it helps reduce the number of characters, which in turn reduces a page's download time.

You see the results as soon as you place the code in the editor. The page is now constrained and centered within the browser window. This is a good time to save the document. Click the Save button in the CSS Editor, and save the style sheet to the stylesheets/layout.css file in your project folder.

Defining the Header and Footer

The header and footer both stretch across the page, but they have different heights and text alignment. Look at your mock-up of the site to determine the height for the header, and you'll find that it's 108px high. Add this code to the CSS Editor:

```
css_layout/layout.css
#header{
  height:108px;
  width:100%;
}
```

This declaration sets the height of the element to the height we need. It also sets the width to 100%. At first glance, you might think that means setting the width to 100% of the screen, but in fact it sets the width of this element to 100% of the width of the parent element, or the width of page, which you've already defined as 900px.

The definition for the footer is almost the same, but we need to change the height to 36px:

css_layout/layout.css

```
#footer{
        width:100%;
        height:36px;
}
```

11.6 Turning One Column into Two

There's nothing spectacular about our page at this point, but that's about to change. One of the most useful features of CSS is its ability to pull elements out of the normal flow and reposition them. Our page has a sidebar and a sidebar part that need to be displayed side-by-side; we'll accomplish that using a simple technique called *floating*.

Document Flow

You learned about the various ways elements are displayed, whether block, inline, or invisible, in the sidebar on page 127. Understanding this difference is the key to using CSS effectively for layout. Using CSS, you can change the default behavior of an element. For example, the div tag is a block element by default. Browsers tend to render this element on a new line with a width that spans the entire available width of the page. However, we can change that by using the display property of CSS:

```
#page{
    display:inline;
}
```

The display property can have several possible values, but we care about only three for now: block, which renders the element as if it were a block element; inline, which renders it as an inline element; and none, which removes the element from the document completely.

Floats

If you've ever read a magazine, a newspaper, or a textbook, you've seen pages where text flows neatly around an image. We can use the float property of CSS to achieve the same result. And we can use the same principle to make two elements sit side-by-side, as if they were columns of text.

When you float an element, you take it out of the normal document flow; the content that remains then wraps around it. If you make two

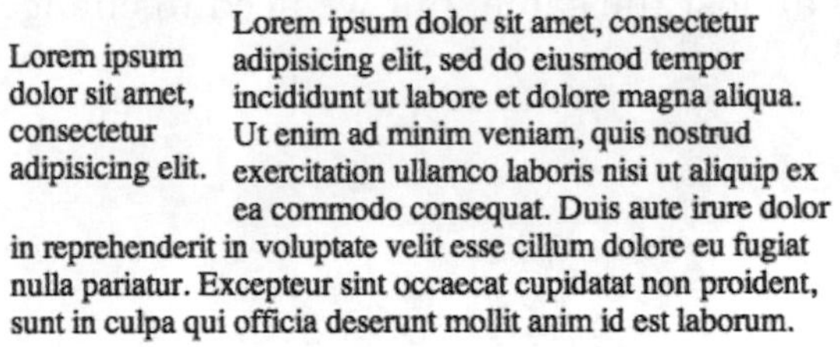

Lorem ipsum
dolor sit amet,
consectetur
adipisicing elit.
Lorem ipsum dolor sit amet, consectetur
adipisicing elit, sed do eiusmod tempor
incididunt ut labore et dolore magna aliqua.
Ut enim ad minim veniam, quis nostrud
exercitation ullamco laboris nisi ut aliquip ex
ea commodo consequat. Duis aute irure dolor
in reprehenderit in voluptate velit esse cillum dolore eu fugiat
nulla pariatur. Excepteur sint occaecat cupidatat non proident,
sunt in culpa qui officia deserunt mollit anim id est laborum.

Figure 11.6: A SINGLE FLOAT CAUSES CONTENT TO WRAP AROUND.

elements float next to each other, you can get the two-column effect you're looking for, as long as you assign widths to each floated element.

Take a look at this simple structure. We have two divs of content: a small callout box and some additional content:

css_layout/float_wrap.html

```
<div class="callout">
  <p>Lorem ipsum dolor sit amet, consectetur adipisicing elit.</p>
</div>
<div class="content">
  <p>Lorem ipsum dolor sit amet, consectetur adipisicing elit, sed
    do eiusmod tempor incididunt ut labore et dolore magna aliqua.
    Ut enim ad minim veniam, quis nostrud exercitation ullamco
    laboris nisi ut aliquip ex ea commodo consequat. Duis aute
    irure dolor in reprehenderit in voluptate velit esse cillum
    dolore eu fugiat nulla pariatur. Excepteur sint occaecat
    cupidatat non proident, sunt in culpa qui officia deserunt
    mollit anim id est laborum.</p>
</div>
```

We can make the main text wrap around the callout box by floating the callout box:

css_layout/float_wrap.html

```
.callout{float:left; width:108px;}
```

The result looks something like Figure 11.6. However, if we float both adjacent regions, they line up as columns, as shown in Figure 11.7, on the facing page:

css_layout/float_columns.html

```
.callout{float:left; width:108px;}
.content{float:left; width:400px;}
```

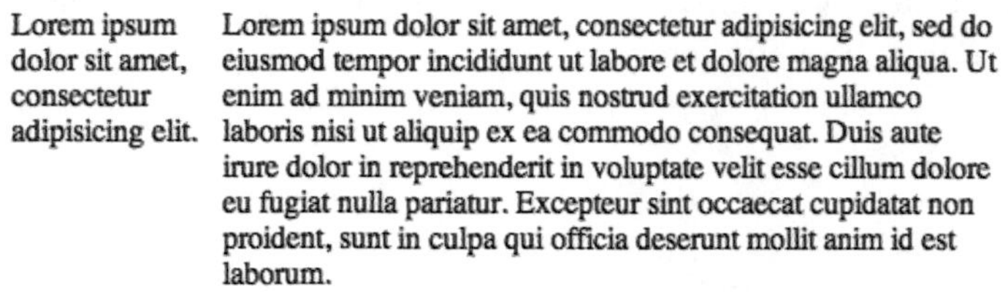

Lorem ipsum dolor sit amet, consectetur adipisicing elit.

Lorem ipsum dolor sit amet, consectetur adipisicing elit, sed do eiusmod tempor incididunt ut labore et dolore magna aliqua. Ut enim ad minim veniam, quis nostrud exercitation ullamco laboris nisi ut aliquip ex ea commodo consequat. Duis aute irure dolor in reprehenderit in voluptate velit esse cillum dolore eu fugiat nulla pariatur. Excepteur sint occaecat cupidatat non proident, sunt in culpa qui officia deserunt mollit anim id est laborum.

Figure 11.7: Two adjacent floats create columns.

To build the sidebar and sidebar section, you need to float the main and sidebar regions. In our HTML code, those two regions are both wrapped by a region called middle, which constrains these two regions.

Define the middle region so it has a width of 100%. If you don't define the width this way, things might not expand as you'd expect:

css_layout/layout.css

```
#middle{
        width:100%;
        float:left;
}
```

Next, define the sidebar. According to your mock-up, the width of the sidebar is to be 306px (use the gridlines!). The float:left directive causes the element to sit to the left of any other elements, which will float around this element. As soon as you place the code in the CSS Editor, you'll notice the sidebar content immediately floats around the sidebar:

css_layout/layout.css

```
#middle #sidebar{
  width:306px;
  float:left;

}
```

You don't want the main region to wrap around the sidebar; you want to make these two elements look like columns. The simplest approach is to float the main region left as well and then give it a width that's not more than the overall width, minus any other elements, margins, borders, or padding. Stop calculating! The answer is 594px—the same width as the pasta image you extracted from Photoshop. That image should fill the entire width of the main region:

css_layout/layout.css

```
#middle #main{
  width:594px;
  float:left;

}
```

All that time we spent with the grid in Photoshop is paying off!

Both of these CSS rules have *scoped selectors*. Any time we have a selector that contains a space, we denote some level of scoping. In the case of #middle #sidebar, the rule is basically saying "the element with the ID of sidebar that is a descendant of the element with the ID of middle." IDs must be unique, so you don't gain too much from scoping here, other than more organized and easier-to-read code. However, scoping becomes more powerful as you go on because you can have rules like this:

```
a{color:#339;}
#sidebar a{color: #fff;}
```

With those rules, links in the sidebar will be a different color than links anywhere else on the page. This is definitely the route you want to take if the sidebar has a background color that is much darker than the main region's color.

Backgrounds and Floats Gotcha

Firefox and other standards-compliant browsers do not apply background colors or borders to any div where all the children have been removed from the normal document flow. Instead, the heights of these containers are collapsed, which means you see no background images, borders, or background colors. For example, take a look at this code:

```
<div id="container">
  <div id="col1">
    <p>foo</p>
  </div>
  <div id="col2">
    <p>bar</p>
  </div>
</div>

#container{
  background-color:#ffe;
}
```

Indent Your Nested Selectors

CSS code is a lot more readable if you group your nested selectors together and indent the elements. For example, this code is fairly easy to read:

```
#navbar {
  height: 36px;
  margin-bottom: 24px;
}
  #navbar ul {
    margin: 0;
    padding: 0;
    list-style: none;
  }
    #navbar ul li {
      float: left;
      margin-right: 20px;
    }

#middle{
  width:100%;
}
```

The following code is bit harder to read than the preceding example:

```
#navbar {
  height: 36px;
  margin-bottom: 24px;
}
#navbar ul {
  margin: 0;
  padding: 0;
  list-style: none;
}
#navbar ul li {
  float: left;
  margin-right: 20px;
}
#middle{
  width:100%;
}
```

The difference is subtle, but the visual guide that indenting gives you can help make it much easier to find something you're looking for.

```
#col1{
  float:left;
  width:400px;
}
#col1{
  float:left;
  width:400px;
  background-color:#eee;
}
```

In this example, you have two columns enclosed in a container. Both columns are floated, which causes the container to collapse—the background color defined in the container is never shown. The solution is simple but not obvious: you need to float the container, as well. Once you do that, the background will appear.[3]

Another well-known solution is to clear the floats before closing the container div by inserting an additional element, such as a break, with a style definition that clears the floats:

```
<div id="container">
  ..
  <br class="clear" />
</div>

...
.clear{
  clear:both
}
```

Both approaches are effective, but the latter approach requires you to place additional markup in your code to fix the problem. I'll leave it up to you to decide which approach you want to take when you run into this problem on your own sites.

11.7 Applying Margins to Content

The basic structure is in place, but things don't look quite readable yet. We've removed all the margins from most of our elements; now we need to put them back. We will define all our new margins in 18 pixel increments, starting with the groups of elements in the sidebar.

---

3. You do have to watch out for Internet Explorer's infamous double-margin bug, in which two adjacent floats can end up adding an additional margin. We'll cover the solution to this problem in Chapter 15, *Working with Internet Explorer and Other Browsers*, on page 215.

Format the Sidebar Elements Quickly

All our sidebar elements have the same structure: subelements wrapped within a parent element. We have a heading and something immediately beneath that heading. We defined our default heading margins in Section 11.5, *Browser Defaults*, on page 176. Now we need to define the margins for the regions themselves:

css_layout/layout.css

```
#browse_recipes, #popular_ingredients, #search{
  margin-left: 18px;
  margin-right:18px;
  margin-top: 18px;

}
```

That should do it for the sidebar. Adding 18px on the left, right, and top should easily clean up the sidebar elements without adding too much additional code. The most important part here is that you were able to share this declaration across three elements. You should strive to do that whenever you can, as long as it makes sense.[4]

11.8 Main Content

The main region consists of the pasta image, followed by two columns, followed by a single column. The pasta image doesn't need any special CSS styling, and the rest of the elements are styled using the same patterns you've already learned. The only thing you need to watch out for is the 18px left margin on all the content in the main region, except for the pasta image. Rather than apply the 18px margin to the main region, we'll make sure to add it to the Get Cookin' and Latest Recipes areas.

The Main Text

The main text needs to float to the left of the Sign Up and Log In buttons, and you already know how to do that because the sidebar works the same way. However, you do need to determine the width of the middle region. The Get Cookin' region and the Sign Up and Log In regions are equal in width, and you know that the width of the main region is 594px. At first glance, you might be tempted to divide 594 in half to get

---

4. Of course, you could end up making more work for yourself. You have to strike a balance between cleverness and readability.

the widths of each section. You would also be wrong to do this because it neglects to take into account the 18px left margin. Remember that margins count as part of the actual width (at least they do in any normal web browser!). The correct formula would look like this: (594 - 18) / 2 = 288.

The Get Cookin' text region gets styled like this:

css_layout/layout.css

```
#main_text{
  float:left;
  width:288px;
  margin-left:18px;


}
```

The Signup Region

The signup region is so close to the main region you could almost group them together. You need to make a few subtle changes to this, though. First, the Sign Up button starts 36px below the pasta image according to your mock-up. You can make this happen by adding a top margin of 36px. Also, the buttons are centered in this column. You can use the text-align:center style to accomplish that. Any elements within this region will be centered, including paragraphs and even div regions:

css_layout/layout.css

```
#signup_login{
  margin-top:36px;
  float:left;
  width:288px;
  text-align:center;
}
```

The Buttons

The buttons need a bit of minor styling, too. By default, anchors and images are inline elements, which means they'll sit side-by-side. In this case, we want the buttons to sit on top of each other with an 18px margin between them. Achieving this is as simple as changing the display type of the anchor tags from inline to block and adding a bottom margin:

css_layout/layout.css

```
#signup_login a{
  width:100%;
  display:block;
  margin-bottom:18px;
  float:left;
}
```

In this situation, you definitely want to scope the style sheet rule to the region. If you don't, every link on the page will be affected by the rule, and you don't want that!

Remember to save your work here so you don't lose anything!

Latest Recipes

At this point, formatting the last section in the main region should be easy because all you need to do is leverage the techniques you have already learned. Each recipe header gets indented 18px, and each recipe description gets indented another 18px. Each recipe has a heading denoted by the h3 tag, and the description is nothing more than a paragraph.

Clearing Floats

Once you float an element, everything after that will wrap around that element until you force an element back into the normal document flow. This is known as *clearing floats*, and this technique is most necessary when you have two columns followed by a single column. To clear floating, you use clear:both within the CSS rule attached to the region that should fall into the normal flow.

You can use scoping to define this region with a tiny amount of code:

css_layout/layout.css

```
#latest_recipes{
    clear:both;
    margin-left:18px;
    margin-right:18px;
    margin-top:18px;
}

  #latest_recipes h3{
    margin-left:18px;
  }

  #latest_recipes p{
    margin-left:36px;
  }
```

This code sets up the indenting and also forces the region into the document flow.

11.9 Revisiting the Footer

Although you might not notice anything wrong with the way the footer looks, you'll definitely want to add a tiny bit of code to the CSS declaration of the footer region to future-proof your design. The footer region comes after a middle region that is floated left. You learned that you should clear floats when you want to force a region back into the normal flow in Section 11.8, *Clearing Floats*, on the previous page. In this particular case, the floating is turned off by the Latest Recipes section, but you might have other pages in the site that don't have a setup like this. I always recommend clearing floats in the footer.

11.10 Summary

We covered a lot of ground in this chapter. At this point, you should have a good understanding of how to do some simple, two-column layouts using CSS. Our home page is starting to shape up. It now has two columns, and it needs only a coat of paint.

## Chapter 12

Replacing the Section Headings Using the Cover-up Method

12.1 The Cover-up Method Explained

The cover-up method doesn't replace the text with an image. As its name implies, it covers the text with a new image by placing the image on a new layer above the text. We haven't covered layers in CSS yet, but CSS basically allows you to place elements wherever you want, as long as you understand how that affects the rest of your site.

Other, simpler replacement methods, such as the Fahrner Image Replacement method, use the display:none CSS property to remove the text from the page and then apply the CSS image to the tag that enclosed the text. Unfortunately, newer versions of screen readers have begun to respect CSS properties and now hide the text from the end user.

This method gets around that issue. The screen reader won't load the image, and the text can still be read. It also looks decent when the style sheets are turned off.

12.2 Preparing the HTML to Be Replaced

To make the cover-up method work, we need to add a span tag within any element we want to obscure. Open your index.html file, and find the Search Recipes header. Next, modify the content so it includes a span tag right before the closing h2 tag:

```
<h2 id="search_header">Search Recipes<span></span></h2>
```

We'll use CSS to load the image into that span tag and then pull it out of the normal flow so it sits on top of the text. Save your file, and validate your code again to make sure you still have solid markup.

12.3 Covering the Text

The first thing we need to do is turn the h2 tag into a container with a width and height that matches the image we will place:

```
#search_header{
    margin:0; padding:0;
    position:relative;
    width:180px; height:36px;
    overflow:hidden;
    }
```

Next, we turn the span element, which is an inline element, into a block element, so that it can have a width and height applied. Now we use position: absolute to position the element using coordinates that are relative to the h2 element (this element's parent), which we just specified to use relative positioning.

Finally, we turn off any margins and padding on this span, just to be safe, and then we load the image into the span as a background image:

```
#search_header span {
    display:block;
    position:absolute; left:0; top:0; z-index:1;
    width:180px; height:36px;
    margin:0; padding:0;
    background:url("../images/search_header.gif") top left no-repeat;
}
```

12.4 Replacing the Other Headings

Now repeat this process for the other headings in the sidebar. Be sure to add the span tag to the HTML document. You can try to reduce the amount of repetition in your style sheets by grouping the common styles using selector groups, which enables you to reduce the amount of code:

```
coverup/style.css
#search_header,
#browse_recipes_header,
#popular_ingredients_header{
    margin:0; padding:0;
    position:relative;
    width:180px; height:36px;
```

```
    overflow:hidden;
}

#search_header span,
#browse_recipes_header span,
#popular_ingredients_header span  {
  display:block;
  position:absolute; left:0; top:0; z-index:1;
  width:180px; height:36px;
  margin:0; padding:0;
}

#search_header span{
  background:url("../images/search_recipes.gif") top left no-repeat;
}

#browse_recipes_header span{
  background:url("../images/browse_recipes.gif") top left no-repeat;
}

#popular_ingredients_header span{
  background:url("../images/popular_ingredients.gif") top left no-repeat;
}
```

Once you replace the headings in the sidebar, follow the same practice
to replace the two headings in the main region. You'll need to make
minor adjustments to the height and width (198px wide by 54px high),
but by now you should have the hang of doing this replacement:

coverup/style.css

```
#get_cooking, #latest_recipes_header{
  margin:0; padding:0;
  position:relative;
  width:198px; height:54px;
  overflow:hidden;
}

#get_cooking span, #latest_recipes_header span  {
  display:block;
  position:absolute; left:0; top:0; z-index:1;
  width:198px; height:54px;
  margin:0; padding:0;
}

#get_cooking span{
  background:url("../images/get_cookin.gif") top left no-repeat;
}

#latest_recipes_header span{
  background:url("../images/latest_recipes.gif") top left no-repeat;
}
```

12.5 Replacing Links

You can use the same approach with hyperlinks. Rather than wrap an empty span, you wrap the linked text with the span. For example, let's say we want to use image replacement on our Foodbox header. The markup would look like this:

coverup/replacedheader.html

```
<h1><a id="foodbox_header" href="/">Foodbox<span></span></a></h1>
```

The CSS code is the same as in the previous example, except that you'll want to make sure that you use display:block on the a and span tags so that the entire image becomes clickable. By default, anchors and spans are inline elements that can't have defined widths and heights.

The corresponding styles look like this:

coverup/stylesheets/replacedheader.css

```
#foodbox_header{
    margin:0;
    padding:0;
    position:relative;
    width:486px;
    height:90px;
    overflow:hidden;
    display:block;
}

#foodbox_header span {
    position:absolute; left:0; top:0; z-index:1;
    width:486px;
    height:90px;
    margin:0; padding:0;
    background:url("../images/banner.png") top left no-repeat;
}
```

Transparency

If you tried this on your page, you might have noticed that the cover-up method doesn't actually cover anything up. The transparent parts of the image let the words show through. We can fix that by stealing a page from another CSS image replacement technique known as Langridge/Leahy Image Replacement (LIR).[1] We can change the height of the span to 0 and then set the top padding of the span to the height of

---

1. http://www.kryogenix.org/code/browser/lir/

the image. A box's height is defined by its height plus its top and bottom padding, so we'll get the desired result, but the text will be hidden:

coverup/stylesheets/replacedheadertransparency.css

```
#foodbox_header{
    margin:0;
    padding:0;
    position:relative;
    overflow:hidden;
    display:block;
    width:486px;
    /*   height:90px; */
    height:0;
    padding-top:90px;
    font-size:10px;
}
```

This code also decreases the font size to make sure that the ascenders don't peek out.

12.6 Downsides of This Method

First, as you might have noticed, we've added markup to our HTML document to get this to work, and we've introduced a large amount of additional CSS code, all so we can have prettier fonts that meet basic accessibility guidelines. It's up to you to decide whether this approach is worth it on your next project.

Also, screen-reading software has rendered other image replacement techniques useless in the past, so you will want to keep an eye on your sites. In other words, this approach might not be as viable down the road. An alternative approach would be to embed the images, use alt attributes, and move on. The only thing you'd lose is the use of the headings, which is important for search engines. You can learn more about that in Chapter 18, *Search Engine Optimization*, on page 257.

12.7 Summary

The methods you used in this chapter provide an accessible and search-engine-friendly way of preserving your type for section headings. You also learned that you could use it for other elements.

## Chapter 13

Adding Styles

You've learned how to position elements and define a layout using CSS, and you've replaced a few images. Now we'll talk about how to make things look pretty. By the time we're done with this chapter, you'll know enough basic CSS to do your next project without assistance.

Some of the things we'll talk about in this chapter might be somewhat familiar to you. For example, you might have used CSS previously to set fonts and colors and perform some basic visual manipulations. We're going to start with fonts and colors but then combine them with some of the things you learned in Chapter 11, *Defining Your Layout with CSS*, on page 165.

13.1 Setting Up the Colors and Fonts

One of the things that annoys programmers when they first use CSS is the complete lack of variables in CSS. CSS provides no way to define variables for reuse later. If we want the header and footer both to use the hex code #FFE500, then we have to put the same hex code in two separate CSS rules or do our best to share that rule using comma-separated selectors. The approach I find most useful is to keep all the color declarations together at the top of the style sheet so I can find them easily later.

The Importance of a Style Guide

Many organizations will have a *style guide* available that might have been developed by someone involved in the branding of the organization. The style guide traditionally dictates what colors and fonts an organization uses in its publications, and it's always a good idea to try

\// Joe Asks. . .

Can't I Generate Style Sheets Dynamically?

Absolutely. You can generate CSS style sheets the same way you generate HTML. You just need to make your web application respond correctly to the request for your style sheets. Although this is a clever approach, it behooves you to implement some sort of caching mechanism so that the styles aren't generated for every request.

It might be tempting to generate style sheets dynamically, but you should look at how much of an impact the lack of variables has. How often will you change your colors? How often do you repeat them? Most of the time, it's not worth the effort to generate this information on the server. Like everything else, it depends on your situation.

to adhere to the established style guide as closely as you technically can if one exists. Foodbox doesn't have one, and a good majority of small companies never think to do one either. Throughout this book, you've done all the groundwork to create a style guide, and this could prove to be useful in your future projects.

A style guide often details how layout, fonts, and colors should look, but it can also dictate how the content should be written. For example, one of my pet peeves occurs when someone uses the words *click here* on a web page. It drives me crazy, and I go out of my way to make sure that some sort of convention exists in the style guide to prevent someone from sneaking it into some copy. Style guides can also prohibit the use of ampersands in favor of spelling out the word *and*, or they can indicate whether to underline your links.

The whole point of a style guide is to create a consistent presentation throughout all of an origination's publications and communications.

The style sheet we'll build in this chapter is the code that implements the style guide.

We've already done a lot of font replacement with images, so we don't have too much to do for our font declarations.

A Word About Class Names

It might be tempting, but you shouldn't include implementation in your class names. I've seen far too many pieces of HTML code that looked like this:

```
<p class="red">An error has occurred</p>
```

When you're looking at the code, it looks nice at first glance. You can tell that the designer intended the error text to be red.

However, when you look at this result in a browser, it might be green instead because someone came along and decided that error messages shouldn't be red, because red is a bad color, and we don't want to scare people. A better approach might go something like this:

```
<p class="critical_warning">An error has occurred</p>
```

You can then document what a critical warning should look like in your style guide. You want to capture intent in your names.

Add this code to your style.css file:

`css_style/stylesheets/style.css`

```
body{
  font-family:Arial, Helvetica, sans-serif;
  font-size:12px;
}
```

Colors, on the other hand, require more work. We need to define not only the colors for our regions but also our links.

Pseudo-classes

Add this code to your style sheet:

`css_style/stylesheets/style.css`

```
#header, #footer{background-color:#FFE500}
#middle{background-color: #ffdd7f}
#main{background-color:#fff8e4}

a{color:#4d3900; text-decoration:none;}
a:visited{color:#806f40;}
a:hover{color:#807940; text-decoration:underline;}
```

The CSS declarations for our colors contain declarations for a:hover and a:visited. These are known as *pseudo-classes*. Up to this point, you've seen how style is applied based on the element's location in the document tree, but the CSS specification allows elements to be styled based on information that's outside the document tree, such as information provided by the browser. By default, web browsers display visited links in a different color than links you haven't clicked yet. This has become a cornerstone of usability over the years because it helps users identify information they've already seen. The visited link color was traditionally set as an attribute on the body tag; as a result, it had to be specified on each page. CSS pseudo-classes let you specify this information in your style sheet instead.

The :hover pseudo-class catches mouse events, and it can be extremely powerful. You can use it to change the color of a link when you hover over it, as our example does, but you can also use it to trigger a drop-down menu or even the display of another region on the page.

Unfortunately, browser issues affect this area of functionality, as well. The :hover pseudo-class works only on links in Internet Explorer 6, although we can attach this functionality to many other elements in other browsers and create some eye-catching effects such as image rollovers or form-field highlighting.

This definition also removes underlines from links unless the user hovers over them. Notice how we remove the underline from the links but add it back using the pseudo-class.

13.2 The Tag Clouds

We can style the tag clouds with a minimal amount of CSS now that we have our well-structured document in place. In the HTML file, we wrapped each tag with a span tag that had a class that ranged from level_1 to level_5. Popular tags got a lower number, and less popular tags got a higher number. To style this, we can make fonts bigger and heavier for the more important tags and made them smaller and lighter for the least important ones:

css_style/stylesheets/style.css

```
.level_1, .level_2, .level_3, .level_4, .level_5{
        margin-bottom:18px;
        margin-left:18px;
        line-height:36px;}
```

> ## Joe Asks...
>
> ### Why Are You Removing the Underlines? Isn't That Bad Usability?
>
> It sure can be. Users look for underlines to figure out whether they should click things. That said, times are changing, and people's habits are evolving; users are learning to look for other cues, such as text with a different color. However, you run the risk of confusing your users. If your headings are different colors than the rest of your text, you start coloring individual words, or you use a color that's not different enough—well, you get the point. It comes down to your audience and what your client wants. The point here is that you now know how to do it. It's up to you to decide when it's appropriate to use this technique.

```
.level_1{font-weight:bolder; font-size:20px;}
.level_2{font-weight:bold; font-size:18px;}
.level_3{font-size:16px;}
.level_4{font-size:14px;}
.level_5{font-size:12px;}
```

13.3 The Search Form

The only thing left is the search form, which at this point looks a little funny next to our nice image button. We need to give the search box a width, height, and border; we also want to control the font we use. We could have defined some of these things, such as the width and height, in the layout style sheet. Rather than split this definition apart, let's put the whole thing in style.css so it's all together:

css_style/stylesheets/style.css

```
#search_form #search_keywords{
        width:200px;
        float:left;
        border:1px solid #000;
        height:16px;
        padding:0;}
```

Pay close attention to the math here. The height of the line is 18px, but the height of the search box is set to only 16px because you have to account for the 1px border on the top and the bottom.

13.4 The Footer

We need to center the text in our footer, and we have to fit two lines within the 36px height we defined in our layout style sheet. Centering the text is easy; it requires only that we apply text-align:center to the footer element.

We can take a few approaches to make the text fit. The first reaction of many developers is to remove the paragraph tags in the HTML document and use a line break, <br>, between the lines, but that makes the page less semantic. It's much easier to change how the browser renders the paragraphs. We can remove the margins from the paragraphs within the footer so that there's no space between the paragraphs. This approach gives us the most flexibility.

Add this to your style sheet:

`css_style/stylesheets/style.css`

```
#footer{text-align:center;}
#footer p{margin:0;}
```

13.5 Cleaning Up Some Loose Ends

The home page is mostly done, but we must address a couple outstanding issues. First, our Sign Up and Log In buttons have borders around them that we need to remove. Second, the yellow color doesn't stretch across the screen as we had originally intended. We need to fix these things before anyone else notices!

Removing Image Borders

Images wrapped by a link automatically get a border around them to let users know they can click the image. In the old days of HTML, a developer would just use the border="0" property in the HTML document; however, that approach mixes design and content, and we don't want to do that. It's also not valid according to our doctype. Fortunately, the solution is easy: we can turn off borders for our images in the style sheet.

Add the following code to your style sheet to turn off borders for all images:

`css_style/stylesheets/style.css`

```
img{border:none;}
```

When you refresh the page, the green borders will be gone.

Stretching the Banner Color

You could use any of several techniques to make the color repeat. For example, you could move the header outside the page wrapper and wrap it with another div, making the wrapping div 100% wide and constraining the header to the same width as your page wrapper. That code would look something like this:

```
<body>
    <div id="header_wrap">
        <div id="header">

        </div>
    </div>
    <div id="page">
        ...
    </div>
</code>
```

```
<p>Some CSS associated with this code would look like this:</p>
```

```
<code language="css">
    #headerwrap{width:100%;
        float:left;
        height:108px;
        background-color:#FFE500;
    }

    #header, #page{
        margin:0 auto;
        width:900px;
    }
```

That is a common approach, and it works for simple situations where all you need is a solid color. However, what if you already have a bunch of pages created, and you can't justify changing the HTML of the page? Or, what if you think adding any more wrappers just to alter the presentation is silly? You can achieve the same results with a repeating background image attached to the body.

Open your mock-up in Photoshop, and select the Slice tool.

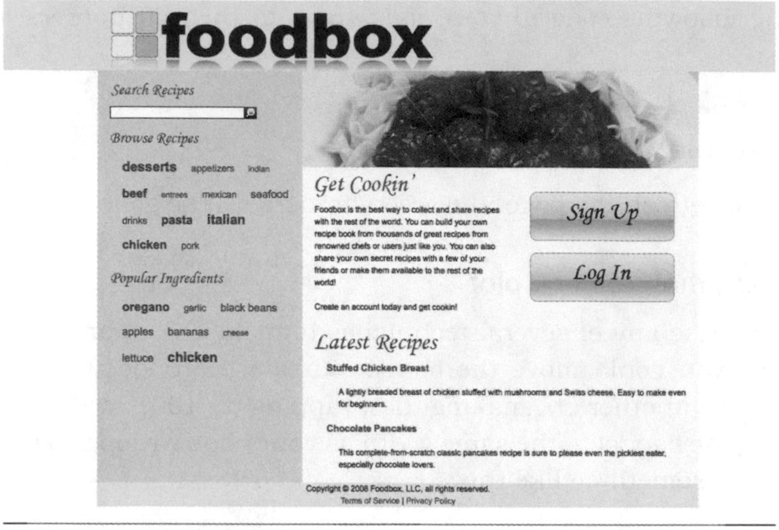

Figure 13.1: FOODBOX IN FIREFOX

Begin by grabbing a small sliver of the background that includes the full yellow banner, as well as a small bit of the white part. Create a new slice in the upper-left corner that is 1px wide by 128px high. You can do this by zooming in, or you can just wing it and adjust the slice properties when you set the slice's name. Speaking of the slice's name, call this slice *background*. Once you set the properties, export the slice to your images folder as a GIF.

In your style sheet, add a rule for the body tag that pulls in the background image and repeats it horizontally:

css_style/stylesheets/style.css

```
body{
        background: #fff url('../images/background.gif') repeat-x;
}
```

When you preview your finished page in Firefox, it should look something like Figure 13.1.

13.6 Summary

You've come a long way in this process, having developed by hand a standards-based page that validates and works in Firefox (and Safari, too; go check!). However, your work isn't done until you've tested it in a few other places, especially that widely used browser from Microsoft.

## Chapter 14

Making a Printer-Friendly Page

Foodbox will be a recipe site, and we expect that the users will want to print the recipes that they find on the site. We can implement this functionality several ways with server-side programming, but this chapter will show you how to use nothing but CSS to change how the page looks when the user prints it.

14.1 Preparing for Print

When a user prints a web page, she is usually concerned only about the information on the page.[1] The sidebar, navigation bars, images, backgrounds, colors, and even the graphical header are largely useless to someone printing the page. Printing these page elements only wastes ink and paper, so the first thing you need to think about when creating a printer-friendly version is how to turn those elements off.

When we attached the layout.css and style.css files, we defined the link to attach only the style sheets when displayed on the screen. As it stands now, our page has no styles applied when we print. This means we can start from the ground up and create a new style sheet designed specifically for printing; we don't have to worry about conflicting with or overriding any existing styles, other than those default styles applied by the user's browser.

---

1. Your clients, however, might be interested in printing pages so they can write on them and hand you back their changes. Ultimately, your clients aren't your primary audience for the site.

14.2 Linking a Print Style Sheet

Create a new file called print.css and place it in your stylesheets directory. Open your index.html file, and add the following code after the existing style tags to attach the style sheet:

css_print/index.html

```
<link rel="stylesheet" href="stylesheets/print.css"
      type="text/css" media="print" charset="utf-8">
```

This time, we set the media type to print instead of screen. Modern browsers will use that style sheet when the user does a print preview or sends the page to the printer. As you work, you'll be able to test your style by using your browser's print preview function; however, you should still run a few tests through a printer if you can.

14.3 Removing Unnecessary Elements

Let's look at the home page and identify certain things that make no sense to print. Printing the sidebar with the search box and tag clouds will only waste ink, so we can safely lose that. The image of pasta isn't that useful to us, either, and the Log In and Sign Up buttons can probably go away, too.

We don't have to worry about the colors we added to the home page because we don't load that style sheet.

The links to the terms of service and privacy policy aren't relevant, either, so we can also take those out.

When marking up the HTML, we designated these regions with unique ID attributes so we could reference these sections easily. All we need to do now is set the display property to none for each of these regions. Add this code to stylesheets/print.css:

css_print/stylesheets/print.css

```
#sidebar, #main_image, #signup_login,
#privacy_and_terms, .noprint{
  display:none;
}
```

The noprint Class

I added a selector to the rule called .noprint. You can use this throughout your content to mark regions that you want to hide when the document is printed. For example, you can hide the logo by adding class="noprint" to the element in your HTML document. This blurs the line between content and presentation slightly more than a purist might like, but it's an effective way to turn off elements dynamically if you use server-side scripting to build your pages.

When you specify display:none for any element, it's not just hidden from view; it's effectively removed from the document.

14.4 Setting Margins, Widths, and Fonts

When we designed our screen layout, we turned off the browser styles and defined our own margins, line-heights, and font sizes. We can do the same thing here, but instead of using pixels, we will define our fonts in terms of points because that's what printers understand.

Add this code to your style sheet:

`css_print/stylesheets/print.css`

```
body, p, h1,h2,h3,h4,h5{margin:0; padding:0;}
p, h1,h2,h3,h4{line-height:18pt;}
p{font-size:12pt; margin-bottom:18pt;}
h1{font-size:18pt;}
h2{font-size:16pt;}
h3{font-size:14pt;}
```

Here we defined font sizes, margins, and line-heights for paragraphs and headings.

Page Margins

One thing you might notice is that we've set the page's margins to 0. We do this because the print margins depend largely on the operating system's printer driver. In many cases, defining a margin in CSS could add more margin space to the edges of a document than you might want.

Choosing a Font Family

Many browsers default to serif fonts, which are easier to read in print, as we discussed in Section 4.2, *Serif Fonts*, on page 54.

Add this code to your print style sheet:

`css_print/stylesheets/print.css`

```
body{
  font-family: Baskerville, Times New Roman, Times, serif
}
```

Dealing with Images in Print

Your images are still measured in pixels. You have two options if you don't hide your images in the print style. The first option is to use CSS to change the height and width of the images to proportionate measurements; the second option is to change the positioning of your text and images so that you don't wrap text around them.

Resizing the images in your print style sheet can be a little dangerous. Increasing the dimensions will make the pixelation much more noticeable when you print the images. But this works only if you give each image its own ID so you can reference it easily.

The second option is better: you use the print style sheet to reorganize your page a bit so the images aren't floated.

Keep in mind that the images you have on your page might not even be suitable for print because they're only 72 dpi. If you need to make high-resolution images available for your content, you might want to consider some server-side PDF generation and use higher-quality, print-ready images.

This rule declares the body style will use the Baskerville font and a couple fallback options. This rule will filter down to any elements within the body of the page, unless those elements have been defined differently.

Adding a Separator

We have no colored separators between our regions. We can separate the header and the content with a thin black line by adding a bottom border to the header:

`css_print/stylesheets/print.css`

```
#header{border-bottom:1px solid #000;}
```

You can use this style rule to add horizontal rules between other sections of your document, rather than adding them to the content.

14.5 Fixing Links

People who read a page printed from a website don't get to see where any of the links go. We can use a little advanced CSS to make this work.

Get Cookin...

Foodbox is the best way to collect and share recipes with the rest of the world. You can build your own recipe book from thousands of great recipes from renowned chefs or users just like you. You can also share your own secret recipes with a few of your friends or make them available to the rest of the world!

Create an account today and get cookin!

Latest Recipes
Stuffed Chicken Breast (#)

A lightly breaded breast of chicken stuffed with mushrooms and Swiss cheese. Easy to make even for beginners.

Chocolate Pancakes (#)

This complete-from-scratch classic pancakes recipe is sure to please even the pickiest eater, especially chocolate lovers.

Copyright © 2008 Foodbox, LLC, all rights reserved.

Figure 14.1: OUR HOME PAGE AS RENDERED WITH OUR PRINT STYLE SHEET

Add this code to your style sheet:

`css_print/stylesheets/print.css`

```
#main a:link:after, #main a:visited:after {
  content: " (" attr(href) ") ";
  font-size: 90%;
}
```

In this case, we use CSS to pull out the href attribute and place it into the content. This little trick works everywhere, except for versions of Internet Explorer prior to IE 8. Those browsers ignore the rule.

That's it for the style sheet. When you print your page, it should look a lot like Figure 14.1.

Forcing Page Breaks

You can force page breaks in your print style sheets. Let's assume you want to print a set of recipes with markup like this:

```
<div class="recipe">
   <h2>Bacon Explosion</h2>
   <ul>
     <li>2 pounds thick cut bacon</li>
     <li>2 pounds Italian sausage</li>
     <li>1 jar of your favorite barbeque sauce</li>
     <li>1 jar of your favorite barbeque rub</li>
   </ul>
   <p>.....</p>
</div>
<div class="recipe">
  <h2>Amazin' Bacon Burger</h2>
  ....
</div>
```

You can make each recipe print on its own page by adding this code to your print style sheet:

```
.recipe {page-break-after: always;}
```

Oh, and if that Bacon Explosion recipe sounds good, you can try making it yourself!*

---
*.   http://www.bbqaddicts.com/bacon-explosion.html

14.6 Dealing with Surprised Users

Some users might expect the printed version of your site to look exactly like the original version. In fact, I've had some clients get upset at the fact that their site doesn't print the same way it does on the screen.

You can mitigate that slightly by placing a visible Print Contents Only link somewhere on the page. That link might look something like this:

```
<a href="#" onclick=" window.print(); return false">Print Contents Only</a>
```

This link uses JavaScript and mixes behavior with content, so you might consider adding the link in using some unobtrusive scripting instead.

You could specify that the layout.css and style.css style sheets be used for the print media type in lieu of a print style, but some browsers have trouble with long, floated elements, so you would need to make your print style override some of your existing styles. However, I don't recommend this approach. Instead, I find that educating users and clients is a lot easier than getting caught in the ugly world of overriding styles. Once your users know the reasons why you serve a different layout for print—to reduce ink, save paper, and focus on content—they might even warm up to the idea.

14.7 Summary

Print styles are easy to implement and can improve the user's experience, as long as you keep them simple. You can use them to present your site's content in an uncluttered, legible way. You can also use the same method to target other devices, such as mobile phones, projectors (when supported), and even assistive technology like screen readers. Of course, this is all possible because we marked up our content properly, and we kept the presentation separate from the content.

Part IV

Preparing for Launch

## Chapter 15

Working with Internet Explorer and Other Browsers

Part of developing on the Web, especially for large audiences, is dealing with browser compatibility. You don't get to pick what browser your customers will use to visit your pages, so you need to make your site usable for the widest-possible audience. Your site looks good on the Firefox browsers; now you will learn how to make your site look good across other browsers, including Internet Explorer. The work you did validating your code and adhering to web standards will pay off here, because most browsers will display your page correctly.

15.1 Deciding What to Support

For about six years, web developers had to contend only with IE 6. That browser had a quirky rendering engine, but six years is a long time in the IT world, so most people discovered the quirks and came up with solutions to get around them. The release of IE 7 caused a whole new bunch of rendering problems for sites, because Microsoft fixed some things and changed others. At the time of writing, IE 8 is nearing completion, and it looks as though it will present some of the same kinds of issues.

In that same time span, Firefox and Safari each went through three versions. Browsers will improve, just as your software improves, and it's not possible for you to make your site look and work the same way in every single version of every single browser; you just won't have the

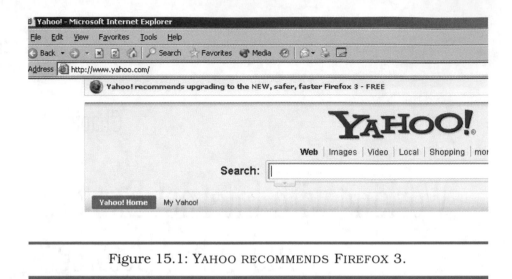

Figure 15.1: YAHOO RECOMMENDS FIREFOX 3.

time and resources to do that. Eventually, you have to decide what browsers and features you will support.

Supporting Browsers

If you're bold, you could just pick a browser and support it exclusively. This might be a great solution if you think your business can support that. For example, assume need to build an intranet site for your business; you will save yourself a ton of time if you can dictate that your users must use Firefox. CHAMP Software, located in Mankato, Minnesota, develops applications for the health-care industry and designs exclusively for Firefox.

You could also do what Yahoo does and recommend a browser to your users. This approach used to be laughed at by professional developers. In the 1990s, tons of amateur websites had "Best Viewed with Internet Explorer" tags on their sites. Yahoo is taking similar steps now, which you can see in Figure 15.1.

Don't think that this is a lazy way out. It's often not *difficult* to make your site work on all platforms, but it might not be the most efficient use of your time, talent, or money. The bottom line is that you should be sure that you take into account any potential customers you might lose because of your decision. Internal business applications can get away with this much more easily than a commercial website can.

Supporting Features

You could decide that certain features of your website won't work in certain browsers. Microsoft serves two versions of Outlook Web Access, a rich version that works only in IE, and a light version that works everywhere else. The rich version has tree controls for your inbox, as well as some other features that require specific IE controls. The light version lacks a lot of advanced features, but it still allows people to check email.

The ultimate goal is to make the site functional enough for anyone who wants to use it.

15.2 Browser Statistics

We can find out what browsers people use by looking at browser statistics. Hitslink.com maintains reports[1] on browser market share, and it seems to provide a decent market snapshot. W3Counter.com[2] and StatOwl[3] also provide statistics that appear to be somewhat accurate, as well. It helps to check multiple sources when making these types of decisions, especially when starting up a new site. Of course, when you've been established for a while, you should have your own logs that you can use to make future decisions.

At the time of writing, Firefox has anywhere from 17% to 26% of the market share. Most users rely on Internet Explorer 7, which comes in at about 42% and climbing, while a surprising 15% to 27% of users still use IE 6. We need to make sure our site works with IE 6 because it would be unwise to ignore 20% of our potential audience.

It's a safe bet that many of your customers—and your customers' customers—use Internet Explorer. The websites you make must be functional, and you must try to make them look equally good in all the browsers you support. It's just good business.

15.3 Internet Explorer: The Evil You Can't Ignore

I don't think there's a standards-focused web developer out there who enjoys dealing with Internet Explorer. Over the course of this book, I've

---

1. http://marketshare.hitslink.com/report.aspx?qprid=0
2. http://www.w3counter.com/globalstats.php
3. http://www.statowl.com/web_browser_market_share.php

Watch Where You Get Your Statistics

W3Schools has a highly referenced browser-statistics page* that details market share for individual browsers. If you looked at that site today, you might see that Firefox has a market share close to that of IE 6 and IE 7 combined; however, you have to remember that this is a site for technical users. That page contains this disclaimer:

"W3Schools is a website for people with an interest for web technologies. These people are more interested in using alternative browsers than the average user. The average user tends to use Internet Explorer, since it comes preinstalled with Windows. Most do not seek out other browsers."

Firefox is a great web browser, and its market share is climbing thanks to support from its users and sponsors. When trying to gather browser statistics, however, you need to make sure you fact-check your sources, especially if you plan to use those statistics in the decision-making process.

---

*. http://www.w3schools.com/browsers/browsers_stats.asp

---

mentioned several of the issues that we face every day, including differences in rendering elements or modes. IE does many things wrong, but it's extremely popular, so you can't ignore it, and your customers don't care about your personal biases.

Every computer that ships with Microsoft Windows has Internet Explorer on it. Users are always free to use a different browser, but the likelihood of the average user installing Firefox, Safari, Opera, or even Google Chrome is low. I make it a point to install Firefox everywhere I can. All my friends and relatives use it because they like the security features. That's not the norm, though, because I'm a techie and so are most of my friends and family. As developers, we have to be mindful that the average computer user doesn't use the same tools we use.

A Little Perspective

Microsoft's browser issues aren't entirely malicious, even though it can feel good to say that they are. Microsoft has its own agenda when it comes to the web browser. It puts more emphasis on its own things working, such as .NET Framework components, ActiveX controls, Out-

> ### Joe Asks...
> #### When Can You Drop Support for a Browser?
>
> That's a decision you and your organization or clients have to make based on usage data you gather from your current or potential customers. Look at the browser statistics for other websites that we talked about in Section 15.2, *Browser Statistics*, on page 217. At the time of writing, IE 6 has more active users than Firefox. If you want to target only Firefox users, then the statistics might not matter; however, if you want to target everyone, you need to make sure you don't shut out a large percentage of potential users.
>
> I use this general rule when deciding which browsers to support: I support the last two major versions of a browser, and then I make sure that the site works and is *readable* in the others. It doesn't have to look the same, but at least my users can use the site.
>
> What browsers and features you choose to support all comes down to how it will impact your income and the income of your clients.

look Web Access, and SharePoint. IE is the delivery vehicle for Microsoft's web-based products.

These products make Microsoft a lot of money, and it has to support those products for the duration of the promised period. This means it can't fix the IE rendering issues we've all come to know and love without completely breaking its own applications.

15.4 Internet Explorer 7

Internet Explorer 7 seems to like our website. Our content is centered, our PNG transparency works as expected, and things line up as they should. This is because we made sure to code a completely standards-compliant page, and we avoided accidentally sending Internet Explorer into quirks mode.

Determine the Rendering Mode

Sometimes you just can't tell what rendering mode you're in, but you can use JavaScript to tell you. Insert this snippet into the head of your page, and you'll see whether you're running in standards mode:

```
<script type="text/javascript" charset="utf-8">
    if(document.compatMode == 'CSS1Compat'){
      alert("Standards mode");
    }else{
      alert("Quirks mode");
    }
</script>
```

Quirks Mode in IE

We discussed quirks mode briefly when we talked about box models in Section 11.5, *Different Box Models*, on page 179; however, it takes more than setting the right doctype to make Internet Explorer use standards mode.

XML Prologs

Some web-page editors (and some templates) place the XML prolog at the top of the document, before the doctype. The presence of the prolog forces IE 6 to render pages in quirks mode. If you see the following in your web documents, you need to remove it:

```
<?xml version="1.0" encoding="iso-8859-1"?>
```

Comments Above the Doctype

Developers often add comments to pages to explain to others what the page does or to place other relevant information that others might need later. Unfortunately, IE 6 and IE 7 both turn on quirks mode if you place comments before the doctype.

In summary, to make IE happy, just don't put anything above the doctype, and things should start working in standards mode.

15.5 Internet Explorer 6

Open the site in IE 6. You'll notice immediately that the banner image doesn't have transparency, the two-column layout is broken, and it

Testing Websites

Cross-browser testing is such an important part of developing sites these days that there are more options than ever for you to try. Here are a few that I've used:

- The website crossbrowsertesting.com* provides online images of various operating system and browser configurations, including Linux and Mac OS, as well as several flavors of Windows.

- Microsoft provides virtual machines[†] of its browsers and operating systems specifically for developers. These images expire quarterly, so you'll need to grab new ones occasionally.

- IETester[‡] allows you to run multiple versions of Internet Explorer side-by-side. It runs only on Windows.

It's easier than ever to check your sites in multiple browsers on multiple platforms. However, if you're looking for the easiest option, I strongly recommend a Mac. With my Macbook Pro, I can run Safari and Firefox during development and easily test other browsers and platforms locally using virtual machines for Windows and Linux.

---

*. http://crossbrowsertesting.com/
†. http://www.microsoft.com/downloads/details.aspx?FamilyId=
21EABB90-958F-4B64-B5F1-73D0A413C8EF\&displaylang=en
‡. http://www.my-debugbar.com/wiki/IETester/HomePage

looks terrible. You can get a sense of the kinds of things that IE can't handle, even though you made sure to work in standards mode, in Figure 15.2, on page 223.

Fixing the Broken Stuff

There are lots of CSS hacks and exploits you can use to get IE to play nice, but using hacks is a bad development approach because hacks get fixed. You need a better way to target the user's browser, and Microsoft provides us with a near-perfect solution: *conditional comments*.

You can use conditional comments to target the use of Internet Explorer in general or to target specific versions of IE. The comments are read only by Internet Explorer; other browsers think they're regular HTML comments and pass them over.

working_with_ie/index.html

```
<!--[if IE 6]>
  <link rel="stylesheet" href="stylesheets/ie6.css"
        type="text/css" media="screen">
<![endif]-->

<!--[if IE 6]>

<style>
   #header img{behavior: url(stylesheets/iepngfix.htc)}
</style>
<![endif]-->
```

In this example, we're instructing the browser to load an additional style sheet. We'll use this approach to correct the rendering issues we've encountered. Add this to your HTML document after the rest of the style sheets, and then create a new file in the stylesheets folder called ie6.css.

Fixing the Columns

The main part of the page appears to be too wide to fit next to our sidebar as it does in the other browsers, so it drops below the sidebar. It just happens that we've encountered an IE 6 bug known as the *double-margin* bug. When an element is floated to the left and then has a left margin, IE doubles the margin. This also happens with the right margin on right-floated elements.

The simplest way to fix the double-margin bug is to add display:inline to the element that is affected by the issue. The problem is actually locating the element that's breaking things.

On close inspection, the culprit behind the double-margin issue is the main_text region. You can fix this by redefining the style in your IE 6 style sheet:

working_with_ie/stylesheets/ie6.css

```
#main_text{display:inline;}
```

Fixing the Transparency

IE 6 doesn't support alpha transparency on a PNG, but there are tons of solutions on the Web. Of course, not all of them are easy to use, but the one I've been the most happy with is the TwinHelix solution.[4]

---

4. http://www.twinhelix.com/css/iepngfix/

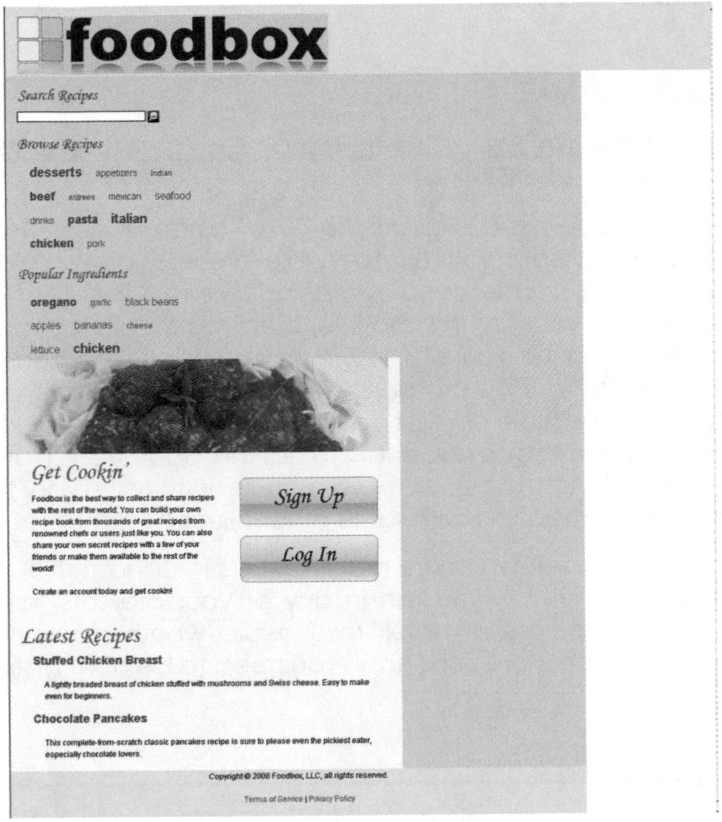

Figure 15.2: IE 6 HAS SIGNIFICANT PROBLEMS WITH OUR SITE.

Download the fix from the company's website, unzip it, and copy the iepngfix.htc and blank.gif files into your stylesheets folder.

Open the iepngfix.htc file, and locate this code:

```
if (typeof blankImg == 'undefined') var blankImg = 'blank.gif';
```

Next, change it to the following:

```
if (typeof blankImg == 'undefined') var blankImg = 'stylesheets/blank.gif';
```

To work properly, the HTC file needs to use a blank .gif file to complete the transparency, and it needs you to provide a link that's relative to the HTML file it's being applied to, not the style sheet.

> ## ᗡᗡ Joe Asks. . .
>
> ### Why Are We Fixing This by Hand? Can't We Use a Well-Established Fix Like IE7-js?
>
> Many developers see projects like IE7-js* as an easy fix. However, as a developer, you're responsible for the code you place in your site. If you understand everything that a project like IE7-js does to make your site compatible, then you should feel comfortable putting it in your site. However, you need to remember that solutions like IE7-js are *generic solutions*. They're intended to handle all possible cases. I don't like introducing more code into my projects than is necessary to get the job done. I'd rather fix the issues I know I have than use a "fix everything" library that might be incompatible with some other things I've done.
>
> Libraries and frameworks are great, but it's important that you understand anything you use in any of your projects. When things break, you are ultimately responsible, whether you wrote the code or not. More important, you need to be able to fix it.
>
> ---
> *.   http://code.google.com/p/ie7-js/

Add this line to your IE 6 conditional comment rule in the index.html file:

`working_with_ie/index.html`

```
<!--[if IE 6]>

<style>
    #header img{behavior: url(stylesheets/iepngfix.htc)}
</style>
<![endif]-->
```

This loads a special CSS behavior, supported only by IE.

Fixing the Space Below the Header Image

The header image has a tiny bit of padding showing up that pushes the rest of the page down, so it doesn't line up with the background we assigned. In standards mode, images are inline content, and they tend to rest on the baseline, leaving some room for descenders. It so happens that *IE 6 follows the specification correctly here*. The problem is that other browser manufacturers have introduced an exclusion to

> ### 〰 Joe Asks. . .
>
> #### How Does This Work for Multiple Pages?
>
> When you put more pages on your site or in your application, the relative paths to the HTC file are going to change depending on the location of your HTML file in the site's structure. You'll need to provide a root-relative link or an absolute link in the HTC file. This might not work on your local computer, but it will work when you deploy your site to a server.
>
> In our case, we'd deploy everything to the server and change the HTC file's reference to blank.gif to this instead:
>
> ```
> if (typeof blankImg == 'undefined')
>     var blankImg = '/stylesheets/blank.gif';
> ```
>
> You could then move the call for the HTC file from your HTML page into the ie6.css file. Just be sure to edit the path there, too.
>
> You could also not use transparent PNGs, but that's no fun!

this one rule, which is sometimes called *almost-strict mode*. The quick fix is to float the image or to change the image's display type to block:

`working_with_ie/stylesheets/ie6.css`

```
#header img{
  display:block;
}
```

It's a simple fix, and it causes everything to line up correctly. We could add this fix to the main layout style, rather than the IE 6 style, but we see the problem only in IE 6, so that's not necessary.

That about does it for the required IE 6 fixes. Everything now works as expected, but now you have the chance to reflect on the work you just did and decide whether supporting IE 6 is really worth all this effort. Your next site might be a lot more complex and require more fixes, but you also may have a different target market. If your next project requires IE 6 support, you'll be familiar with the more common issues and solutions.

15.6 Internet Explorer 8

Microsoft is becoming increasingly friendly toward developers who want to work within the realm of web standards. Internet Explorer 8 (IE 8) lets developers specify the rendering mode they want to use. IE 8 includes several modes to choose from, including modes that cause the browser to emulate IE 5 and IE 7. According to Microsoft, the IE 8 mode "provides the highest support available for industry standards, including the W3C Cascading Style Sheets Level 2.1 Specification, and the W3C Selectors API, with limited support for the W3C Cascading Style Sheets Level 3 Specification (Working Draft)."

That sounds amazing, but there's one significant downside: this rendering mode doesn't respect the doctype, and the doctype is the method that the rest of the browsers use to determine how to render pages. Fortunately, Microsoft has included another mode called *IE 8 emulation*[5] that respects the doctype and uses IE 8 rendering mode for standards-compliance and IE 5 mode when it encounters quirks mode. You should review this list of the possible compatibility values for IE 8.[6]

Value	Description
IE=8	The web page supports IE 8 mode, which is also called *IE 8 standards* mode.
IE=7	The web page supports IE 7 mode, which is also called *IE 7 standards* mode.
IE=EmulateIE8	If the web page specifies a standards-based DOCTYPE directive, the page supports IE 8 mode; otherwise, it supports IE 5 mode (*quirks* mode).
IE=EmulateIE7	If the web page specifies a standards-based DOCTYPE directive, the page supports IE 7 mode; otherwise, it supports IE 5 mode (*quirks* mode).
IE=Edge	The web page supports the highest mode available to the version of Internet Explorer used to display the page. This option is generally intended for testing purposes.

We can make IE 8 implement things correctly for us by adding this code snippet to the header of the HTML document, right after the head tag:

working_with_ie/index.html

```
<!--[if IE 8]>
  <meta http-equiv="X-UA-Compatible" content="IE=EmulateIE8" >
<![endif]-->
```

---

5. http://msdn.microsoft.com/en-us/library/cc288325(VS.85).aspx#
6. Source: http://msdn.microsoft.com/en-us/library/ms533876(VS.85).aspx

Figure 15.3: OUR SITE LOOKS GREAT IN GOOGLE CHROME!

Notice that we place this tag at the top of our document, right after the opening of the head element. You need to set the compatibility mode as soon as possible, before any style sheet links or JavaScript includes, so that your CSS and scripts will be interpreted correctly. Once you apply this fix, IE 8 behaves quite nicely. In fact, it even supports the advanced CSS features we used in our print style.

Problems with This Approach

With IE 8, Microsoft finally supports many of the same standards that other browsers have had for a few years; however, it still doesn't do this by default, and you have to add this content to every page in your site to make it behave nicely. Fortunately, you're adding a meta tag, so this approach is less kludgy than implementing some CSS or JavaScript workaround. That said, it's still an extra step, and purists will scoff at the additional markup. I'm not a fan of this implementation, but I'll take this simple, one-line fix over hours of hacking my scripts to make them work any day.

15.7 Other Browsers

It doesn't hurt to take a look at how your site appears in other browsers. Fortunately, Foodbox looks great in Safari on the Mac, which you can

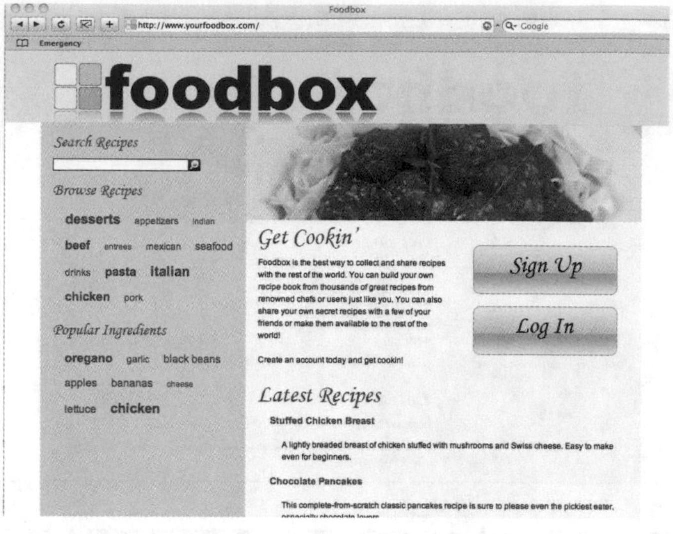

Figure 15.4: OUR SITE LOOKS JUST FINE IN SAFARI, TOO!

see in Figure 15.4. And it appears as though Google implemented a standards-compliant rendering engine in Chrome because we don't have to fix anything in that browser, either (see Figure 15.3, on the preceding page).

I want to point out that it's not like we got lucky. This is the way things work when you follow web standards and work with valid documents. For this reason, I'll reiterate that you shouldn't waste time developing in Internet Explorer; instead, you should develop in a standards-compliant browser and fix things in the oddball browsers later.

15.8 Summary

Developing sites for multiple browsers is important for reaching a wide audience, and I'm pleased to say this is getting easier. If you embrace standards, things just work. As IE 6 fades away and IE 7 gets replaced by IE 8, the differences between various browsers become less and less. That's good news for developers and great news for users.

Chapter 16

Accessibility and Usability

You need to consider all segments of your audience. Can a color-blind user make good use of your site? How about someone who's blind? What about someone who can't physically use a mouse? Are your links in your tag cloud too close together, making it hard for someone with impaired motor skills to navigate?

And what about people on slow Internet connections? Do your pages still load quickly for them? How does your site work on a mobile device, such as a cell phone?

The terms *accessibility* and *usability* are often foreign to application developers. It's a topic that, until recently, hasn't been popular. This chapter will make you aware of the various types of issues that you might encounter with different types of users, as well as show you ways to improve your site for everyone.

16.1 What Does Accessibility Mean to You?

Whenever I talk to web developers, I like to ask them what they think of when they hear the term *accessibility*. I find the different responses to this question quite interesting. Some people have no idea what this means at all, and others think it applies only to access for the disabled. Accessibility is so much more than that—it's about access in general.

You should consider an application or website to be accessible if it can be viewed and used by any user using any possible means of interaction. This includes assistive technologies but also users who access your site via older computers, slow Internet connections, cellular phones, PDAs, and game systems. Your site doesn't have to work the same on all these platforms, but it should be usable enough that users can achieve their goals, whether it's finding information, reading documents, or buying products.

If your site works only when JavaScript is enabled, it's not accessible. Not every device supports JavaScript, not every user enables it, and not every browser handles JavaScript the same way.

If your site *requires* your users to have Flash installed to work, it's not accessible, no matter how awesome the animations on the menu might look. If users can't click those menu items because their iPhones doesn't come with Flash, you've lost potential customers.

If your site has so many graphics that it's unusable to someone on a slow Internet connection (yes, those still exist), then your site is not accessible.

If you're like many programmers, your first reaction is probably that you need to be able to use things like Flash and JavaScript to make your sites appealing, usable, and competitive. That is a valid argument; Gmail without Ajax is a lot more difficult to use than its robust counterpart. But Gmail *works* without Ajax; it's just not *as* functional. Rather than make its service unavailable, Google has implemented something that works well enough to be functional and useful, even if it's more cumbersome than the normal version.

Your site should be readable and functional to everyone. It doesn't have to look as awesome or work as slickly, but it does have to let people complete their tasks.

16.2 Basic Accessibility Issues

This section covers basic accessibility issues.

People Who Are Blind

Users who are completely blind most often rely on software called *screen readers*, special software that uses a computerized voice to read the text on the page to a user. There are several screen-reading software packages available, including the popular JAWS, but all have their strengths and weaknesses when it comes to what they support.

Screencasts, Videos, and Tours

It seems as though every new site has some sort of tour, whether it's a bunch of application screenshots or a video walk-through. When designing a tour or a screencast, you need to think about how useful that screen cast would be for a blind user. When you're doing the voiceover track for a screencast, treat it as sports announcers treat televised games: describe what's happening to the viewer. Don't just say "click here"; say "select the New Recipe link." A little description goes a long way, even for your sighted users.

The same rule applies to your tour images. Be descriptive in your captions, and you'll make many users quite happy.

Color

If your users can't see, then they obviously won't notice any of the color you used in your website. We spent a chapter on color in this book, and we talked about the ways that you can use color to evoke emotion in your users. Unfortunately, none of that applies when dealing with blind users, so you should make sure that you find other ways than to convey important information to them. For example, if you use color to denote an error on a form submission, you might also consider listing and describing the problems at the top of the form. Additionally, you might want to wrap these elements with the strong or em elements. Many screen-reading tools will audibly draw attention to content marked up with those elements.

Alternative Text Attributes

We talked about alt attributes a bit in the sidebar on page 130. It's one of the best-known ways to make a site accessible; however, it can also be extremely annoying to users of screen readers if used incorrectly.

The purpose of the alt attribute is to provide descriptive content information about an image. Unfortunately, many web developers treat alt attributes as just another thing they need to do, so they put in some arbitrary content or, worse, the filename again.

Most people who use screen readers aren't interested in hearing "bullet," "check mark," or "lady with a red sweater."

If you have an image that's on the page simply for decoration, consider using a blank alt attribute:

```
<img src="/images/circle.gif" alt="">
```

A better solution is to move these purely aesthetic items into your style sheets, keeping only images that are truly content in your HTML document. For example, you can use CSS to apply images to lists:

```
ul{
  list-style-image: url("/images/circle.gif");
}
```

But your users do want to hear words you've placed inside an image or inside your graph that shows usage of your products by country. Make sure your alternate text describes the content of your image—or leave it blank. Don't leave the alt attribute off, though! Many screen readers know to ignore blank alt attributes.

One last thing: please don't start your alternative text with "An image of..." The user will already know the content is an image because the screen reader will announce that fact when it reads the alt attribute.

Graphs and Charts

Charts and graphs displayed as images are basically worthless to blind users unless you provide some description of them. In addition to the aforementioned alt attribute, the img tag also supports an attribute called longdesc. You can use this attribute to describe a graph or chart. Describing a figure helps every one of your users, especially if it's very complex.

Spelling and Grammar

The screen reader works best when the text on the page is readable. When writing your content, you should take special care to ensure it is well-defined, spell-checked, and grammatically correct. Screen readers have to pronounce the words they see, and this makes grammar and structure important. Think about words that you write the same way, but pronounce differently, such as the word *read*. Read the previous sentence aloud and then laugh at what you read. Which version of *read* did you think I referred to? The one that sounds like *reed* or the one that rhymes with *red*? You'll never know. If you're not careful with your sentence structure, a screen reader won't either. It will do its best to figure it out based on the tense and context of the sentence, but it's on you to use correct grammar and spelling!

Spelling individual words correctly is also important. Imagine how much trouble a screen reader would have if you left a letter out of a word by accident.

> ## Brian's Rules for Proofreading
>
> I write a lot, whether it's for internal documentation, for my blogs, or for books like this one. I also make tons of mistakes while doing so. To account for this, I have developed a proofreading strategy that, if used continuously, can be extremely effective.
>
> First, read what you write out loud. If you can get through it without laughing, you're a third of the way there.
>
> Second, read the sentence backward. Reading your text out of context can help you spot misspelled words or duplicate words.
>
> Finally, get someone else to read your content aloud. This is important. You'll get to hear your content, and you'll get feedback from that person on how to make it better.

Finally, punctuation is important. Pay attention to how you use periods, commas, and other punctuation marks! Some screen readers use different vocal inflections when they encounter different kinds of punctuation. For example, a comma might cause a screen reader to pause for a second, which makes comprehension much easier.

My solution to a lot of this is to spell-check content with a computer first and then get someone else to proofread my content for me. It's even better if you can get someone else to write the content, but you still have to look it over yourself for spelling errors. If your clients write the content, they'll still blame you for typos, grammatical errors, and spelling mistakes.

JavaScript and Ajax

JavaScript and Ajax enable developers to create much richer user interfaces. For example, we can use this combination to allow our users to edit things in-place instead of jumping to a different form. You can use this combination to show and hide regions of a page based on data entered by the user. Or you can use it to implement fake pop-up windows like Lightbox[1] to load pages and content instead of using regular browser windows as pop-ups.

---

1.   http://www.huddletogether.com/projects/lightbox2/

The problem is that, although many screen readers claim to support some JavaScript and Ajax functionality, few screen readers support this functionality *well*. It's often hard for a screen reader to tell exactly what changed on the page. You should develop your site so that all its features work without JavaScript, but then go back and add the fancy JavaScript-based features you desire. This way you can build in graceful degradation through progressive enhancement, rather than leaving it as an afterthought.

For example, consider forms that post via Ajax. It'd be easy for you to make those forms perform a regular post, after which you could go back and use JavaScript to modify the form unobtrusively so it performs an Ajax request. You'd then use server-side code to determine whether you had received a regular request or an Ajax request. The regular request might display a new page, while the Ajax request would return a JavaScript response that modifies the existing page's contents. This implementation wouldn't take long to implement, but it would make your site usable to a lot more people.

You should keep testing different versions of screen-reading software to see how they handle your site. The companies behind the screen readers are working to make the Web friendlier to their users.

If you keep these types of things in mind as you build a site, you will make things better for all your users. Images with long descriptions might provide users with a better understanding of the graph. Checking your grammar and spelling is something you should be doing anyway. Graceful degradation of your user interface also makes it possible for your app to be used by less sophisticated browsers. I can surf the Web with my cell phone, but some of my favorite Web 2.0 websites don't work on it, yet.

Google Is Blind, Too!

It's easy to forget this fact, but Google and other search engines interpret your web page the same way a blind user's screen-reading software would. Certain content, such as videos, images, graphs, and Flash, might not be interpreted. Your site's structure might also cause problems for your users.

One way I recommend testing your site for accessibility is to use a text-based browser like Lynx (see Figure 16.1, on the facing page). You might also try turning off all CSS, JavaScript, and images in your browser. Navigate around your site, and you'll get a quick idea of how good or

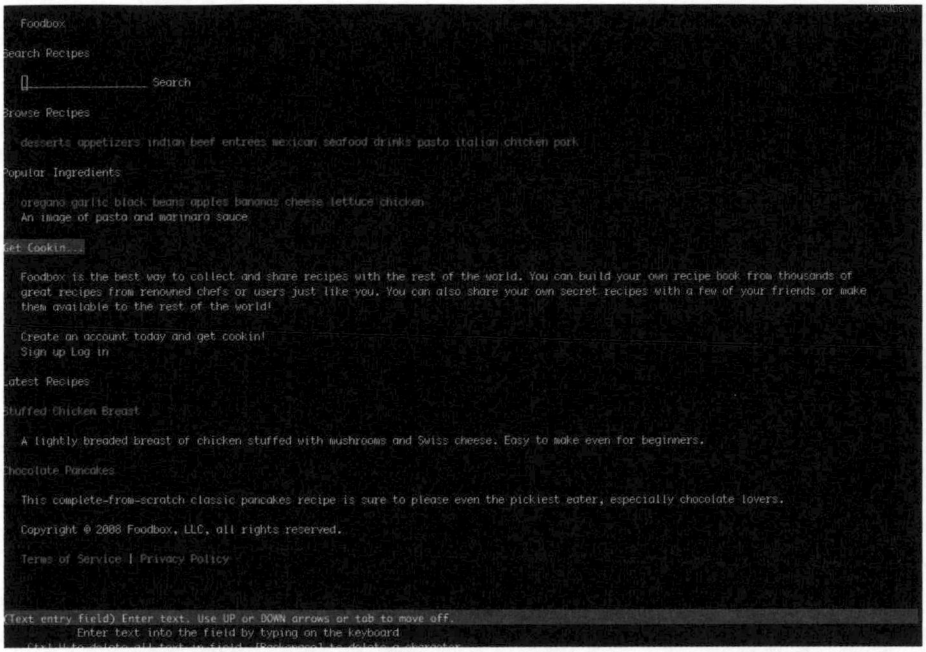

Figure 16.1: FOODBOX ON LYNX, A TEXT-BASED BROWSER

bad your site is in terms of accessibility; you'll also get a feel for how search engines will interpret your site.

Color-Blind Users

Color-blind users might encounter difficulty on your site if you've used color to convey important information. Color-blind users have difficulty distinguishing between certain types of color. For example, many color-blind users cannot distinguish red from green or red from black.

You should take care that you choose colors with enough contrast to make charts, graphs, and other areas of your site readable. For example, red text on a black background could be almost invisible to a color-blind user.

Protanopia and Deutanopia

Protanopia and deutanopia are two of the most common types of colorblindness. People with these forms of colorblindness have difficulties distinguishing between red and green.

Figure 16.2: Foodbox as seen through the eyes of someone with protanopia

You can see how the Foodbox site looks to users with protanopia in Figure 16.2. Notice how the red sauce on the meatballs shows up as almost dark gray, while how the rest of the site looks extremely brown. Red actually appears quite dark to people with protanopia, so it's important to think carefully about how you use this color in your designs.

Deutanopia is similar to protanopia, except that reds and greens often appear to be the same color. The Foodbox site also looks quite different to people afflicted with deutanopia, as shown in Figure 16.3, on the facing page.

Tritanopia

Tritanopia is a rare form of colorblindness in which yellow and blue are virtually indistinguishable. Our site looks quite pink to people with this disability, as shown in see Figure 16.4, on the next page.

People with Visual Impairments

People with visual impairments have their own unique issues that might not be immediately apparent. Visually impaired users often use

Figure 16.3: FOODBOX AS SEEN THROUGH THE EYES OF SOMEONE WITH DEUTANOPIA

Figure 16.4: FOODBOX AS SEEN THROUGH THE EYES OF SOMEONE WITH TRITANOPIA

magnification software such as ZoomText or the built-in zooming feature of OS X, so it's not especially important that you worry about the size of your fonts. However, you should avoid using extremely small fonts.

Magnification tools have a drawback, though. Visually impaired users focus on the region they've zoomed in on and will miss content outside the zoomed window. Imagine looking at your computer screen through a paper towel tube. You have to move the tube around to see everything, so you might not see everything the site designer intended. As the developer, you have no control over how people use their accessibility tools, so how do you combat this problem? You should construct your site so your users don't have to use magnification.

Visually impaired users, especially older users, do not want a separate site. Like other people with disabilities, they want to be treated equally, and a big fear with a separate site is that you, the developer, won't keep it updated. I've run into that a few times, and it's extremely frustrating.

As a daily user of assistive technologies like screen magnification, my advice to you would be to let the user worry about zooming in. What you should worry about is keeping important pieces of content together. Anyone who needs them probably has the magnification tools already. When it comes to the Web, IE 7, Firefox, and Opera all allow scaling of the entire page, and full-screen magnification software on Macs and PCs make it possible to increase the size of the entire workspace, not just the browser.

People with Hearing Impairments

The Web is primarily a visual medium, but an increasing number of websites use videos to show off site features or to share information. Your hearing-impaired users can certainly watch the video, but if you don't provide a transcript, some captioning, or subtitles for your video or screencast, you could be leaving such users out in the cold. If you run a podcast, consider providing transcripts of your program with clickable links so that hearing-impaired users can follow along with your broadcast.

Senior citizens, veterans, Baby Boomers, and a shockingly growing percentage of younger people have hearing difficulties,[2] so it's important

---

2. MiracleEar, the hearing-aid company, reports that "15% of recent college graduates have as much or more hearing loss than their parents."

that you don't leave these users out of your plans. If you post video clips with audio, ensure that the audio is loud enough and of sufficient quality to be heard at low volumes. Doing so will ensure that your users can increase the volume to meet their needs.

Motor Impairments and Mouseless Users

As everyday users of computers, it's easy for us to forget that users of our services and products don't have the same setups we do. For example, some users must use alternative input devices in lieu of a mouse because they don't have hands or lack the muscle control to operate a mouse. Of course, your blind users won't be working with a mouse, either.

How do these people navigate? Some use special tubes that can manipulate a pointer when the user blows or sips. Other users rely strictly on a keyboard. And let's not forget that many developers prefer keyboard shortcuts to using a mouse.

Your keyboard users will rely on keyboard shortcuts and tabs, so try to act like them. Navigate your site only using a keyboard, and take note of any problems you encounter. Do you use slider controls? Make sure that users can type in a value instead. Do you use in-place editors that make the user click a region to activate the text area? The bottom line is simple: don't make your application dependent on the use of a mouse.

Finally, please, please avoid the use of the word *click*, as in *click here*. This text implies that your user has a mouse, and it's unnecessary, anyway. For example, a *Click here for more information* link would work better if you changed it to a *More information* link. If you've followed rules for good usability, it should be obvious how the user should access the additional information you provide. Personally, I think the only reason people use the phrase *click here* is because they see others do so; I call upon you to break that cycle.

16.3 Being All-Inclusive!

An accessible site should work for everyone who wants to use it. If you use lots of JavaScript and Flash or Silverlight on your site, you should think about how people might interact with the site if they were unable to use any of those technologies. You shouldn't feel as though you have to be held back by the *lowest common denominator* when you build your new application—it's important to be competitive. However, you should strive to provide access to every user you possibly can.

At the time of writing, one of my favorite sites, Hulu,[3] uses Flash to play videos of my favorite shows. Unfortunately, I can't watch those shows on my iPod because the iPod doesn't support Flash yet. On the other hand, YouTube, which also uses Flash to play videos, has been making its videos available on the iPod and iPhone since the iPhone's launch, as do other video sites. Hulu made a good choice in using Flash; it's available in many more places and on more platforms than QuickTime or Windows Media. However, if YouTube can make its videos work on non-Flash devices, so can Hulu.[4]

Admittedly, Hulu doesn't have any say in how the iPod plays its videos, but its example does illustrate how your technology choices can accidentally leave out a segment of your audience. Whenever you implement some flashy new technology, you should consider how it impacts the various segments of your audience.

Navigation

One of the easiest ways for you to kill your website or web application is to make unintentional choices that limit the ability of your users to navigate around your site. Navigation is critically important. If you plan to use pull-down menus for your navigation, make sure that the entries within the pull-down menus are available through another method. Users with older browsers or screen readers might not be able to pull the menus down and will see only the top-level menu items. To get around this, you can create *landing pages* for those top-level menu items. These landing pages should contain the links that appear in the pull-down menu. The idea of an extra set of pages might not appeal to you at first, but aside from the accessibility benefits, this approach gives you or your marketing people another chance to plug some quality keywords and content into the site.

I've seen tons of sites that use Flash movies as menu systems. Although many people have Flash on their home computers, this approach can cause issues for the occasional user with a screen reader, mobile phone, or PDA browser. Users shouldn't have to download or install anything to move around your website. I'm not saying you shouldn't use Flash

---

3. http://www.hulu.com/
4. Of course, there might be legal issues that might prevent this.

> \\/ Joe Asks. . .
> ?ʃ
> ⌣ __But Flash Is Accessible, Isn't It?__
>
> If you ask Adobe, it is. That company has been conscious about accessibility since it merged with Macromedia, which has always worked hard to incorporate accessible features into its tools. However, even though Flash movies *can* be accessible, it's up to the person building the Flash movie to make sure that it is accessible. Even then, screen-reading software doesn't always work well with it, and some platforms don't support Flash. If you plan to use Flash, get some people to test it. Get a trial copy of JAWS or Window-Eyes, install it, and see how well it works with your site. There's nothing new here: test, test, and test again.

for navigation; rather, I'm saying you should make sure that people can get around your site without it.

Handling Errors

How do you display error messages in your applications? If you use pop-up boxes, you should be aware that users with motor impairments might have more difficulty clicking them away. If you use a different colored font such as red to indicate an error, color-blind users might not notice the message. If you use Ajax to handle validation, some screen-reading software won't notice the changes. So, what options do you have, after all?

You can see one of the better examples of how to handle form validation properly in the built-in scaffolding from Ruby on Rails. When your user enters invalid data, the form is redisplayed, and a new region is placed on the page that lists each field that contained an error. The message also gives a brief description of the problem. The scaffolding also outlines each form field with an error in red. Color-blind users might not see the red text, but they will notice the new error-message region on the page, and they will also see the thicker border that surrounds the affected form fields.

This approach could be greatly improved if the error messages were displayed *next to* the form fields containing the erroneous data; however, it's still a good approach because it doesn't rely solely on color to denote that a problem occurred.

Cross-browser Testing

We covered testing your site on multiple browsers in Chapter 15, *Working with Internet Explorer and Other Browsers*, on page 215. In a similar vein, we'll cover how to work with mobile devices in Chapter 19, *Designing for Mobile Devices*, on page 265. There isn't much to add about cross-browser compatibility at this point, other than to say that it's a big part of accessibility in general. Your ultimate goal should always be to include as many people as you can.

16.4 Critical Business Issues

Building sites in a competitive market can often impact your ability to make web pages and applications accessible to your users. If you want to develop an application that is compelling, state-of-the-art, innovative, and commercially appealing, then you will likely find yourself embracing a technology that is not highly accessible. You need to compete with others, but you also need to reach the 90% of the market that could use your application right away.

Regardless, you need to keep accessibility in mind from the start. I understand that releasing your site and getting users is important to your clients, but you're in for a big surprise if you think you can build a site first and add in accessibility later. Once your site has tons of users, you'll have new features to roll out and new trouble tickets to address. Accessibility is like test-driven development: if you don't do it from the start, it will never get done because you'll hate doing it. If you can't get accessibility into the plan because it's the right thing to do, then you need to frame it in terms the stakeholders understand: money. Talk to the stakeholders about how much of their target market they will exclude if they don't embrace the importance of accessibility. The number of people excluded could be far higher than your stakeholders have imagined.

If you work on a project for a government agency, university, or public school, you need to be aware of the laws that govern how technology can be purchased. Some government agencies cannot purchase appli-

> ### ⚡ Joe Asks...
>
> #### If Accessibility Is So Important, Why Are We Waiting Until Now to Implement It?
>
> That's a fair question. I left off covering this topic until now because I had so much material to cover, and this is not a book on accessibility. However, if you look back, you'll notice that I brought up accessibility topics all along, including alternative text, validation, semantic markup, dyslexia, and some color issues. Implementing accessibility features for the Foodbox site will be easier for us because the site's design has taken such issues into account from the outset. When building your next site, you'll want to take all the things mentioned in this chapter into consideration when you *begin* development.

cations that don't comply with the Section 508 guidelines. If your target market includes those types of agencies, you need to make sure they can use your product.

Visit http://www.section508.gov/ for more information about those guidelines and how they affect you. Following these guidelines can help you create highly accessible websites and applications; personally, I find these guidelines more helpful than the guidelines put forth by the W3C when it comes to working with disabled users.

16.5 Improving Our Site's Accessibility

When we look at Foodbox with a text-based browser, we can see that, because of the way we structured the site, a blind user with a screen reader (or even a mobile user who doesn't have the ability to load style sheets) will have to scroll down quite a bit to read the site's content or to sign in. The search box and tag clouds are both in the way.

We'll get past this slight irritation by creating some links to skip over the navigation, hiding these links with our main and print style sheets so regular users won't see them but screen-reading software will still announce them.

Adding the Skip Links

Open your index.html file, and add the code in bold immediately beneath the banner image:

accessibility/index.html

```
<div id="header"> <!-- start of header -->
  <img src="images/banner.png" alt="Foodbox">
▶ <ul id="skiplinks" class="noprint">
▶   <li><a href="#main_text" accesskey="0">Skip to Content</a>
▶ </ul>
</div> <!-- end of header -->
```

The Skip to Contents link references our page's main text region. Adding id attributes to our sections makes it extremely easy to provide accessible navigation.

Access Keys

You might have noticed another attribute on our *Skip to content* link—the accesskey attribute.

This attribute allows you to specify a keyboard shortcut that users can use to activate links, buttons, or form fields. This is particularly helpful for users with screen readers, but it's also helpful for people who can't or don't want to use a mouse. Of course, you'll need to provide some way to inform your users that these keys exist because few of them will inspect your code to figure this out.

At first glance, my choice of 0 (zero) for a value here might not make sense. I assigned this value to the *Skip to Content* link for the same reason the developers of Twitter did: it works great for mobile-phone users. See? Accessibility *is* about more than assisting disabled users.

Screen Readers and display:none

You learned that we can use display:none in a corresponding CSS rule to remove regions and elements from the page in Chapter 14, *Making a Printer-Friendly Page*, on page 205. However, many screen-reading software packages have started respecting this property. Many articles on accessibility advocate using display:none to hide the skip links, but this is no longer a valid solution. Instead, we can use some positioning tricks to push the links well outside the page.

How Access Keys Work

When a user presses the access key, how the browser responds is determined by the element attached to that access key. When you assign an access key to a link, the link is activated when the user presses the key.* If you assign an access key to a label tag that's bound to a form field, the user's cursor is placed within that form field.

An access key basically replaces a mouse click, and it can speed up a user's workflow significantly.

---

*. Internet Explorer focuses the link rather than activating it.

Hiding Skip Links with Negative Positioning

The CSS to hide our content contains only a few lines. First, we need to use *absolute positioning*, where we specify the X and Y coordinates of the element using CSS. Once we enable absolute positioning, we specify that we want to position the item at -9999px. This means that we want to position the item 9999px to the left of the browser's left edge.[5]

Add this CSS rule to your stylesheets/layout.css file:

accessibility/stylesheets/layout.css

```
#skiplinks{
  position:absolute;
  left:-9999px;
}
```

We applied the class="noprint" attribute to the skip links list so our print style sheet will hide it automatically.

Labels for Forms

We can improve the usability for mobile users, blind users, and users with motor impairments even further if we use access keys to help users navigate our pages. We can even attach an access key to a form field. To do that, we need to modify our form just a bit and add a label field to the form. A label field gives us a way to bind a text label to a form field

---

5. If you specify a containing element as position:relative, then any absolutely positioned elements within the containing element are positioned using the containing element's top-left corner.

The Power of Labels

The label tag enables you to enhance the usability of your site's forms for all your users. For example, if you associate a label tag with a radio button or checkbox, a user can select the text of a label to "check" a checkbox or "click" a button. This approach benefits those users who aren't as accurate with a mouse or trackpad.

You associate a label by referencing an element's ID like this:

```
<input type="checkbox" value="yes" id="user_active"
       name="user[active]" />
<label for="user_active">Activate User</label>
```

Taking advantage of label tags when you build your forms can make things much easier on the users who interact with your forms.

---

and is often used by screen readers to help associate form field names with values.

Labels can help associate text labels with form fields, but you can also use them to link keyboard shortcuts to form elements. If we add a label to our form and set the for attribute of the label to match the ID of the search box, then the user's cursor will be placed inside the search field when the access key is pressed:

accessibility/index.html

```
<form id="search_form" method="get" action="/recipes/">
  <div>
    <label for="search_keywords" accesskey="s">Keywords</label>
    <input type="text" id="search_keywords" name="keywords">

    <input type="image" alt="Search" src="images/search.png">
  </div>
```

We use $\boxed{\text{S}}$ as the access key in this snippet, but the actual key combination will differ, depending on the user's browser and the OS. Safari and Firefox on the Mac require you to press $\boxed{\text{Ctrl}}$+$\boxed{\text{S}}$. On Windows, that combination calls up the Save dialog box. Instead, use $\boxed{\text{Shift}}$+$\boxed{\text{Alt}}$+$\boxed{\text{S}}$ in Firefox and $\boxed{\text{Alt}}$+$\boxed{\text{S}}$ in Internet Explorer.

\\// **Joe Asks...**

Wait: If Every Browser Has a Different Keyboard Shortcut, How Do Users Know What to Use?

Screen readers for the blind like JAWS will actually announce the access keys to the user when it encounters them. It's incredibly useful for those users. However, the access keys you defined won't just automatically appear in most web browsers.

You should consider some sort of accessibility statement on your page. Within your skip links navigation, you could link to the accessibility statement and show a list of your access keys, as well as provide other useful information to help disabled users navigate your site. You could also provide a simple accessible form on that page where users could give you feedback so you can find out whether things are working in a useful way.

The label tag we incorporated adds the text *keywords* to our search form. We don't want that, but we can use CSS to hide it, just as we hid the navigation skip links:

accessibility/stylesheets/layout.css

```
#search_form label{
  position:absolute;
  left:-9999px;}
```

For extra credit, you can try combining both rules into one.

So far we've made a couple changes to the page that have improved its accessibility significantly. You could expand upon these improvements further by adding some additional jump links to your navigation. In fact, you might want to do that for your mobile audience anyway.

16.6 Tabbing

The site doesn't have any complex forms yet, but it's only a matter of time until you'll create one. When you do, it's important to think about how a keyboard user might navigate your form. When a user presses the Tab key, the cursor jumps from element to element; however, the tab order might behave unexpectedly if you've done a poor job of designing your form. In the event that you find yourself with a form that doesn't tab properly, you can use the tabindex attribute to gain tighter control over the form fields.

The tabindex attribute lets you control the tab order on an interface. Simply increment the tabindex attribute for each field on a form. You can specify the tabindex on any interactive element, including links, drop-down lists, text areas, checkboxes, and radio buttons.

Let's mock up the Foodbox sign-up form using a proper, accessible form:

```
<form id="signup" action="/signup" method="get">
  <p>
    <label for="account_login">Login</label><br>
    <input id="account_login"
           name="account[login]"
           size="30" type="text" tabindex="1">
  </p>

  <p>
    <label for="email">Email</label><br>
    <input id="account_email"
           name="account[email]"
           size="30" type="text" tabindex="2"></p>

  <p>
    <label for="password">Password</label><br>
    <input id="account_password"
           name="account[password]"
           size="30" type="password" tabindex="3">
  </p>

  <p>
    <label for="password_confirmation">
           Confirm Password
    </label><br>
    <input id="account_password_confirmation"
         name="account[password_confirmation]"
         size="30" type="password" tabindex="4">
  </p>

  <p>
    <label
      <input class="button" name="commit"
             type="submit" value="Sign up"
             tabindex="5">
    </label>
    or <a href="/" tabindex="6">Cancel</a>
  </p>

</form>
```

The Vertical Bar (and Other Special Characters)

If you use the pipe character in your site to separate items, as we did in our footer, you might be in for a shock when you test it on a screen reader. Here's our footer, as interpreted by a screen reader:

"Copyright copyright two thousand eight Foodbox, LLC, all rights reserved. Link Terms of Service vertical bar Link Privacy Policy."

The screen reader read the copyright symbol as a word, so *copyright* is read aloud twice. Notice that it also interpreted the pipe character as *vertical bar*.

This is fine in small doses, but imagine if we had six things in our footer, separated by these bars. When you develop sites, please be mindful of how you use special characters for things that aren't directly content related. Can you think of a better way for us to do the footer?

Avoiding tabindex

You might be thinking this is a colossal hassle. Don't worry; that's perfectly normal. Specifying tabindexes can be painful, especially when you have complex forms with lots of fields and you have to insert new fields in the middle. You can avoid using tabindexes if you're careful about how you design your forms. If you allow your web forms to flow naturally in a linear fashion, you won't need to worry about this much. However, you will want to test your forms by trying to fill them out with only a keyboard on every browser you can get your hands on.

16.7 Accessibility Testing Checklist

Before you launch your site, you should do a quick audit of all your pages. Things that should be in your list of acceptance criteria include the following:

- Check that all pages in the site have valid markup.

- Verify that all style sheets are valid.

- Ensure that all image tags have *useful* and descriptive alternative text.

- Test that all pages are legible and usable in a text-based browser such as Lynx.

- Check to see whether your pages are legible in older browsers.

- Turn off JavaScript and see whether your pages are usable.

- Throttle your connection and see how fast your pages load, or use a speed-testing tool to catch large, unoptimized images.

- Turn off images and test every page to ensure that no important text is rendered solely as an image.

- Install the Fangs Firefox extension to see how a screen reader might interpret your page.

- Get a demo of JAWS[6] or Window-Eyes,[7] turn off your monitor, and try to navigate your site.

- Have a third party review your site's content for spelling, grammar, and other issues.

- Search and remove any references to *click here* because not every user has a mouse. Also, people know what to do with hyperlinks these days, and if you haven't made your links obvious enough, then you need to review how you implemented them.

- Use a service such as the Colorblind Web Page Filter[8] or the wonderful cross-platform desktop application to Color Oracle[9] to test your site for various forms of colorblindness.

- Ensure that you don't have any rapidly flashing elements on your pages that might cause trouble for users with epilepsy.

- Ensure you've implemented a skip navigation option on your site so that users with screen readers can skip over your repetitive navigation.

- Ensure that users can tab easily between form fields.

- Make sure you have transcripts or captioning for any videos on your site, so hearing-impaired users can follow along.

---

6. http://www.freedomscientific.com/
7. http://www.gwmicro.com/
8. http://colorfilter.wickline.org/
9. http://colororacle.cartography.ch/

16.8 Summary

Accessibility and usability are too important to ignore. Even if you don't deal with disabled users, the techniques you use to ensure that your site is accessible for the disabled can make your site more usable for everyone. Always remember that accessibility doesn't mean *accessible for the blind*; rather, it means that your site can be used by anyone from any device. You should strive to achieve that goal whenever you develop.

## Chapter 17

Building a Favicon

A *favicon* is a little icon that shows up next to the address bar of most browsers and is often displayed alongside the bookmark for the site. In browsers that support multiple tabs, the favicon appears in the tab containing your site. This constant exposure helps you reinforce your site's brand. Most popular sites use favicons, and Foodbox should be no exception.

17.1 Creating a Simple Icon

To create an effective favicon, we need something that will reflect our branding. Let's create a simple icon for Foodbox by taking the four squares from the Foodbox logo. Open Photoshop, and create a new document, setting the dimensions to 64px wide by 64px high. Use 72px for the resolution, and be sure to choose the RGB color space. Set the background color to white.

Import the foodbox.ai logo file you built by using File > Place. After you import the image, use the resize handles to size the image so that only the squares fit on the canvas, as shown in Figure 17.1, on the next page. Hold down the $\boxed{\text{Shift}}$ key while resizing to constrain the transformation so you don't distort the logo.

17.2 Creating the Favicon

A favicon is a 16px-by-16px Windows .ico file, and Photoshop doesn't have a built-in filter to export that type of file. However, you can get a

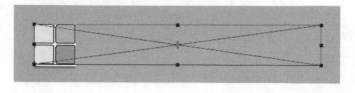

Figure 17.1: RESIZE THE FOODBOX LOGO SO THAT ONLY THE SQUARES ARE WITHIN THE CANVAS.

free filter from Telegraphics that works for almost all versions of Photoshop.[1] We will also use a command-line program called png2ico,[2] which converts PNG files to ICO files. Windows users can download a binary version, while Linux and Mac users might want to check their package manager for the program instead.

Resize the image in Photoshop to 16px by 16px using Photoshop's Image Size command, which you can access at Image > Image Size. Choose the Bicubic Sharper option to get the best results when reducing an image.

Now save the file as favico.png. Favicons support transparency, so you could save this as a transparent PNG.

Open a terminal or command prompt, navigate to the folder containing the PNG you just saved, and run this command:

```
png2ico favicon.ico favicon.png
```

Place the favicon.ico file in the root of your website, not in the images folder, and most browsers will automatically find the file. You won't see the favicon on your local file system, so you must upload your files to your server. You might also have to restart your web server to make the favicon show up in the address bar. You can see the final result in Figure 17.2, on the facing page.

Safari, Firefox, and Internet Explorer 7 support favicons natively, but Internet Explorer 6 might need a little help from you to display the icon.

---

1. http://www.telegraphics.com.au/sw/
2. http://www.winterdrache.de/freeware/png2ico/index.html

Figure 17.2: OUR FAVICON

Add this code to your home page in the head section if you can't get the favicon to show up:

```
<link rel="shortcut icon" href="favicon.ico">
<link rel="icon" type="image/ico" href="favicon.ico">
```

17.3 Summary

A favicon is an important part of your site's branding, and it can go a long way toward helping users remember your brand, because they'll see it in their browser while they visit your site and in their bookmarks bar when they're somewhere else. A favicon is especially effective when you incorporate existing logos or imagery into your icon.

## Chapter 18

Search Engine Optimization

Foodbox is ready for launch, and everyone thinks it looks great. Nothing feels better than finishing up a project that you've put a lot of effort into. However, getting the site up doesn't mean you're done. The site's not worth much if nobody can find it, so we need to talk about the necessary steps you can take to improve your visibility but also keep your site user-friendly.

18.1 Content Is King

I've mentioned this a few times already, but I want to drive this point home: no matter how good your site looks, your users will not stick around long if you don't have content. Look at Flickr.[1] That site has a plain, conservative, and clean design with minimal color because its developers know that people come there to look at user-uploaded photos. Those photos are Flickr's content.

Search engines think your content is important, too. They want you to have content that is relevant to the keywords you've selected.

Scamming the Search Engines

First, a disclaimer: if you're looking at this section and thinking that you can use any of these techniques to improve your ranking, you're mistaken. The search engines already know all these dirty tricks, but I'm listing them here so you can identify them and stay away from them. It's easy to do some of these things accidentally, while other techniques

---

1. http://www.flickr.com/

are implemented by unscrupulous SEO companies or by developers responding to the demands of their clients. These techniques sometimes work in the short term, but they will almost certainly result in your website getting whacked with the ban stick.

Keyword Overloading

Keyword overloading basically means that you throw in a ton of keywords for your site. Sometimes people do this accidentally because they don't count the number of keywords they enter; other times people enter an abundance of keywords because they want to get noticed. Generally, you want to avoid repeating the same keyword more than a couple of times, and you want to keep the number of keywords to around thirty to forty-five per page.

Irrelevant Keywords

Using keywords that have absolutely nothing to do with your site's subject or content can get you into trouble. Some sites pick popular keywords ripped out of the headlines or use some of the top search terms from Google to attempt to trick users into visiting them.

Some good keywords for Foodbox might be *chicken*, *turkey*, *recipes*, *dinner*, and *pasta*. Some less than appropriate words might include *Free mp3s*, *videos*, *free iPod*, and *Paris Hilton*.

Don't laugh. It happens a lot, often because stakeholders make developers do it. When that happens, you have to decide whether that's something you are willing to do. I won't because I don't want to be responsible when Google blacklists the website a few months after it goes online.

Alternate Content

This technique relies on some (usually server-side) technology to detect a search engine and serve different content than what the users see. The search engines crawl your site and grab the content, indexing it for keywords, content, and links that get thrown into their databases. If you serve them different information, you're being dishonest, and eventually the search engines will detect that, usually because someone complains. Remember that the search engines are a business, too, so it's in their best interests to make sure that their search results return relevant information.

Hiding Content

This is one of the older cheats, but I remain amazed at how popular this one is, especially among novice web developers. This method involves taking a ton of nonrelevant keywords and phrases, placing them in the content of the site, but then using some technique to hide the content from the site's users. In the past, developers would just set the text color so it matched the background color. Once the search engines got wise to this technique, developers started to use CSS to position content off the page by using negative margins and other types of positioning tricks.

What Is Content?

Content is anything that your users come to see. Your text is obviously content, but so are your images, videos, music, and downloadable files. Generally speaking, search engines are interested in all these items, so you want to make sure you do what you can to help them find it.

You already know that you should provide alternative text for all images using the alt attribute for your img tags. What you might not know is that, because a search engine can't see your images, it relies on this alternative text for descriptive information, just as a screen reader would. It's important that you make your alternate text relevant and descriptive.

18.2 Choosing Keywords

Foodbox definitely needs some keywords, but it's so hard to figure out what people will use to find your site. Here are a few ways that you and your team can use to build a list of keywords.

Guess How They Will Find You

Write down a few obvious words that you think people might use to search for your site. When I think of this site, I could see people searching for *food*, *baking*, *cooking*, *recipes*, *quick dinners*, *snacks*, *desserts*, and *cookbooks*.

Decide How You Want to Be Found

Next, write down a few keywords that you want people to use to find your site. The keywords in the previous section are a good start, but you can always think of a few more. A local client might want you to

> ### Joe Asks...
> #### What About Flash?
>
> Google and Adobe have partnered together* to make index-ing of Flash movies possible, but the effectiveness of this depends largely on how the original author constructed the Flash movie. For example, if the Flash movie contains text and links, Google will likely be able to see those. Flash is served within an HTML page, so you can always use the meta tag to define keywords and a brief description.
>
> Flash might be searchable by more search engines in the future—it has already come a long way in terms of its acces-sibility. These things change all the time; as a web developer, you're expected to keep yourself up-to-date on this stuff.
>
> ---
> *.http://searchengineland.com/google-now-crawling-and-indexing-flash-content-14299

use the city, state, or region in the keywords so that a user could find them when searching for *wrecking yards in Secaucus, New Jersey*.

Spy on the Competition

Find out what your friends or enemies are doing for their keywords. You can view the source of any of web page as easily as you can view your own, so find out what others use. Don't steal their keywords, though, and don't try to hijack their phrases. I once had a client who kept asking me to use a competitor's name in his keyword list, which is completely unethical. As you do more web development, especially as you become more comfortable with the design and content aspects, you'll learn to be a great diplomat as you talk your clients down from strange and sometimes dangerous positions.

Adding Keywords

Open your index.html file, and add a new meta tag to the head section:

```
<meta name="keywords" content="foodbox, recipes, cookbook, desserts,
entrees, dinner, share, browse, ingredients, mexican, italian, community">
```

The name attribute defines the type of the meta tag, and the content attribute specifies the content or value. You enter your keywords or keyword phrases by separating them with commas.

Joe Asks...

Are Keywords Even Important Anymore? My Competitors Don't Seem to Have Any, and They're Doing Great!

Keywords matter if you use them correctly. You just have to reconcile them with the content of your site. A lot of search engines have dramatically lowered the weight they give keywords in search position because people would try to cheat by placing irrelevant keywords in their lists.

Your sites of your competitors might have high search-engine rankings without keywords because of many other factors. CodingHorror* doesn't have any keyword tags, but the site constantly publishes new articles and get lots of hits via trackbacks. Links to your content far outweigh keywords when it comes to attaining a high search-engine ranking.

You're not CodingHorror, and you don't have their traffic or inbound links to rely on yet. If you want to optimize your site, you can't go wrong with keywords. You're definitely not going to be penalized for using them, as long as you make sure you match them to your content.

---

*. http://www.codinghorror.com/

18.3 Reconciling Our Content

Now that you have a few keywords selected, you need to think about how you can revise your main content so that you can sprinkle those keywords throughout. A good copyeditor comes in handy here, but often you must do this work yourself. Take a few stabs at working some keywords into the Foodbox main content. When you think you're done, try these two surefire proofreading tricks:

- Read your text backward, from the end of the paragraph to the beginning. This often helps you catch spelling and punctuation mistakes because you're not reading the words in context.

- Read your text aloud. If you can get through it without laughing, you're off to a good start. You should also read it aloud to a couple of other people and get their feedback.

To strengthen your position within search engines, you need to make sure that you have been consistent with not only your content but also with your keywords and your page elements.

Each page of your site should have a specific title. The title should contain the current page's title, followed by the name of the website. This way, the most important information, the page title, will show up in the search results. The page title is almost always displayed in the search results.

Second, each page of your site should have at least one h1 tag that matches the page title you specified in the title tag. This consistency helps search engines determine the strength of the content; you could have forgotten to change the title tag.

Third, your keywords should contain words used within the title of the page or at least in some of the links on the page, as well as in the paragraphs of your content.

18.4 Don't Optimize Your Users Away!

All this reconciliation of your content can lead to something undesirable: lost users. Remember that your content is king here, and you should be careful not to sacrifice your content for the sake of throwing in a few extra keywords. You should write your content for people first and robots second.

18.5 Links and You

The number of links on your site can help or hurt your search-engine ranking. If you have a lot of links on a page, especially links that point away to other sites, the search engines might think the page doesn't have any relevant content. The search engines might give the page a lower score because you're linking away to everyone else.

Also, keep an eye on how other places link to you. Generally, you want to get other people linking to you because search engines will see other sites sending traffic to you and assume this is because you have more relevant content. Some sites, including link farms, link exchanges, and, as Google puts it, *bad neighborhoods*, can reduce your search ranking because the engines might think your site is a spam destination.

You can't do too much to prevent people from linking to you, but some less-than-reputable people will try to get you to exchange links with them. Before you exchange links with anyone, you should make sure that doing so will benefit you as much as it benefits them.

18.6 It All Comes Down to Common Sense

If you've read this chapter and thought "There's nothing new here that I couldn't have already figured out on my own," then you're on the right track. There's no real magic to SEO. There's no way to instantly get to the top of Google's search listings and stay there. You might find some people who can game the system for a short while, but really, we're talking about search engine *optimization*, not search engine *scamming*.

Good, well-written, regularly updated content that's relevant to your audience gets people to link to your site. Those links improve your search engine ranking. So, the next time your boss or client wants to hire an "SEO expert," suggest that he or she investigate hiring a good copy editor to improve the writing on the site instead. The rest of the optimization stuff should fall into place for you, especially if you've developed something that people really care about and want to link to.

18.7 Summary

In this chapter, we briefly touched on a few things you can do to improve your site's visibility to the search engines without sacrificing usability. Search engine optimization is something you'll need to do frequently, because the rules change constantly.

## Chapter 19

Designing for Mobile Devices

The Foodbox stakeholders call you back in. Everywhere they go, they see people using BlackBerry devices, iPhones, Windows Mobile devices, and other handheld devices to access websites. Your stakeholders would like you to provide a mobile version of the Foodbox site so that people can access recipes from the grocery store while they're shopping.

To implement a design that will work for mobile devices, you need to understand the mobile audience. Once you think you have a bead on this audience, you need to familiarize yourself with some mobile platforms so you can determine which platforms make the most sense for you to support. Completing this pair of steps will help you implement a mobile strategy that will work.

19.1 Mobile Users

Mobile users have different needs than desktop or laptop users.

First, mobile user often have different reasons for using a site. They probably won't use their tiny keypad to enter a recipe into the site, but they are likely to look up what ingredients they need to make tonight's dinner when visiting the grocery store. Therefore, you might choose to focus on making only a subset of your site's features available to your mobile users.

Second, the connection is often slow, so mobile users need pages to load quickly. At the time of writing, 3G service isn't available in many parts of the United States, and most of the other mobile data plans remain quite slow.

Figure 19.1: FOODBOX ON THE IPHONE'S MOBILE SAFARI

Third, users looking to use the site from a mobile device need to be able to read your content easily on a small screen. The Foodbox site's design is preserved on the iPhone, but it can be hard to read without zooming in, as shown in Figure 19.1. On the other hand, the Opera mobile browser maintains some of the design, but you can't read much of anything (see Figure 19.2, on the facing page).

Finally, users need to be able to find the information they're looking for easily. The navigation structure you designed for your regular audience might be too cumbersome to navigate using a cell phone's keypad.

We'll need to address all these issues to create a version of the Foodbox site for mobile users.

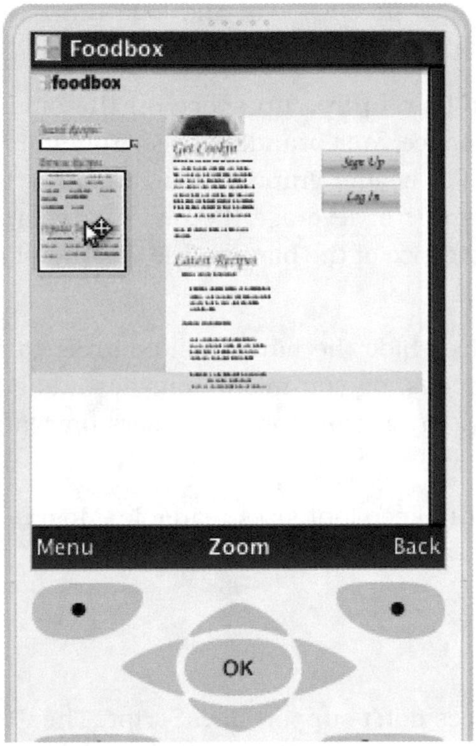

Figure 19.2: FOODBOX ON THE OPERA MOBILE BROWSER

19.2 Thinking About the (Very) Small Screen

If everyone had an iPhone, web developers wouldn't have to do too much to make their sites work. The iPhone comes bundled with a browser that does a great job of rendering pages, *and* it even supports JavaScript. However, most people don't have iPhones. Instead, most people who use their phones to browse the Web do it on a 2- to 3-inch screen using a proprietary browser that has no scripting support. The small screen doesn't give you much of a canvas to present information, which means we'll have to jettison some portions of the existing site.

For example, it's common practice to reproduce your navigation menu on every page of your site when targeting a full-sized browser. But this menu will have to go because it takes up too much room. Of course, users need to get around your site, but you can replace the navigation menu with a link to a simple, unstyled list of pages. Keeping the page plain will reduce its download and load times, and you'll free up important real estate on the rest of the site.

While considering how to free up space on the smaller screen, don't forget how much space your branding uses. You should definitely consider using a smaller header graphic. You can either use a text banner instead of this graphic or leverage the resizing technique you learned earlier to shrink the size of the banner (see Chapter 17, *Building a Favicon*, on page 253).

Some mobile devices hide the navigation controls to get more content on their small screens, so you might consider adding your own Back button on the page to simplify how your users navigate the mobile version of your site.

Finally, remember to keep font sizes readable. Most users would rather scroll than squint, and most devices can't zoom yet.

19.3 JavaScript

Many mobile devices don't support JavaScript. The iPhone does, and it relies on it heavily, but most of the current BlackBerry models don't support it at all. However, I don't consider this to be a huge issue because I don't advocate using JavaScript for critical parts of a site unless you provide an alternative method anyway—remember that screen-reading software often has trouble with JavaScript as well.

19.4 Serving Mobile Content

You can use a few methods to provide mobile-friendly content to your users. For example, you might use a style sheet designed for mobile devices, you might take advantage of user agent detection to serve different content to different audiences, or you might host your mobile content at a different URL.

Mobile Style Sheets

The CSS specifications provide the handheld media type, which was designed to be used by handheld devices. You designed a style sheet specifically for printing in Section 14.2, *Linking a Print Style Sheet*, on page 206; you could take a similar tack here and design a style sheet specifically for mobile devices. At first, this might seem to be the best and easiest way to deliver content, but it has one big disadvantage: they're hardly used.

The iPhone, iPod touch, and Windows Mobile devices try to provide a "real" Internet experience to their users, so they load up the style sheets intended for use on a typical computer screen.

User Agent Detection

Many developers use user agent detection in conjunction with a server-side technology or web-server configuration to serve different designs based on what device a person uses. This might seem like a great idea, but some of your users might disagree.

For example, Apple's developer guidelines encourage iPhone developers not to serve different pages to iPhone users. This way, users won't be surprised by seeing a different page than they expected to see. Instead, Apple recommends that a website should detect the use of an iPhone and then provide a link to an optimized site. This way, users can decide for themselves if they want to use the optimized or regular version of the site. Twitter and Amazon both provide a mobile version of their sites with a link to visit the regular site. When users visit the Foodbox site using a mobile device, you could set a cookie that you could use to redirect users to the site's mobile version automatically the next time they visit your site.

Using a Different Subdomain

You could also host your mobile pages on a different subdomain. This approach requires that users know the address of your mobile site, which means you have to do a good job of advertising it on your main site.

To pull this off without duplicating files, you would point your mobile address at your main site and then detect the subdomain using a server-side script. If you detect that a user requested the mobile domain, you would serve the appropriate style sheets or possibly a completely different layout that you optimized specifically for mobile users. I recommend this approach.

19.5 Deciding What to Support

Many different mobile browsers exist, and they all seem display pages differently. You have to decide which ones you will focus on and which

Testing Mobile Designs

You might have a real mobile phone or device handy to test your site, but you can also find emulators for many of the popular platforms.

- BlackBerry

  http://www.blackberry.com/developers/downloads/simulators/index.shtml*

- Google Android

  http://code.google.com/android/reference/emulator.html

- iPhone

  http://marketcircle.com/iphoney/†

- Opera Mini

  http://www.opera.com/mini/demo/

- Windows Mobile

  http://www.nsbasic.com/ce/info/technotes/TN23.htm

---

*. BlackBerry provides simulators for many of its phones, but it doesn't label which simulator goes with each phone.

†. At the time of writing, iPhoney works only on a Mac. Windows users with Safari installed can use http://www.testiphone.com/ to get a decent simulation, but user agent detection doesn't work.

ones you will ignore. I recommend going about this the same way you might choose what regular web browsers to support: choose the popular ones. You should also find out what your boss or client uses and include support for that one, too!

AdMob provides some great statistics[1] you can use to determine the most popular mobile platforms. AdMob lets developers embed ads within mobile software and on mobile sites. AdMob isn't the only company that provides this type of service, but it's one of the biggest. As is always the case when relying on third-party statistics, you should use these statistics as a guide until you can gather your own usage stats.

---

1. http://www.admob.com/s/solutions/metrics

The largest chunk of the audience is made up of iPhone users, according to the stats from AdMob. However, let's implement something that has a chance to work across most devices in our first pass.

We know that most devices can't support JavaScript, and they have a small screen. We also know they need to download content quickly.

Mirroring Your Site Without Duplicating Content

One of the surest ways to lose customers is to make a mobile site that doesn't stay up-to-date with the latest information. Throughout this book, we've built a design in straight HTML without any consideration for any server-side technologies; however, I am working under the assumption that you're a developer, and you probably have some idea of how to go about building dynamic websites.

With that in mind, let's set up a new domain for our site, point it at our main domain, and then use some server-side logic to detect which URL the user requested. In this book, I'll walk you through how to use PHP to transform our static pages for use on mobile devices. Depending on your site design, you might be able to swap out templates based on the host name.

This book doesn't really cover system administration, so how you set up your site to respond to multiple domains depends largely on your web host. You could create a new record in your DNS that points the domain to the same IP address as your primary address:

```
www.yourfoodbox.com  A  12.34.56.78
m.yourfoodbox.com     A  12.34.56.78
```

Some web hosts, including Dreamhost,[2] provide an easy way to mirror domains. Consult your web host, your sysadmin, or your web server's documentation on how you might mirror your domain name. Essentially, all you need to do is make two domains point to the same server.

If all you're doing is testing on your local machine, you could modify your local hosts file like this:

```
127.0.0.1 localhost www.yourfoodbox.dev   m.yourfoodbox.dev
```

You can find this file at c:\windows\system32\drivers\etc\hosts on Windows; on most Linux and OS X systems, you can find it at /etc/hosts. You need to have administrative privileges to make changes to this file.

---

2. http://www.dreamhost.com

Transforming Content

We can choose from a few approaches to reformat our content for mobile devices, but these approaches start to fall apart when we look at them closely. We can't just use a handheld style sheet because most of the browsers out there will try to read the screen style sheets anyway, which eliminates that option. We already discussed the facts that the mobile users are much more focused on content, and they often have slow connections (at least in the United States), so we need to minimize the amount of data we send to them, which in turn will enable them to load our site more quickly. We need a way to strip out all the cruft and show a basic page.

If we disable style sheets altogether, our site is surprisingly usable on a mobile phone. We could also disable the images and replace any images that have links with regular links. It turns out that all the way back in 2005 a developer named Mike Davidson came up with an extremely clever solution that will meet our needs perfectly.[3]

Mike's solution relies on a mechanism that uses PHP to preprocess all HTML pages and strip out content, but *only* when the mobile domain is used. With some slight modifications, his technique gives us exactly what we need to make a quick mobile version of our site. To do this, you need to use Apache and have it configured to serve PHP pages. From this point on, I'll assume you have that working.[4]

To use this method, we have to ensure that the web server is using the Apache PHP module to process PHP pages; we also have to ensure that PHP is properly enabled. This method won't work if PHP is running as a regular CGI program. You can test your setup if you create a file in your web space called info.php and place this content in the file:

mobile/info.php

```
<?php phpinfo(); ?>
```

You should see something similar to Figure 19.3, on the next page. The Server API value should be Apache 2.0 Module.[5]

---

3. http://www.mikeindustries.com/blog/archive/2005/07/make-your-site-mobile-friendly
4. Dreamhost (http://www.dreamhost.com/) offers cheap hosting plans that support the concepts in this book if you don't feel like setting this up yourself. I've even set up a coupon code. Use *WDFD* to get a discount.
5. If you don't know PHP, you should learn it. It's far from my favorite language, but I think anyone who develops web applications should at least be familiar with it because it's quite versatile, very powerful, and widely supported.

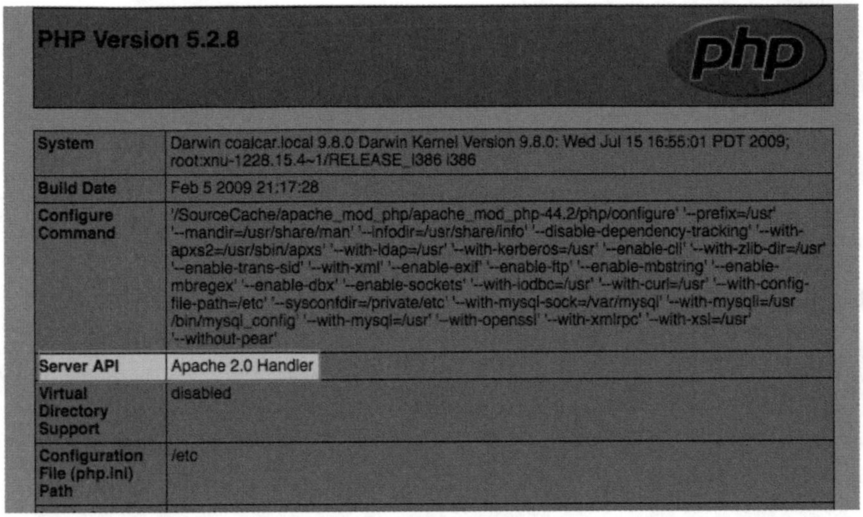

Figure 19.3: PHP CONFIGURED TO USE THE APACHE MODULE

We need to add a special directive to tell Apache to send all HTML files through the PHP interpreter so that the filter will work. We can do that by modifying the .htaccess file in the root directory of our website. Add this line to that file:

`mobile/.htaccess`

```
AddType application/x-httpd-php .html .htm
```

From this point on, the PHP interpreter will read all your HTML files.

Writing the Handlers

We will use an extremely useful feature called *autoprepend* and *autoappend*. This feature lets you trigger scripts to run before and after each page request. You could use this technique to do some logging or set up some variables for later use; you could also use this technique to capture the buffered response from the server and parse it.

Let's begin by writing the prepend script, basing it on the example code that Mike Davidson provided in his initial example.

Create a file called global_prepend.php, and add this code:

```
mobile/global_prepend.php
<?php
function callback($b) {

  $mobile_domain = "m.yourfoodbox.com";
  $web_domain = "www.yourfoodbox.com";

  if ($_SERVER['SERVER_NAME'] == $mobile_domain) {

  // replace www.yourfoodbox.com with m.yourfoodb.com
  $b = str_replace($web_domain, $mobile_domain, $b);

  // replace all hyperlinked images with regular links, using the alt text
  $b = preg_replace('/(<a[^]*>)(<img[^]+alt=")([^"]*)("[^]*>)(<\/a>)/i',
    '<p class="link">$1$3$5</p>', $b);

  // replace images with paragraph tags
  $b = preg_replace('/(<img[^]+alt=")([^"]*)("[^]*>)/',
    '<p class="image">[$2]</p>', $b);

  // strip out stylesheet calls
  $b = preg_replace('/(<link[^]+rel="[^"]*stylesheet"[^]*>|style="[^"]*")/i',
    '', $b);

  //remove scripts
  $b = preg_replace('/<script[^]*>.*?<\/script>/i', '', $b);

  // remove style tags and comments
  $b = preg_replace('/<style[^]*>.*?<\/style>|<!--.*?-->/i', '', $b);

  // add robots nofollow directive to keep the search engines out!
  $b = preg_replace('/<\/head>/i',
    '<meta name="robots" content="noindex, nofollow"></head>', $b);

  }
  return $b;

}
ob_start("callback");
?>
```

Line 2 defines a function that takes in the contents of the HTML page as a string. The next two lines define variables for our regular domain and our mobile domain. Line 7 compares the domain requested by the user with the mobile domain. If they match, we'll start filtering out content.

On line 10, we replace all occurrences of the regular domain with the mobile domain. Doing this means any hard-coded links will always use the mobile domain, eliminating any chance of accidentally sending the user to the wrong domain. Next, line 12 replaces all linked images, such as our sign-up and login images, with regular links that use the images' alt text. On line 16, we handle the rest of the images by replacing them with the alt text in square brackets.

Starting at line 20, we strip out style sheet links, calls to scripts, inline styles, and comments. This will significantly improve performance on mobile devices by reducing the amount of data kicked down to a device; this should especially please users who have plans where they pay by the amount of data they transfer to and from their device.

The final transformation occurs on line 30. It adds a directive to the page's header that stops search engines from indexing this page or any of its links. We don't want to be penalized by having two versions of our site listed in the search engines.

When we finish transforming the page, we return the string. The call to ob_start on line 38 turns on the output buffer, and we pass the callback function to the buffer so it can be executed at the end of the response. To write out the content, we need to create the global_append.php file, which we append to the end of the response:

mobile/global_append.php

```php
<?php
  ob_end_flush();
?>
```

This file flushes our transformation from the content buffer, rendering the page. If we miss this step, our users won't see anything at all. All we need to do now is activate the filters. We can do this by adding these two lines to the .htaccess file:

mobile/.htaccess

```
php_value auto_prepend_file /home/yourfoodbox/yourfoodbox.com/global_prepend.php
php_value auto_append_file /home/yourfoodbox/yourfoodbox.com/global_append.php
```

The paths for each of these scripts need to be a full path on the server to the scripts. Once you upload these files to the server, you're ready for the mobile traffic!

Further Improvements

The mobile version of the site looks good at this point, but we can improve the usability a little. Right now, the skip link at the top lets us jump right down to the content, but we could make it easier for members if we also put the Log In and Sign Up links in the skip links section. In fact, it would be a good idea to implement this functionality for screen-reader users, too.

> ### PHP Under FastCGI
>
> You can still use the techniques outlined here if your server is not using the Apache module to serve PHP pages. However, you can't use the .htaccess file to define the auto_prepend lines. Instead, those directives need to be in your server's php.ini file.
>
> ```
> auto_prepend_file =
>     /home/yourfoodbox/yourfoodbox.com/global_prepend.php
> auto_append_file =
>     /home/yourfoodbox/yourfoodbox.com/global_append.php
> ```
>
> Finally, ensure that your HTML pages are being served via FastCGI. In your .htaccess file, do this:
>
> ```
> AddType php5-cgi .html .htm
> ```
>
> The specific AddType depends entirely on how your web server is configured, so check your documentation, ask your system administrator, or contact your web host for specific details if you run into trouble.

19.6 Restructuring for Mobile Users

The solution in this chapter is a quick fix, but it might not go far enough for complex sites. We discussed how mobile audiences are different and how you just don't need some things in a mobile version of a website. We might want to use a server-side technology to serve different views to the end user based on the user agent. That's beyond the scope of this book, but it would not be difficult to do, especially if your site uses a content management system or is at least backed by a database.

19.7 Summary

Mobile users have completely different needs than desktop users, and this audience segment continues to expand rapidly. As mobile technologies such as the phones from Google and Apple become more common, we'll be able to provide even richer, more interactive solutions for these users. In the meantime, you now have the tools and knowledge required to craft a usable mobile site that most mobile users can use, regardless of the mobile device they use.

## Chapter 20

Testing and Improving Performance

A great design won't overcome a poor implementation. We spent a lot of time working to build a solid site, and it would be a shame if our end users had to wait while our site loads. We can improve our performance if we can identify potential problem areas.

20.1 Strategies for Improving Performance

When we talk about improving performance, we're talking about making the page load faster for our readers. On the server side, you might use techniques such as caching dynamically built pages. However, once you've squeezed out all the performance you can from your web server, you can investigate a few things related to site's design that can affect its performance on the client. Fortunately, it's easy to identify and fix these things.

First, look at the file sizes of your HTML, CSS, and JavaScript files. The number of characters these documents contain impacts how long they'll take to transfer to the end user. You want to keep their sizes to a minimum. You might not think it matters that much, but every little bit adds up when you serve thousands of requests per day.

Next, look at the sizes of all the images you load on your page. We talked about image optimization earlier, but sometimes it's easy to forget to resize and compress a photograph before adding it to the website. Also, some types of images can be compressed beyond the compression that Photoshop provides.

You need to investigate the number of files a user's browser will request. If you have one page that has links to three style sheets, two JavaScript scripts, and five images, you're looking at a total of eleven hits to your server. The user's browser will download the HTML file and then start making additional requests to your site to grab the other files it needs.

Your users probably won't be doing that constantly, because many of your images and scripts will be cached on their machines. However, they could be faced with at least the appearance of a slow site if you have too many assets, especially because some browsers limit simultaneous connections to two hits at a time, as recommended by the HTTP 1.1 specification.[1]

Finally, you need to identify files that won't change often so you can employ strategies to keep the user's browser from constantly checking to see whether a new version exists. If you just finished a redesign, you could safely instruct the clients to cache the logo, style sheets, and scripts for an extended period of time.

Let's take a look at Foodbox and see how we stack up.

20.2 Determining Performance Issues

It's never a good idea to optimize prematurely, but it's also foolish to not at least be aware of potential performance problems you might encounter. You can use a couple methods to look at your page for potential issues from an external perspective.

Note that both these methods assume that you've placed your pages on a server that's accessible to the Internet.

Speed Test

WebSiteOptimization.com runs a service that can scan any URL and determine the size and download times of a page and its individual assets, which gives you a great starting point. You can perform this speed test by visiting your site with Firefox and selecting Tools > Speed Test on the Web Developer toolbar.

---

1. http://www.w3.org/Protocols/rfc2616/rfc2616-sec8.html#sec8.1.4

Running this speed test shows that we have about 59KB of images on our site. For comparison, a speed test run against Microsoft's home page shows that it has about 61KB of images; running the test against Adobe's home page reveals that it has about 156KB of images. We stack up well against those sites on this front.

The speed test also shows us that we can save some space by compressing our CSS and JavaScript files. It also shows us that we forgot to identify the heights and widths of some of our images. That's something we should fix in our content document. It's not incredibly important to fix those issues (because we have included many images in the style sheets as well), but it's something that can make a site appear to load faster because the browser doesn't have to determine the dimensions of the images on its own. Defining heights and widths for all images in the HTML document can also allow browsers to display the text while the images load. Use the height and width attributes for the img tag to specify the dimensions of your images.

The real eye opener is seeing how long the speed test says dial-up users will have to wait for our full page to load. According to the report, someone using a 56Kbps dialup connection might have to wait up to 15.59 seconds for all the images, styles, and content for the home page to load. That seems like a long time, but compare that to Microsoft's home page, where a dial-up user with a slow connection might have to wait more than 56 seconds![2]

YSlow

The speed test gives us a lot of good information, but it doesn't provide too many suggestions for fixing the problems it finds. Yahoo provides YSlow, an extension for the Firebug extension (yes, an extension for an extension), which grades your page and provides you tips on why it's slow.

The YSlow extension grades your page and gives you suggestions for improving its performance. You might not have the ability to address all the items that YSlow points out, but you can address some common issues that can have a huge payoff.

An initial report of the Foodbox site shows that we should investigate implementing ETags, look into using compression, minify scripts, and

---

2. Don't fool yourself into thinking those people aren't out there. High-speed internet isn't prevalent in poor and rural areas yet.

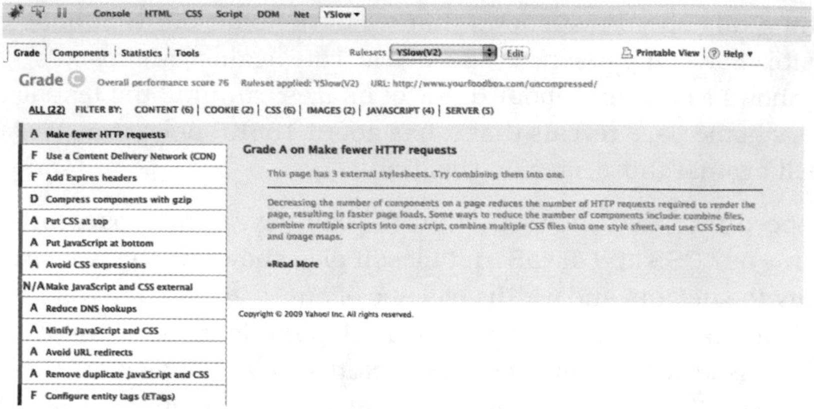

Figure 20.1: YSLOW FOUND SEVERAL PROBLEMS WE MIGHT WANT TO ADDRESS.

look into cache expiry (see Figure 20.1). We'll cover these suggestions in the next few sections.

20.3 Addressing Performance

You have some measurements, but now you need to make some decisions about how you want to approach potential problems. As is always the case, you must balance costs against the benefits here; each of the solutions in this chapter has its pros and cons.

Set Expires Headers

If your content rarely changes, you can set the content to expire well into the future or even several hours from the present.

If you using Apache with mod_expires, you can use this code to cache all JPEG, GIF, and PNG files for one hour from the last-modified date:

```
ExpiresActive On
ExpiresDefault A0

<FilesMatch "\.(jpg|png|gif)$">
  ExpiresDefault A3600
</FilesMatch>
```

The ExpiresDefault directive sets the default caching expiry to 0. The *A* means *from first access*.

The ExpiresDefault value is set in seconds. This example sets the expiry to 3600 seconds from the last-modified date of the file. As you can probably guess, this rule is useless unless these images are changing on the server every hour.

You could be more verbose and do something like this instead:

```
ExpiresActive On
ExpiresByType text/html "access plus 30 seconds"
ExpiresByType text/css "access plus 1 hour"
ExpiresByType text/javascript "access plus 1 hour"
ExpiresByType image/png "access plus 1 day"
ExpiresByType image/jpg "access plus 2 months"
ExpiresByType image/gif "access plus 1 year"
```

This method lets you specify a header based on the MIME type rather than the extension; this could be beneficial if you use a server-side scripting language to send files.

It makes more sense to set a *far-future Expires header*, which sets the Expires header to some point in the distant future:

```
<FilesMatch "\.(jpg|png|gif|css|js)$">
  Expires A31536000
</FilesMatch>
```

This rule sets the expiry to be one year from the browser's first access of images, style sheets, and JavaScripts on our site. This rule will go a long way toward reducing hits on our server from browsers.

One drawback to a far-future expiration date is that you have to change the name of the file or reference the file with a querystring when you want to change it because you can't force users to clear their cache. If you create a static website, I don't recommend setting far-future headers for things that might change frequently. Fortunately, many web-application frameworks handle the creation of far-future headers for you by altering the filename during deployment or rendering. If your framework doesn't handle this expiry for you, you need to change the names of your files when you create new versions. It's impossible to invalidate your users' cache.

Investigate ETags to Improve Caching

Modern web servers support a request header called an Entity Tag, commonly referred to as an *ETag*. When a browser makes a request, it records the ETag for a URL. When the user requests the same URL a second time, the ETag's hash for the new request is compared to the one the browser already knows about. If the ETags match, the page content isn't downloaded, and the browser is instructed to use the cached copy. This saves bandwidth and improves the user experience.

You can compute ETags using the file size and last-modified date, a checksum, or pretty much anything you want. The implementation of an ETag is completely up to the web server that generates it. If you use a server-side framework, you can generate your own ETags, which is especially valuable for things like RSS feeds and dynamic CSS and JavaScript that don't have last-modified dates.

Improperly generated ETags can end up causing users to request the full page each time a user visits; in extreme cases, using them improperly can accidentally prevent users from seeing new content. If you have load-balanced servers serving up your pages, it's possible for each of the back-end servers to generate different ETags. Apache and IIS generate completely different ETags for the same page, so you want to avoid balancing requests between those two servers unless you've set up your ETags correctly.

If you serve your pages with Apache, you can set the ETag header by adding this line to your website's .htaccess file:

```
FileETag MTime Size
```

This creates the ETag by using the file's last-modified time and file's size.

When to Use ETags

Sometimes—as in the case of an RSS feed, a web service, or a blog—you might not be saving files to disk, so you won't have a modified date to use. In these cases, you'd set the ETag header in your scripts. If you use clustering to serve your files, it's possible that your last-modified times can be different, causing clients to think that files aren't cached when they are because both servers won't be generating identical ETags for identical content.

If you can't trust that the last-modified time is accurate or if you simply don't have a last-modified time, you'll want to create your own ETags by creating a hash of the content or another unique mechanism.

ETags are useful if you have a caching mechanism in front of your website. The front-end server can use the ETags to determine whether it needs to fetch content from the back end or it should serve its own cached content.

Disabling ETags

For static sites, especially those that make use of expires headers, ETags might not be necessary and might actually *decrease* load times. When ETags are used, the client still makes a request to the server. Although the server might not send back the entire response body, it still creates traffic.

For now, we're going to disable ETags completely for our site, and we will rely entirely on the Expires headers we have set. Add this to your .htaccess file:

```
FileETag None
```

YSlow will give you a good score for your ETags if you've properly configured them for your site instead of ignoring them. Eventually, the home page and other pages will probably be built from a database, but you won't want the servers to rebuild the page on every request. At that point, you'll generate your own ETags or set your own Expires headers from your server-side code, and you'll have your code use the ETag to decide whether new content needs to be sent out.

Use Asset Servers to Distribute Requests

Relative links for images, style sheets, and scripts might not always be the best approach for a larger website. Many browsers limit the number of concurrent connections to any given web server, and if you have 20 external assets linked on your page, Internet Explorer 7 will make 20 connections to your server, two connections at a time. That will make your site appear slow. Some browsers use a higher number, which means more concurrent requests to your server and increased server loads. You want to serve your content as fast as possible, and one of the best ways to do that is to split your assets onto different servers. For example, consider this approach:

```
<img src="images/banner.jpg"/>
<script src="scripts/prototype.js"></script>
```

A better approach might look something like this:

```
<img src="http://images.foodbox.com/banner.jpg"/>
<script src="http://scripts.foodbox.com/js/prototype.js"></script>
```

The latter approach does have some downsides. First, it requires you to find or maintain more servers. It also creates external dependencies. Finally, you have to remember that absolute links include the protocol, which is either HTTP or HTTPS. If you do e-commerce on the site, then pages you serve to the user with SSL need to be coded so that any external assets are also requested via SSL. This means that your asset servers need SSL enabled, and you have to change your absolute links from http:// to https://. If you forget to do this, your end users will receive security warnings, and some things might not display properly.

You also need to decide if it's worth it. Aside from the extra servers (not to mention the extra work involved in deploying your assets to multiple machines), assets are usually cached by the end user's browser, so the end user won't be downloading the same style sheets and images with every request. This approach is a great option for high-traffic sites because it will make a noticeable difference in how first-time users experience their first visit to your site. It's also a good approach for relieving the strain on your application servers, because you can delegate the serving of static images and scripts to a dedicated web server.

Pushing your assets to cloud services like Amazon S3 is popular now, and it's something I recommend you investigate if you need that level of distribution.

Compress Files

Modern web servers can serve compressed content, reducing download times. If you use Apache, you can enable mod_deflate and use a few rules in your .htaccess file to enable compression:

```
AddOutputFilterByType DEFLATE text/html text/css \
    application/x-javascript
BrowserMatch ^Mozilla/4 gzip-only-text/html
BrowserMatch ^Mozilla/4\.0[678] no-gzip
BrowserMatch \bMSIE !no-gzip !gzip-only-text/html
```

The first two Browsermatch rules in this particular example disable serving compressed files to old versions of Netscape, and the last rule turns compression back on in case Internet Explorer identifies itself as Netscape.

Minifying Scripts

If you have JavaScript and CSS libraries that tend to be quite large, you should *minify* them, or reduce the file size by stripping out comments, line breaks, and whitespace. You can also obfuscate JavaScript by shortening variable and function names to reduce the number of characters.

You might think that minification is an unnecessary step if you already use the web server to compress your files. However, minification allows you as a developer to ignore how many comments or extra spaces you put in your files; the minification process removes them, and you will reduce your file sizes because the compressor won't be compressing as many characters.

Yahoo provides the YUI Compressor,[3] a command-line utility that can minify CSS and JavaScript files. Using the tool is as simple as this:

```
java -jar yuicompressor-2.4.2.jar \
    --type js prototype.js > prototype.min.js
```

You can keep your nicely formatted styles and scripts in your working directory and still deploy minified ones to your site. Just make copies of your CSS and JS files and then use the YUI compressor to shrink them. Upload the minified copies to your site instead of the originals.

Minification and Automated Deployment

Professional web developers automate the deployment of websites. It's tedious to do manual uploads, especially if you do them all the time. Automating deployment lets you define the workflow once and let the computer handle things from there. Automating the process ensures that you won't forget a step or file.

If you already have an automated deployment system in place, you can easily make minification part of that process. You don't even have to use a complicated deployment framework. For example, the following Ruby script lets us minify our CSS and JavaScript files and then upload the whole site to a web host. Note that this script requires the net-scp gem.[4] All you need to do is configure the remote server settings and give the script the location of the YUI compressor. I recommend placing all the YUI Compressor's JAR files within a bin folder of your project folder:

performance/deploy.rb

```
# Scans your project for CSS and JS files and
# runs them through the Yahoo Compression utility
# and then uploads the entire site to your web server via SCP.

# Configure your settings below and be sure to supply the proper path
# to the Yahoo compressor. Set the COMPRESS flag to false to skip compression
```

---

3. http://developer.yahoo.com/yui/compressor/
4. Install the gem with this line: sudo gem install net-scp.

```ruby
COMPRESS = true
WORKING_DIR = "working"
REMOTE_USER = "homer"
REMOTE_HOST = "yourfoodbox.com"
REMOTE_PORT = 22

REMOTE_DIR = "/home/#{REMOTE_USER}/yourfoodbox.com/"

FILES = ["index.html",
         ".htaccess",
         "global_append.php",
         "global_prepend.php",
         "favicon.ico",
         "stylesheets",
         "images"
         ]

COMPRESSOR_CMD = 'java -jar bin/yuicompressor-2.4.2.jar'
# DONE CONFIGURING

require 'rubygems'
require 'net/scp'
require 'fileutils'

@errors = []

FileUtils.rm_rf WORKING_DIR
FileUtils.mkdir WORKING_DIR
FILES.each do |f|
  if File.directory?(f)
    FileUtils.cp_r f, WORKING_DIR
  else
    FileUtils.cp f, WORKING_DIR
  end
end

# Upload files in our working directory to the server
def upload(files)
  Net::SCP.start(REMOTE_HOST, REMOTE_USER, :port => REMOTE_PORT) do |scp|
    files.each do |file|
      puts "uploading #{file}"
      if File.directory?(file)
        scp.upload! "working/#{file}",  REMOTE_DIR, :recursive => true
      else
        scp.upload! "working/#{file}",  REMOTE_DIR
      end
    end
  end
end
```

```ruby
# Minify all CSS and JS files found within the working
# directory
def minify(working_dir)
  files = Dir.glob("#{working_dir}/**/*.{css, js}")

  files.each do |file|
    type = File.extname(file) == ".css" ? "css" : "js"
    newfile = file.gsub(".#{type}", ".new.#{type}")
    puts "minifying #{file}"
    `#{COMPRESSOR_CMD} --type #{type} #{file} > #{newfile}`

    if File.size(newfile) > 0
      FileUtils.cp newfile, file
    else
      @errors << "Unable to process #{file}."
    end

  end
end

minify(WORKING_DIR) if COMPRESS

if @errors.length == 0
  puts "Deploying"
  upload(FILES)
else
  puts "Unable to deploy."
  @errors.each{|e| puts e}
end
```

You can take this a step further and use a script like this to combine all your CSS scripts together into a new file. You can then replace the calls to the style sheets in all the HTML documents with a single call to the newly created style sheet. This results in a single compressed file and reduces the number of requests the user will make to your site.

20.4 Image Optimization

You learned how to use Photoshop to optimize your images in Chapter 10, *Creating Assets from Our Mock-Up*, on page 151. But you can optimize your images further in some cases. For example, Yahoo's Smush-It! service can optimize images using several open source tools, and the YSlow extension can automatically send all your images to this service to be optimized. I ran the Foodbox site through Smush-It!; you can see the results in Figure 20.2, on the following page.

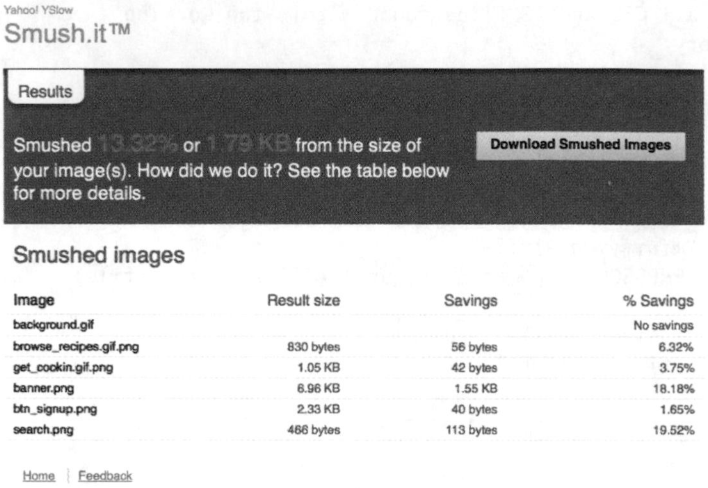

Figure 20.2: SMUSH-IT! WAS ABLE TO REDUCE OUR IMAGES BY AN ADDI-
TIONAL 13%, OR A LITTLE UNDER 2KB.

According to the report, Smush-It! was able to reduce the size of all our images by 13%. At first glance, that sounds like a big deal. On closer inspection, it looks as though it managed to save us a little less than 2KB. Worse, it requests that we change some of our files from GIFs to PNGs, which means we'd have to change our style sheets and markup if we were to use the images it provided. In this case, I'm happy to leave things as they are.

Doing It Yourself

Smush-It uses Pngcrush[5] to optimize PNG files, ImageMagick[6] to detect image types and convert GIFs to PNGs, and JPEGTran[7] to remove meta-data from JPEGs.

As a simple experiment, I'll take our get_cookin.gif and convert it to a PNG file that I'll optimize with Pngcrush:

```
convert get_cookin.gif tmp.png
pngcrush -rem alla -reduce --brute tmp.png get_cookin.png
```

---

5. http://pmt.sourceforge.net/pngcrush/
6. http://www.imagemagick.org/script/index.php
7. http://sylvana.net/jpegcrop/jpegtran/

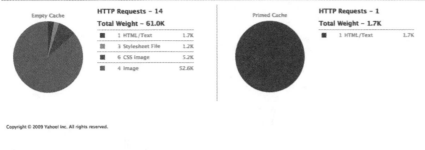

Figure 20.3: WITH OUR OPTIMIZATIONS, PEOPLE WHO VISIT OUR PAGE
REPEATEDLY WILL NEVER HIT OUR SERVERS.

When I compare the two files, the file size ends up being identical. In this case, the extra step wasn't worth the effort. Photoshop's filters were adequate.

However, I get a different result if I optimize the Sign Up button:

```
pngcrush -rem alla -reduce --brute btn_signup.png btn_signup2.png
```

The original file is 2.4KB, and the new file is 2.3KB. So, the sizes aren't identical, but the difference isn't much.

Further image optimization isn't necessary to improve performance in this case, but it's something you should be aware of when working on your own sites. If it turns this technique would benefit you, be sure to script the conversion so it's a transparent part of your deployment process.

20.5 Summary

Our users will experience much faster load times after their first visit once we implement the techniques discussed in this chapter (see Figure 20.3. We've only scratched the surface of performance optimization, but now you should have a better understanding of what you can do to improve the responsiveness of the site if you run into trouble. Proper use of ETags, compression, minification, and Expires headers can go a long way toward reducing requests and, consequently, the amount of bandwidth your site uses.

Chapter 21

Where to Go Next

You've finished creating the Foodbox site. Now you might be looking at the finished product and wondering what you should do next or what you might do differently next time. This chapter will explore a few ideas you can investigate to improve the development process in the future.

21.1 Additional Pages and Templates

We spent an entire book designing a site, but we built only one page. Your typical site will have more than one page, and its interior pages probably won't look exactly like the home page for the site.

Second-Level Pages

It's common practice for sites to have more than one design. The home page is usually unique, and all subsequent pages have a design that's similar in style to the home page but with a smaller banner, modified navigation, and often changes to the content of the sidebar. This second-level template is usually designed to frame the content. Let's quickly create a simple second-level template and use it.

Creating a Second-Level Template

Create a new file called level2.html by copying your index.html file. Next, locate and remove this file, including all its contents:

```
<div id="middle">
  ...
</div>
```

Now replace that file with this one:

final/level2.html

```
<div id="middle">
  <div id="leftcol">
  </div>

  <div id="rightcol">
  </div>

</div> <!-- end of middle container -->
```

Next, we need to apply class="level2" to the body tag. We can use the new class to scope CSS selectors that are specific to our second-level template.

For the layout, we'll shrink the heading so that it's only 54px high. We'll then use the floating technique we used earlier to define our two columns:

final/stylesheets/layout.css

```
.level2 #header{height:54px;}
#middle {width:100%;}
#leftcol, #rightcol{
  margin:18px;
  float:left;
  display:inline;
}
#leftcol{width:558px;}
#rightcol{width:270px;}
```

We've shrunk the header, so we have to create new graphics for our background and our logo. We could open Photoshop, but we can quickly create the images we need using ImageMagick,[1] open a Terminal window or command prompt, and navigate to our images directory.

Make the new banner 36px high:

```
convert -geometry x36 banner.png banner_small.png
```

Now change the name of the image in your level2.html template to use banner_small.png instead of banner.pmg.

The header is 54px, so we want our background to be the same height. We can use ImageMagick's crop command to take care of that.

---

1. Get ImageMagick at http://www.imagemagick.org/script/index.php. If you're a Mac user, you can grab it via MacPorts; if you're a Linux user, your distribution's package manager probably has it available.

```
convert -crop 1x54+0+0 background.gif background_level2.gif
```

The arguments for crop include the width and height of the new image we want to create, followed by the starting X and Y coordinates of the offset, or the top-left corner with respect to the original image.

To style the page, we change the background color of the middle region and the filename for the background image:

`final/stylesheets/style.css`

```css
.level2 #middle{background-color:#fff8e4}
body.level2 {background: #fff url('../images/background_level2.gif') repeat-x;
}
```

It takes only a few small steps to create a simple template that we can use to build additional pages.

Creating a Login Page with the Template

You can make the login page using the level2.html template. Create login.html by copying the level2.html page you just made. Add this code to login.html:

`final/login.html`

```html
<div id="leftcol">
  <h2>Log in</h2>

  <form id="login" method="post" action="/user_sessions">
  <table>
    <tr>
      <th><label for="username">Username</label></th>
      <td>
        <input type="text" name="username"
               id="username" class="text">
      </td>
    </tr>
    <tr>
      <th><label for="password">Password</label></th>
      <td>
        <input type="password" name="password"
               id="password" class="password">
      </td>
    </tr>
    <tr>
      <th> </th>
      <td>
        <input type="checkbox" name="remember" id="remember" class="checkbox">
        <label for="remember">Remember me</label></td>
      </th>
    </tr>
```

Figure 21.1: A SIMPLE LOGIN PAGE USING OUR SECOND-LEVEL TEMPLATE

```
    <tr>
      <th> </th>
      <td><input type="submit" value="Log in"></td>
    </tr>
   </table>
  </form>
</div>
<div id="rightcol">

  <h2>Already have an account?</h2>
    <a href="/signup/">
      <img src="images/btn_signup.png" alt="Sign up">
    </a>
</div>
```

You'll also need to add this code to layout.css:

```
final/stylesheets/layout.css
```

```
form {margin-left:36px;}
form table{border:0px;}
form table tr{height:36px;}
```

When you finish, you end up with something like Figure 21.1.

That worked out pretty well, but you can probably see that this workflow won't scale if the site has hundreds of pages.

21.2 Advanced Templating

If you keep copying this template and creating pages from it, you will quickly create a maintenance nightmare for yourself. Color and font changes are all handled in the CSS, but what do you do if links in the footer need to change? If you've created twenty pages by copying and pasting, you will have to manage all those links and content. Also, links to other documents get more difficult to manage, especially as you start building a hierarchy of links.

If you are developing a static website, you can use Adobe Dreamweaver to track templates. You associate pages to your template, and Dreamweaver will automatically change any associated pages when you change your template. Dreamweaver can be a terrific asset if you work with ColdFusion or PHP, because it can track your links to pages and images automatically. For example, if you move a page to a new folder, Dreamweaver can update all the relative links to style sheets, images, and other files. However, the product can also be pricey, and it might be overkill for what you need to do. Of course, Dreamweaver isn't the only solution for static-page creation.

StaticMatic[2] and Nanoc[3] are two flexible and simple website management tool for static sites. Both are written in Ruby, are extremely easy to use, and feature excellent documentation. Best of all, they're free.

Of course, most sites today aren't static. But you should have no problem transforming the templates you develop into something you can use with your framework or language, whether you use PHP, ColdFusion, Ruby on Rails, Django, Perl, .NET, or any other type of web-based framework.

Most modern web frameworks have a built-in templating mechanism. Building the design is the hard part; turning it into a usable template usually takes no time at all.

21.3 Grid Systems and CSS Frameworks

In this book, I deliberately steered you away from using some of the popular CSS frameworks out there because I wanted you to build your own grid. Now that you understand how grid systems work, you might want to investigate a few of the open source layout frameworks.

---

2. http://staticmatic.rubyforge.org
3. http://nanoc.stoneship.org/

YUI Grid

The Yahoo! User Interface Library (YUI) has a grid builder[4] called YUI Grid that makes it almost too easy to set up your grid. The code for a simple Foodbox template generated with the grid builder might look like this:

`final/yui_foodbox.html`

```
<!DOCTYPE HTML PUBLIC "-//W3C//DTD HTML 4.01//EN"
 "http://www.w3.org/TR/html4/strict.dtd">
<html>
<head>
   <title>YUI Base Page</title>
   <link rel="stylesheet"
href="http://yui.yahooapis.com/2.7.0/build/reset-fonts-grids/reset-fonts-grids.css"
type="text/css">
</head>
<body>
<div id="doc2" class="yui-t3">
   <div id="hd" role="banner"><h1>Foodbox</h1></div>
   <div id="bd" role="main">
       <div id="yui-main">
       <div class="yui-b"><div role="main" class="yui-g">
        <p>Lorem ipsum dolor sit amet, consectetur adipisicing elit,
        sed do eiusmod tempor incididunt ut labore et dolore
        magna aliqua. Ut enim ad minim veniam, quis nostrud
        exercitation ullamco laboris nisi ut aliquip ex ea commodo
        consequat. Duis aute irure dolor in reprehenderit in voluptate
        velit esse cillum dolore eu fugiat nulla pariatur.
     </p>
   </div>
</div>

       </div>
       <div role="search" class="yui-b">
        <p>Lorem ipsum dolor sit amet, consectetur adipisicing elit,
        sed do eiusmod tempor incididunt ut labore et dolore
        magna aliqua. Ut enim ad minim veniam, quis nostrud
        exercitation ullamco laboris nisi ut aliquip ex ea commodo
        consequat. Duis aute irure dolor in reprehenderit in voluptate
        velit esse cillum dolore eu fugiat nulla pariatur.
     </p>
     <p>
        Excepteur sint occaecat cupidatat non proident,
        sunt in culpa qui officia deserunt mollit anim id est laborum.
         </p>
       </div>

       </div>
```

---

4. http://developer.yahoo.com/yui/grids/builder/

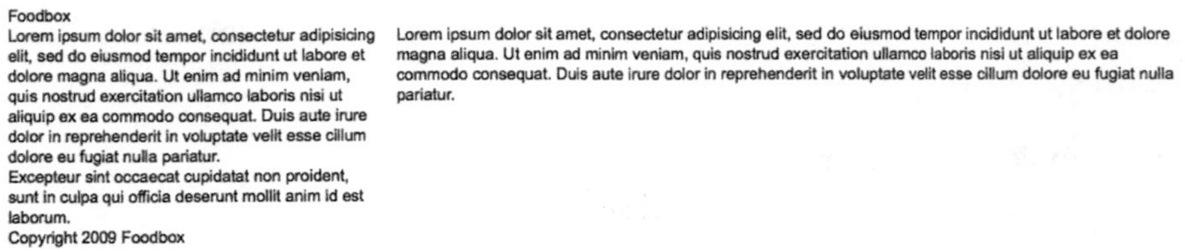

Foodbox
Lorem ipsum dolor sit amet, consectetur adipisicing elit, sed do eiusmod tempor incididunt ut labore et dolore magna aliqua. Ut enim ad minim veniam, quis nostrud exercitation ullamco laboris nisi ut aliquip ex ea commodo consequat. Duis aute irure dolor in reprehenderit in voluptate velit esse cillum dolore eu fugiat nulla pariatur.

Lorem ipsum dolor sit amet, consectetur adipisicing elit, sed do eiusmod tempor incididunt ut labore et dolore magna aliqua. Ut enim ad minim veniam, quis nostrud exercitation ullamco laboris nisi ut aliquip ex ea commodo consequat. Duis aute irure dolor in reprehenderit in voluptate velit esse cillum dolore eu fugiat nulla pariatur.
Excepteur sint occaecat cupidatat non proident, sunt in culpa qui officia deserunt mollit anim id est laborum.
Copyright 2009 Foodbox

Figure 21.2: OUR UNSTYLED FOODBOX YUI GRID LAYOUT

```
  <div id="ft" role="contentinfo"><p>Copyright 2010 Foodbox</p></div>
</div>
</body>
</html>
```

The grid builder will style this appropriately. With this framework, you essentially program to YUI's interface. Use the right IDs and classes, and everything just works. In this example, the doc2 ID on the outermost div specifies that the width should be 960px wide, and the yui-t3 class states that the left column should be 300px wide. The tool includes lots of configurable options; you can read more about them in the documentation.[5]

This particular version also resets all the elements, as shown in Figure 21.2. For example, notice how small the Foodbox heading is. You will need to add your own style sheet after the YUI styles to size your headings.

960 Grid System

The popular 960 Grid System[6] is a simpler alternative to YUI Grid. The 960 Grid System uses a predefined width of 960px for the page and divides it into either 12 or 16 columns. When you build a layout on this grid, you use classes to determine how many columns each region will contain.

If you choose the 12-column grid, then you define the header and footer to be 12 columns wide, the sidebar to be four columns wide, and the main content to be eight columns wide. The spacing between

---

5. http://developer.yahoo.com/yui/grids/
6. http://960.gs/

the columns is automatically handled for you, so you don't even have to think about it.

Take a look at the markup:

```
final/960_foodbox.html
```

```
<!DOCTYPE html>
<html lang="en">
<head>
<meta http-equiv="content-type" content="text/html; charset=utf-8" />
<title>960 Grid System &mdash; Demo</title>
<link rel="stylesheet" href="http://960.gs/css/reset.css" />
<link rel="stylesheet" href="http://960.gs/css/text.css" />
<link rel="stylesheet" href="http://960.gs/css/960.css" />
</head>
<body>

  <div class="container_12">

    <div id="header" class="grid_12">
      <h1>Foodbox</h1>
        </div>


        <div id="sidebar" class="grid_4">
      <p>Lorem ipsum dolor sit amet, consectetur adipisicing elit
        sed do eiusmod tempor incididunt ut labore et dolore magna aliqua.
        Ut enim ad minim veniam, quis nostrud exercitation ullamco
        laboris nisi ut aliquip ex ea commodo consequat. Duis aute irure dolor
        in reprehenderit in voluptate velit esse cillum dolore eu fugiat nulla
        pariatur.
      </p>
      <p>Excepteur sint occaecat cupidatat non proident, sunt
        in culpa qui officia deserunt mollit anim id est laborum.
      </p>

        </div>

    <div id="main" class="grid_8">
      <p>Lorem ipsum dolor sit amet, consectetur adipisicing elit
        sed do eiusmod tempor incididunt ut labore et dolore magna aliqua.
        Ut enim ad minim veniam, quis nostrud exercitation ullamco
        laboris nisi ut aliquip ex ea commodo consequat. Duis aute irure dolor
        in reprehenderit in voluptate velit esse cillum dolore eu fugiat nulla
        pariatur.
      </p>
      <p>Excepteur sint occaecat cupidatat non proident, sunt
        in culpa qui officia deserunt mollit anim id est laborum.
      </p>
    </div>
```

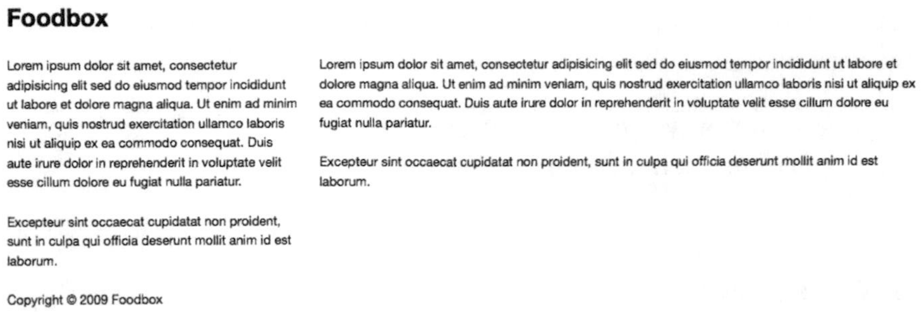

Foodbox

Lorem ipsum dolor sit amet, consectetur adipisicing elit sed do eiusmod tempor incididunt ut labore et dolore magna aliqua. Ut enim ad minim veniam, quis nostrud exercitation ullamco laboris nisi ut aliquip ex ea commodo consequat. Duis aute irure dolor in reprehenderit in voluptate velit esse cillum dolore eu fugiat nulla pariatur.

Excepteur sint occaecat cupidatat non proident, sunt in culpa qui officia deserunt mollit anim id est laborum.

Lorem ipsum dolor sit amet, consectetur adipisicing elit sed do eiusmod tempor incididunt ut labore et dolore magna aliqua. Ut enim ad minim veniam, quis nostrud exercitation ullamco laboris nisi ut aliquip ex ea commodo consequat. Duis aute irure dolor in reprehenderit in voluptate velit esse cillum dolore eu fugiat nulla pariatur.

Excepteur sint occaecat cupidatat non proident, sunt in culpa qui officia deserunt mollit anim id est laborum.

Copyright © 2009 Foodbox

Figure 21.3: OUR UNSTYLED FOODBOX 960 GRID SYSTEM LAYOUT

```
<div id="footer" class="grid_12">
  <p>Copyright &copy; 2010 Foodbox</p>
    </div>

  </div>

</body>
```

This grid enables you to build simple layout with only a few lines of code, as shown in Figure 21.3. The 960 Grid System uses a base font size of 13px and a line-height of 1.5, which is a relative measure that means 1.5 times the font size. In this case, the line-height would be 19.5px, which would be difficult to work with when cropping images. So, modify the line-heights and font sizes of the elements by adding your own style sheet.

If you want to integrate the 960 Grid System into your workflow, you can get printable sketching paper from the 960 Grid System website, along with Photoshop templates to help you design your site.

Frameworks Don't Solve Everything!

Although these frameworks make it extremely easy to get a grid-based layout working, you still have to use your knowledge of the baseline grid when you choose fonts and spacing and when you place your images. You'll also notice that these systems bring in a lot of additional CSS that you might not even need. Also, the 960 Grid System requires you to include multiple files, which can decrease performance, so be sure to make good use of minification techniques and caching if you use this framework.

If you use them only when you understand how the code works, you can get enormous benefit from CSS frameworks.

21.4 CSS Alternatives

As a programmer, working with CSS probably feels a little unstructured and redundant. CSS lacks inheritance and variables, so you end up typing the same code over and over.

Code like this gets awfully difficult to manage:

```
#latest_recipes{
   clear:both;
   margin: 18px 18px 0 18px;
}

#latest_recipes h3{
  margin-left:18px;
}

#latest_recipes p{
  margin-left:36px;
}
```

Repeating the latest_recipes selector just for scoping seems wrong.

Several open source projects have created CSS generators that transform their special markup into static CSS files that you can push out to your applications. I'll cover Less, a simple but powerful CSS preprocessor implemented using the Ruby language.[7]

Less CSS

You can use Less[8] to leverage Ruby and your existing knowledge of CSS syntax to build CSS style sheets easily.

---

7. You might also be interested in Sass, which is similar to Less but has slightly different syntax. You can learn more about it at http://sass-lang.com/.
8. http://lesscss.org/

You can nest declarations in a logical fashion, so the previous example would look like this:

```
final/less_examples.less
#latest_recipes{
   clear:both;
   margin: 18px 18px 0 18px;

   h3{
     margin-left:18px;
   }

   p{
     margin-left:36px;
   }
}
```

When the Less file is converted into a CSS file, the h3 and p selectors will be properly scoped.

The real benefit of using Less comes from its support for variables and expressions. This support makes it possible to do something like this:

```
final/less_examples.less
@text_color: #fff;
@width: 900px;
@font_size: 12px;
@line_height: @font_size * 1.5;
@margin: @line_height;
@sidebar: @width / 3;
@main: @width - @sidebar - @margin;

body {color: @text_color; }
#page { width: @width; margin: 0 auto; }
#middle { width: @width; }
#main { width: @main; }
#sidebar { width: @sidebar; }
```

Of course, browsers won't understand the style sheets in this form. You need to run your files through the Less preprocessor to convert the files into standard CSS files:

```
less source/style.less stylesheets/style.css --watch
```

The --watch switch monitors the source file for changes. When you save, it regenerates your CSS files. This makes testing a breeze, and it can simplify style sheet management tremendously. You can also integrate this approach into your automated deployment workflow without much effort.

21.5 Don't Forget to Buy the Stock Images!

The pasta logo we used in this book is a stock image available at iStock-photo.[9] We're using the watermarked version in the examples, but when we go to production, we need to pay for the final version.[10] This might seem like common sense, but you can take a look at the Photoshop Disasters blog[11] to see lots of examples of people releasing watermarked stock images in production, even in print publications! So, don't forget to secure the rights to any stock images or other assets you use in your application. Remember, you don't get to use an image for free just because it shows up in a Google Image search!

21.6 Visual Effects

Visual effects such as fading and animations used to require Flash. But now you can implement a lot of effects using JavaScript libraries such as jQuery, Prototype, and Scriptaculous. These tools are open source JavaScript frameworks aimed at simplifying element manipulation, animation, effects, and Ajax. Let's use jQuery to make the pasta image on our page transition to other images with a crossfade.

First, we need to collect and resize some images for the crossfading. The images need to be 594px wide by 144px high to fit into that area of our page. I'll use three images from Flickr that are licensed under the Creative Commons Attribution license. That means we need to be sure to credit the image to its creator when we display it. I've chosen three images:[12]

- http://www.flickr.com/photos/pencapchew/3108612635/

- http://www.flickr.com/photos/stevendepolo/3523644703/

- http://www.flickr.com/photos/denniswong/3486409564/

---

9. http://www.istockphoto.com
10. I had to purchase the rights to reproduce this image in this book so you could use it in the examples.
11. http://www.photoshopdisasters.com/
12. If you can't access these URLs, you can find the images in the book's companion source code.

Resizing the Images

We need to resize the images so they all have a width of 594px; this will enable them to fit in the same space as the pasta image. We can use ImageMagick's Geometry option to pass only the width parameter. This code constrains the proportions of the width and height so our images don't get distorted:

```
$ convert -geometry 594x originals/tacosalad.jpg tacosalad.jpg
$ convert -geometry 594x originals/phadthai.jpg phadthai.jpg
$ convert -geometry 594x originals/chickenmac.jpg chickenmac.jpg
```

Next, we need to perform a crop, grabbing whatever is in the middle of the image. Let's begin by finding the image's height:

```
$ identify tacosalad.jpg
tacosalad.jpg JPEG 594x394 594x394+0+0 8-bit DirectClass 146kb
```

According to this, the height is 394px. We can take that number and subtract 144, the height we need for our images. Next, we take that result and divide by two. In this case, we need to start cropping at 9px across and 125px down:

```
$ convert -crop 594x144+0+125 tacosalad.jpg tacosalad.jpg
$ convert -crop 594x144+0+125 phadthai.jpg phadthai.jpg
$ convert -crop 594x144+0+125 chickenmac.jpg chickenmac.jpg
```

Building the Script

To crossfade images, we need to make one image disappear as we bring in the next image. Programs like Flash use a timeline to control the effects. Each image is on its own layer, and you overlap the layers on the timeline for the duration of the crossfade. JavaScript doesn't have the concept of a timeline, but it does give us the ability to fade things in and out.

We'll start with our array of images. For this example, we'll keep things simple and not modify the alternate text on the crossfade:

`final/javascripts/crossfade.js`
```
images = [
"images/pasta.jpg",
"images/tacosalad.jpg",
"images/phadthai.jpg",
"images/chickenmac.jpg"
]
```

The order of the items in the array is important here because it determines the order in which the images will crossfade.

Next, we need to put all the images on the page and stack them on top of one another. The crossfade script will start with the top image and fade it out to reveal the second image. After five seconds, it'll repeat this process with the next image, and so on. When it gets to the end, it will reset the process.

We will use a combination of CSS and JavaScript to stack the images on the page within the banner:

`final/javascripts/crossfade.js`

```
Line 1   var image_box = $("#main_image");
     2
     3   image_box.css({'position' : 'relative', 'height': '144px'} );
     4   var image_html = "";
     5   for(var i = 0; i < images.length; i++) {
     6     image_html += '<img style="position:absolute;top:0; z-index:' +
     7     (images.length - i) + '" src="' + images[i] + '" id="image_' + i + '"/>';
     8   };
     9
    10   image_box.html(image_html);
```

We begin by grabbing the container that will hold the images. Next, we use JavaScript to set the positioning of the element to relative and enforce a specific height so that it won't collapse. Next, we create a new string that will hold the HTML for the images we want to stack. We loop over the array of images, creating each image's markup. We set each image to be absolutely positioned on top of the one beneath it using the top, left, and z-index CSS properties that we attach using an inline style.[13] The top and left attributes are both set to 0, and the z-index, or stacking order, is set so that each image in the array is stacked below the previous image.

We also give each element in this stack of images its own ID using the image_i format, where i is the position of the image in the array. We'll need this later, when we need to identify the element to fade out.

Once we build up the HTML for the images, we can pass the HTML string to the html() method of the container, as shown on line 10.

We need to initialize a counter variable so we can keep track of the image in the stack. We need the images to transition every five seconds,

---

13. Previously, I said that inline styles are bad. However, they're somewhat necessary here. Although the position, top, and left attributes could be set in the CSS file and attached to these images by class name, the z-index needs to be unique for each image. So, here I defined all the definitions using the style attribute.

> **Absolute Positioning in a Relative Area**
>
> Normally, you use the top-left corner of the browser window as the reference point when you want to position things by coordinate position. Thus you would define something you need to place 100px from the top and 18px from the left like this:
>
> ```
> .box{
>   position:absolute;
>   top:100px;
>   left:18px;
> }
> ```
>
> When we define an element with relative positioning, we can use it as a reference point for any absolutely positioned elements contained within the relatively positioned element. This makes it easier for us to stack our banner images on top of each other because we can specify their top and left positions as 0, relative to the container.

so we'll use the setInterval() method, which invokes a method at a given interval:

`final/javascripts/crossfade.js`

```
Line 1  var i = 0;
     2  var delay_in_miliseconds = 5000;
     3
     4  setInterval(function(){
     5    $("#image_" + i).animate({ opacity: 0}, 3000);
     6    i++;
     7    if(i == images.length) i = 0;
     8    $("#image_" + i).animate({ opacity: 1}, 3000);
     9  },delay_in_miliseconds);
```

On line 4, we pass an anonymous function to setInterval(), which uses our counter variable to grab the image to fade. After we fade the image, we increment our counter variable so that we can make the next image appear. However, before we activate the next image, we check to see whether we are out of images; if so, we reset the counter variable back to 0. Essentially, we shuffle the images around like a deck of cards, fading one into the next.

Getting It on Our Home Page

Our crossfading script won't do much unless we call it from our home page. To do that, we need to load both the jQuery library and our script.

Open the index page, and add the following code immediately before the closing body tag:

final/index.html

```
<script type="text/javascript"
   charset="utf-8"
   src="http://ajax.googleapis.com/ajax/libs/jquery/1.3.2/jquery.min.js">
</script>

<script type="text/javascript" charset="utf-8"
  src="javascripts/crossfade.js">
</script>
```

Here we load the jQuery library and our own custom crossfader. I've often thought that if browsers were to cache files based on the originating URL, then we could increase the performance of our sites if everyone included common libraries like jQuery from the same source. Visitors who come to my site from another site could already have the library loaded. It turns out that Google provides exactly this service via its Ajax Libraries API.[14] We can load jQuery from there, and there's a good chance our visitors will already have jQuery in their local cache.

Finally, we need to make a small change to our main image's markup. Our script injects several stacked images into a container with the ID of main_image. In our index page, however, the main_image ID is attached to the pasta image. Remove the ID from the pasta image, and wrap it with a div, placing the main_image ID on the new div:

final/index.html

```
<div id="main_image">
  <img src="images/pasta.jpg" alt="Pasta and marinara sauce">
</div>
```

That's it! We now have an extremely simple image crossfader, and it's completely unobtrusive. When JavaScript is turned off, people will see only the original pasta image. When you use JavaScript, always make sure you keep your JavaScript code out of your content document. Use event observers or other techniques to apply behavior to your pages. Also, never use an onclick or onmouseover because this mixes interaction with presentation, is completely unnecessary, and can end up being an accessibility problem if you didn't provide an alternative path.

---

14. http://code.google.com/apis/ajaxlibs/documentation/

Unobtrusive JavaScript

Unobtrusive JavaScript describes JavaScript that is completely separated from the content progressively. This approach provides an easy method to enhance your site, while still providing functionality for people who can't use JavaScript.

Traditionally, you might do this if you wanted to make a link open in a new window:

```
<a href="#" onclick="window.open('help.html');">Help</a>
```

However, that approach prevents people from getting to your links if they don't have JavaScript enabled. A better way would be to use the link as intended, letting the href attribute hold the URL for the link and then using JavaScript to observe the link. When someone clicks the link, the script will take the value of the href and open it in a new window.

Unobtrusive JavaScript has another advantage: you can easily reuse it. Let's say we wanted every link on our page with the class of popup to open in a new window. This tiny bit of jQuery code will do exactly that:

```
(document).ready(function(){
  var links = $("a.popup");

  links.click(function(event){
  event.preventDefault();
  window.open($(this).attr('href'));
  });
});
```

For more on unobtrusive JavaScript, visit http://onlinetools.org/articles/unobtrusivejavascript/.

JavaScript can make your pages come alive, and you can improve everyone's user experience if you use it correctly. Make your code unobtrusive, make sure things work without it, and don't forget to minify your scripts!

21.7 Experiment and Practice!

In this book, we used a conservative color scheme and design, but now that you have gone through the process, you should go back to the beginning and try to reimplement this site using your own ideas. Make your own sketch, create your own logo, choose your own colors and fonts, and use a grid system to build your site. Look at other sites for inspiration, and use Firebug to inspect how the designers built the pieces. Learn from others, and practice, practice, practice some more. Like programming, web design is something you can spend a lifetime mastering.

So, keep learning, exploring, and experimenting. And be sure to have fun throughout the process.

Chapter 22

Recommended Reading

It's no secret that programmers read a lot of books and websites to keep their skills sharp. This chapter lists some resources that I think will help you further explore the elements of design that I've gone over in this book.

22.1 Color Resources

Color is a complex topic, and a good understanding of color will help you convey your message and capture your audience's attention. I've found these resources valuable, although you may need to scour your local library for a few of these titles.

- Albers, Josef. *The Interaction of Color* [Alb75]

- Itten, Johannes. *The Elements of Color* [Itt97b]

- Itten, Johannes. *The Art of Colour: The Subjective Experience and Objective Rationale of Color - Revised Edition* [Itt97a]

- Morton, Jill. *A Guide to Color Symbolism* [Mor97], Colorcom, 1998.

22.2 Books on Fonts and Typography

A good understanding of fonts and typography is crucial to your success as a web developer, so I encourage you to investigate further these resources. These two books do an excellent job of showing you how to effectively use type and grid systems in your designs.

- Ruder, Emil, *Typography* [Rud81]

- Muller-Brockmann, Josef, *Grid Systems in Graphic Design* [MB96]

22.3 Technical Books

This book gets you started on the path towards mastering web development, but if you're looking for the next step, you will find these resources quite useful.

- Ash, Tim. *Landing Page Optimization The Definitive Guide to Testing and Tuning for Conversions* [Ash08]

- Clifton, Brian. *Advanced Web Metrics with Google Analytics* [Cli08]

- Goto, Kelly and Cotler, Emily. *Web ReDesign 2.0: Workflow that Works* [GC04]

- Krug, Steve. *Don't Make Me Think! A Common Sense Approach to Web Usability* [Kru04]

- Meyer, Eric. A. *Cascading Style Sheets: The Definitive Guide, Third Edition* [Mey06]

- Sydik, Jeremy. *Design Accessible Web Sites* [Syd08]

- Veen, Jeffrey. *The Art & Science of Web Design* [Vee00]

- Zeldman, Jeffrey, *Designing With Web Standards* [Zel06]

22.4 Web sites

The Internet is full of guides and tutorials to help you build web sites, but here are some of the best resources I've found related to the topics we covered in this book.

About Hearing Loss . . . . http://www.miracle-ear.com/abouthearingloss.aspx
The Miracle-Ear web site contains good information about hearing loss, including types and causes.

A List Apart: CSS @ Ten: The Next Big Thing. . .
. . . http://www.alistapart.com/articles/cssatten
Håkon Wium Lie discusses using @font-face in your stylesheets.

A List Apart: Going to Print . . . . http://alistapart.com/articles/goingtoprint
An article from Eric Meyer on using CSS to provide printer-friendly stylesheets for your site.

Brandcurve: "Color Meanings Around the World". . .
. . . >http://www.brandcurve.com/color-meanings-around-the-world/
A list of colors and their international meanings.

Lighthouse International - " Making Text Legible Designing for People with Partial Sight"...

. . . http://www.lighthouse.org/accessibility/legible/

Basic guidelines for making effective legibility choices that work for nearly everyone.

Safalra: "The Myth of Web-Safe Fonts"...

. . . http://safalra.com/web-design/typography/web-safe-fonts-myth/

Provides a good background in fonts and CSS.

Unit Interactive: "Better CSS Font Stacks"...

. . . http://unitinteractive.com/blog/2008/06/26/better-css-font-stacks/

Discussion of font stacks, with some excellent examples.

WebAim: "CSS in Action: Invisible Content Just for Screen Reader Users"...

. . . http://www.webaim.org/techniques/css/invisiblecontent/

Explanation and examples on how to provide additional content to screen readers, such as navigation skip links.

Appendix A

Bibliography

[Alb75]   Josef Albers. *Interaction of Color*. Yale University Press, New Haven CT, 1975.

[Ash08]   Tim Ash. *Landing Page Optimization: The Definitive Guide to Testing and Tuning for Conversions*. Sybex, New York, 2008.

[Cli08]   Brian Clifton. *Advanced Web Metrics with Google Analytics*. Sybex, New York, 2008.

[GC04]   Kelly Goto and Emily Cotler. *Web ReDesign 2.0: Workflow that Works*. Peachpit Press, Berkeley, 2004.

[Itt97a]   Johannes Itten. *The Art of Color: The Subjective Experience and Objective Rationale of Color - Revised Edition*. Wiley, New York, 1997.

[Itt97b]   Johannes Itten. *The Elements of Color*. Wiley, New York, 1997.

[Kru04]   Steve Krug. *Don't Make Me Think! A Common Sense Approach to Web Usability*. Peachpit Press, New York, 2004.

[MB96]   Josef Müller-Brockmann. *Grid Systems in Graphic Design*. Niggli, Sulgen, Switzerland, 1996.

[Mey06]   Eric Meyer. *CSS: The Definitive Guide*. O'Reilly Media, Inc., Sebastopol, CA, third edition, 2006.

[Mor97]   Jill Morton. *A Guide to Color Symbolism*. Colorcom, Broomfield CO, 1997.

[Rud81]   Emil Ruder. *Typography*. Niggli, Sulgen, Switzerland, 1981.

[Syd08]   Jeremy Sydik. *Design Accessible Web Sites: 36 Keys to Creating Content for All Audiences and Platforms.* The Pragmatic Programmers, LLC, Raleigh, NC, and Dallas, TX, 2008.

[Vee00]   Jeffrey Veen. *The Art and Science of Web Design.* New Riders Press, Upper Saddle River NJ, 2000.

[Zel06]   Jeffrey Zeldman. *Designing Web Standards.* Peachpit Press, New York, second edition, 2006.

Index

The Pragmatic Bookshelf

Available in paperback and DRM-free PDF, our titles are here to help you stay on top of your game. The following are in print as of November 2009; be sure to check our website at pragprog.com for newer titles.

Title	Year	ISBN	Pages
Advanced Rails Recipes: 84 New Ways to Build Stunning Rails Apps	2008	9780978739225	464
Agile Coaching	2009	9781934356432	250
Agile Retrospectives: Making Good Teams Great	2006	9780977616640	200
Agile Web Development with Rails, Third Edition	2009	9781934356166	784
Augmented Reality: A Practical Guide	2008	9781934356036	328
Behind Closed Doors: Secrets of Great Management	2005	9780976694021	192
Best of Ruby Quiz	2006	9780976694076	304
Core Animation for Mac OS X and the iPhone: Creating Compelling Dynamic User Interfaces	2008	9781934356104	200
Core Data: Apple's API for Persisting Data on Mac OS X	2009	9781934356326	256
Data Crunching: Solve Everyday Problems using Java, Python, and More	2005	9780974514079	208
Debug It! Find, Repair, and Prevent Bugs in Your Code	2009	9781934356289	232
Deploying Rails Applications: A Step-by-Step Guide	2008	9780978739201	280
Design Accessible Web Sites: 36 Keys to Creating Content for All Audiences and Platforms	2007	9781934356029	336
Desktop GIS: Mapping the Planet with Open Source Tools	2008	9781934356067	368
Developing Facebook Platform Applications with Rails	2008	9781934356128	200
Enterprise Integration with Ruby	2006	9780976694069	360
Enterprise Recipes with Ruby and Rails	2008	9781934356234	416
Everyday Scripting with Ruby: for Teams, Testers, and You	2007	9780977616619	320
FXRuby: Create Lean and Mean GUIs with Ruby	2008	9781934356074	240
From Java To Ruby: Things Every Manager Should Know	2006	9780976694090	160
GIS for Web Developers: Adding Where to Your Web Applications	2007	9780974514093	275
Google Maps API, V2: Adding Where to Your Applications	2006	PDF-Only	83
Grails: A Quick-Start Guide	2009	9781934356463	200

Continued on next page

Title	Year	ISBN	Pages
Groovy Recipes: Greasing the Wheels of Java	2008	9780978739294	264
Hello, Android: Introducing Google's Mobile Development Platform	2009	9781934356494	272
Interface Oriented Design	2006	9780976694052	240
Land the Tech Job You Love	2009	9781934356265	280
Learn to Program, 2nd Edition	2009	9781934356364	230
Manage It! Your Guide to Modern Pragmatic Project Management	2007	9780978739249	360
Manage Your Project Portfolio: Increase Your Capacity and Finish More Projects	2009	9781934356296	200
Mastering Dojo: JavaScript and Ajax Tools for Great Web Experiences	2008	9781934356111	568
Modular Java: Creating Flexible Applications with OSGi and Spring	2009	9781934356401	260
No Fluff Just Stuff 2006 Anthology	2006	9780977616664	240
No Fluff Just Stuff 2007 Anthology	2007	9780978739287	320
Practical Programming: An Introduction to Computer Science Using Python	2009	9781934356272	350
Practices of an Agile Developer	2006	9780974514086	208
Pragmatic Project Automation: How to Build, Deploy, and Monitor Java Applications	2004	9780974514031	176
Pragmatic Thinking and Learning: Refactor Your Wetware	2008	9781934356050	288
Pragmatic Unit Testing in C# with NUnit	2007	9780977616671	176
Pragmatic Unit Testing in Java with JUnit	2003	9780974514017	160
Pragmatic Version Control Using Git	2008	9781934356159	200
Pragmatic Version Control using CVS	2003	9780974514000	176
Pragmatic Version Control using Subversion	2006	9780977616657	248
Programming Clojure	2009	9781934356333	304
Programming Cocoa with Ruby: Create Compelling Mac Apps Using RubyCocoa	2009	9781934356197	300
Programming Erlang: Software for a Concurrent World	2007	9781934356005	536
Programming Groovy: Dynamic Productivity for the Java Developer	2008	9781934356098	320
Programming Ruby: The Pragmatic Programmers' Guide, Second Edition	2004	9780974514055	864
Programming Ruby 1.9: The Pragmatic Programmers' Guide	2009	9781934356081	960
Programming Scala: Tackle Multi-Core Complexity on the Java Virtual Machine	2009	9781934356319	250
Prototype and script.aculo.us: You Never Knew JavaScript Could Do This!	2007	9781934356012	448
Rails Recipes	2006	9780977616602	350

Continued on next page

Title	Year	ISBN	Pages
Rails for .NET Developers	2008	9781934356203	300
Rails for Java Developers	2007	9780977616695	336
Rails for PHP Developers	2008	9781934356043	432
Rapid GUI Development with QtRuby	2005	PDF-Only	83
Release It! Design and Deploy Production-Ready Software	2007	9780978739218	368
Scripted GUI Testing with Ruby	2008	9781934356180	192
Ship it! A Practical Guide to Successful Software Projects	2005	9780974514048	224
Stripes ...and Java Web Development Is Fun Again	2008	9781934356210	375
TextMate: Power Editing for the Mac	2007	9780978739232	208
The Definitive ANTLR Reference: Building Domain-Specific Languages	2007	9780978739256	384
The Passionate Programmer: Creating a Remarkable Career in Software Development	2009	9781934356340	200
ThoughtWorks Anthology	2008	9781934356142	240
Ubuntu Kung Fu: Tips, Tricks, Hints, and Hacks	2008	9781934356227	400
iPhone SDK Development	2009	9781934356258	576